Ray Baker

Beyond Narnia:
The Theology of C.S. Lewis

Beyond Narnia:

The Theology of C.S. Lewis

Ray Baker

Christian Publishing House
Cambridge, Ohio

Cover image: Phil Mendez

Cover design: Margareta Brisell Axelsson

Beyond Narnia: The Theology of C.S. Lewis by Ray Baker

ISBN-13: **978-1-949586-16-9**

ISBN-10: **1-949586-16-2**

Table of Contents

Dedication

For my brother-in-law Gary who keeps nagging me to write something in English!

Abbreviations

1&2T	*First and Second Things*
Abolition	*The Abolition of Man*
Comp	*Compelling Reason: Essays on Ethics and Theology*
CR	*Christian Reflections*
Dawntreader	*The Voyage of the Dawn Treader*
Discarded	*The Discarded Image*
Divorce	*The Great Divorce*
Dock	*God in the Dock* (abridged)
Dock+	*God in the Dock* (unabridged)
DT	*The Dark Tower*
Dymer	*Dymer*
EC	*Essay Collection and Other Short Pieces*
EC1	*Essay Collection*, vol. 1
EC2	*Essay Collection*, vol. 2
ExCrit	*Experiment in Criticism*
Faces	*Till We Have Faces*
FE	*Fernseeds and Elephants*
GM	*The Grand Miracle and Other Selected Essays on Theology and Ethics*
Grief	*A Grief Observed*
Hideous	*That Hideous Strength*
I&I	*Image and Imagination: Essays and Reviews*
Lady	*Letters to an American Lady*
LBattle	*The Last Battle*
Letters1	*Collected Letters, Vol. 1, Family Letters, 1905–1931*
Letters2	*Collected Letters, Vol. 2, Books, Broadcasts and the War, 1931–1949*
Letters3	*Collected Letters, Vol. 3, Narnia, Cambridge and Joy, 1950–1963*
LettersWHL	*The Letters of C.S. Lewis* (W.H. Lewis, ed.)
Lion	*The Lion, the Witch and the Wardrobe*

Magician	*The Magician's Nephew*
Malcolm	*Letters to Malcolm: Chiefly on Prayer*
MC	*Mere Christianity*
OOW	*Of Other Worlds*
OS	*On Stories*
OTOW	*Of This and Other Worlds*
Paper	*They Asked for a Paper*
PC	*Present Concerns*
Perelandra	*Perelandra*
PRegress	*The Pilgrim's Regress*
ProbPain	*The Problem of Pain*
Psalms	*Reflections on the Psalms*
Rehab	*Rehabilitations*
Reunion	*Christian Reunion and Other Essays*
Screwtape	*The Screwtape Letters*
SE	*The Seeing Eye and Other Selected Essays from Christian Reflections*
SLE	*Selected Literary Essays*
SMRL	*Studies in Medieval and Renaissance Literature*
Surprised	*Surprised by Joy*
Temporum	*De Descriptione Temporum*
Timeless	*Timeless at Heart: Essays on Theology*
Toast	*Screwtape Proposes a Toast and Other Pieces*
Trans	*Transpositions*
Und	*Undeceptions*
WLN	*World's Last Night and Other Essays*
WoG	*Weight of Glory and Other Addresses*

"Which of the religions of the world gives to its followers the greatest happiness? While it lasts, the religion of worshipping oneself is the best."[1]

"A Confession"
I am so coarse, the things the poets see
Are obstinately invisible to me.
For twenty years I've stared my level best
To see if evening – any evening – would suggest
A patient etherized upon a table;
In vain. I simply wasn't able.[2]

[1] C.S. Lewis, "Answers to Questions on Christianity" in *Dock+*, p. 58. Also in *EC*, p. 325.

[2] Lewis wrote this parody of T.S. Eliot's famous poem "The Love Song of J. Alfred Prufrock". C.S. Lewis, "A Confession" in *Poems* (London: Geoffrey Bles, 1964), p. 1.

The Nerd of Nerds: Introduction to C.S. Lewis

I promise I am not a fanatic. You know the type – the guys who "nerd out" on a subject with a depth that both frightens and fascinates at the same time. They somehow manage to steer every conversation to the one love of their life with a speed and skill that takes one's breath away. I've met Lewis-nerds like that. I hope I'm not one of them.

Lewis was the "nerd of nerds" – a frumpy bachelor who loved stories of gods and fairies, who quoted other writers whom no one else has ever heard of, who peppered his conversations with sometimes byzantine explanations of a word's etymology, and who read literature in obscure languages like Icelandic.[3]

Few professors of literature have managed to sell books in such large numbers as C.S. Lewis.[4] Few theologians have succeeded in forming the faith of so many people as C.S. Lewis. Theologian Richard John Neuhaus comments on Lewis's influence:

> The first thing I should say is that I am not a Lewis scholar. The second thing is that, from what I understand of the man, he would likely be amused that there are people called Lewis scholars. There are simply those who can stop reading Lewis, and those who can't. After a while, some of the latter find that they are thought to be Lewis scholars.[5]

I don't think I would call myself a person who can't stop reading Lewis, but I appreciate his humor, his masterful use of the English language and his eagle-eye insights into human nature and humanity's relationship with God.

---

[3] OK – OK! I admit it: I'm a nerd too. I love etymology and even speak Icelandic.

[4] What about Dan Brown you may say? We'll just have to wait and see how well his books are selling 50 years after his death!

[5] Richard John Neuhaus, "C.S. Lewis and Postmodernism" *First Things* (December 1998).

Acclaim and scorn

C.S. Lewis gained popularity with a broad public after the success of *The Screwtape Letters* in 1942. Shortly after that, Lewis presented the basics of Christian faith in a series of popular radio broadcasts on the BBC during World War II. At a time before the invention of television, and when the BBC was the only radio station in England, an estimated 600,000 people listened to Lewis's weekly talks.[6] The broadcasts were so popular that Lewis's voice was said to be second only to that of Prime Minister Winston Churchill as the most recognizable voice in the United Kingdom.[7]

In the Spring of 1993 *Christianity Today* surveyed a large number of Christian leaders as to the most influential Christian books of the twentieth century. They published a list of one hundred titles with the comment:

> By far, C.S. Lewis was the most popular author and *Mere Christianity* the book nominated most often. Indeed, we could have included even more Lewis works, but finally had to say, 'Enough is enough, give some other authors a chance.'[8]

During his lifetime he published approximately forty books. A large number of additional books have been released posthumously, many of which are collections of essays, sermons, poems, letters and other short texts.[9] More than fifty years after his death, between two and three million copies of his books are sold each year – just in English. His books continue to appear in new translations in languages around the world.[10] Many devotional guides have been published with excerpts from his work;[11] C.S. Lewis societies exist around the world and the number of websites dedicated to Lewis's works is seemingly infinite.

---

[6] Anonymous, "Don v Devil" *Time* 50/10 (September 8, 1947): 65.

[7] Art Lindsley, *C.S. Lewis's Case for Christ* (Downers Grove: InterVarsity Press, 2005), p. 15.

[8] Michael Maudlin, "1993 Christianity Today Book Awards" *Christianity Today* (April 5, 1993), p. 28. See also John G. Stackhouse, "By Their Books Ye Shall Know Them" *Christianity Today* (September 16, 1996), pp. 58–59.

[9] See the bibliographies and compilations at the end of this book.

[10] Kathryn Lindskoog, *Sleuthing C.S. Lewis: More Light in the Shadowlands* (Macon, GA: Mercer University Press, 2001), p. 6.

[11] Among others we may mention: *The Business of Heaven – Daily Readings; Daily Readings with C.S. Lewis;* and *A Year with Aslan*. See bibliographies for details.

Lewis joins the saints and apostles as a motif for stained glass windows in at least three churches: St. George's Episcopal Church in Dayton, Ohio; St. Luke's Episcopal Church in Monrovia, California; and St. David of Wales Episcopal Church in Denton, Texas.

In addition to a large quantity of secondary sources that analyze Lewis's literature, his books have inspired at least three theatrical plays. *Shadowlands,* the story of C.S. Lewis's love and marriage to Joy Davidman has been filmed twice, once by the BBC with Joss Ackland and Clare Bloom in the leading roles (1985) and once in a Hollywood version starring Anthony Hopkins and Debra Winger (1993). Both versions have their artistic and biographical strengths and weaknesses.

Dramatist Mark St. Germain penned *Freud's Last Session,* a clever play about an imaginary tête-à-tête between Lewis and a weathered Sigmund Freud shortly before the latter's death in London in 1939.[12]

As this book manuscript was approaching its final form, actor David Payne began touring the United States and Great Britain with the solo performance *My Life's Journey: An Evening with C.S. Lewis* where "Lewis" sits in his wing chair with a pot of tea and tells amusing anecdotes as he reflects on various aspects of life and faith.

Filmed versions of some of *The Chronicles of Narnia* have introduced a new generation to Aslan and the other magical figures of Narnia.

British Prime Minister Winston Churchill wanted to honor Lewis as a Commander of the Most Excellent Order of the British Empire (CBE) in 1947, but Lewis declined, not wanting to lend his support to any specific political party or ideology.

Lewis was portrayed on the cover of *Time* magazine on September 8, 1947 as "the apostle to the skeptics." Lewis was generally not so keen on modern journalism and commented on the article in a letter to a pen pal:

> The review is of course a tissue of muddles and direct falsehoods – I don't say 'lies' because the people who write such things are not really capable of lying. I mean to lie = to say what you know to be untrue. But to know this, and to have the very idea of truth and falsehood in your head, presupposes a clarity of mind which they haven't got. ... To call them liars would be as

[12] A filmed version is available on YouTube: <https://www.youtube.com/watch?v=keuKx_mA3bk>.

> undeserved a compliment as to say that a dog was bad at arithmetic.[13]

As Lewis grew in popularity with a broad public, he was often the target of unfair criticism from within the world of British academia. Much of the criticism focused on Lewis's theology. He was a conservative Christian at a time when logical positivism was the dominant philosophy at British universities. He believed in the supernatural when theologians like Rudolf Bultmann questioned – and even rejected – belief in miracles and called the church to demythologize the Bible and the Christian faith.

Atheist philosopher Ayn Rand scribbled in the margins of her copy of *The Abolition of Man* that Lewis was an "abysmal bastard," a "monstrosity," a "cheap, awful, miserable, touchy, social-metaphysical mediocrity," a "pickpocket of concepts," and a "God-damn, beaten mystic."[14]

> C.S. Lewis lived through a period in English life when the intellectuals and the esthetes were anti-Christian and certainly highly critical of the role of the church. But the temper of that disparagement was not like that of the American scene. England never suffered the indignity of H.L. Mencken and the Scopes trial. The extremes were muted. Besides, the evangelical Christian movements in England were and are of very long standing, and they never quite produced the popular forms of fundamentalism and anti-intellectualism that America spawned ... Instead there was an accelerated erosion of that gentle kind of English social and political humanism that assimilated Christianity into an ordered society, a society characterized by mutual interdependence and public service.[15]

Lewis was also the target of criticism from within the literary establishment. He was not so interested in modern English literature. He was well aware of the trends in contemporary literary theory where one attempted to psychoanalyze a writer from his or her works, but thought that there was no sense in trying to show *why* a writer was wrong if one

---

[13] Personal letter to Mary Willis Shelburne dated February 8, 1956 in *Lady*, p. 51. Also in *Letters3*, p. 702.

[14] Robert Mayhew, ed. *Ayn Rand's Marginalia: Her Critical Comments on the Writings of over 20 Authors* (Second Renaissance Press, 1998).

[15] Paul L. Holmer, *C.S. Lewis: The Shape of His Faith and Thought* (New York: Harper & Row, 1976), p. 92.

had not first established *that* he or she was wrong.[16] Lewis called the tendency to dismiss classical works of literature "chronological snobbery" – the idea that the innovative, new and avant-garde should be prioritized over works which have stood the test of time.

> A man who has lived in many places is not likely to be deceived by the local errors of his native village; the scholar who has lived in many times is therefore in some degree immune from the great cataract of nonsense that pours from the press and the microphone of his own age.[17]

Lewis believed that one should read at least one old book for every new book one reads.

> It's a good rule after reading a new book never to allow yourself another new one till you have read an old one in between. If that is too much for you, you should at least read one old one to three new ones. ... Every age has its own outlook. It is especially good for seeing certain truths and especially liable to make certain mistakes. We all therefore need the books that will correct the characteristic mistakes of our own period. ... None of us can fully escape this blindness, but we shall certainly increase it, and weaken our guard against it, if we read only modern books. ... The only palliative is to keep the clean sea breeze of the centuries blowing through our minds and this can only be done by reading old books.[18]

He presented the same idea in a creative manner in *The Screwtape Letters*, where the demon Screwtape instructs his disciple Wormwood in the art of temptation.

> Only the learned read old books and we have now so dealt with the learned that they are of all men the least likely to acquire wisdom by doing so. We have done this by inculcating The Historical Point of View. The Historical Point of View, put briefly, means that when a learned man is presented with any statement in an ancient author, the one question he never asks is whether it is true. He asks who influenced the ancient writer,

---

[16] C.S. Lewis,"Bulverism" in *Dock+*, p. 273. Also in *EC*, p. 588.

[17] C.S. Lewis, "Learning in War Time" in *WoG*, pp. 58–59. Also in *EC*, p. 584.

[18] C.S. Lewis, "On the Reading of Old Books" in *1&2T*, pp. 27–28. Also in *Dock+*, p. 201–202 and *EC*, p. 439.

> and how far the statement is consistent with what he said in other books, and what phase in the writer's development, or in the general history of thought it illustrates, and how it affected later writers, and how often it has been misunderstood (specially by the learned man's own colleagues) and what the general course of criticism on it has been for the last ten years, and what is the 'present state of the question'. To regard the ancient writer as a possible source of knowledge – to anticipate that what he said could possibly modify your thoughts or your behaviour – this would be rejected as unutterably simple-minded. And since we cannot deceive the whole human race all the time, it is most important thus to cut every generation off from all others...[19]

The devil's reluctance to allow people to discover the wisdom to be found in old books is an idea that fits exceptionally well with Lewis's distaste for modernist literature.

Although T.S. Eliot was another star in the literary firmament who made a parallel journey to Christian faith, Eliot and Lewis never became friends. Lewis simply lacked appreciation for the modernist literature Eliot was writing. Lewis preferred fantasy, fairy tales and older medieval and renaissance literature. Lewis's friend and biographer Roger Lancelyn Green described Lewis's frustration over the fact that no editor would publish his poems. He and his friends decided to launch a "literary dragonade" where they parodied Eliot and other modernist poets by penning "pseudoeliotic" poems which they then sent to bastions of modernist literature like the journals *Dial* and *Criterion* (where Eliot was editor). Even so, they failed to dupe the editors.[20] Much later Lewis criticized Eliot and Pound in "Poetry" in *Experiment in Criticism.* He claims that no one reads their poems, but even if someone against all odds might do so, they would still come up with wildly differing interpretations. The reader is left with "what the poem means to me", a precursor to some postmodern theories within literary criticism.

Then there's the possibility that some of the criticism directed against Lewis is based on jealousy and other irrational reasons. Petty rivalries

[19] *Screwtape*, letter 27, pp. 139–140.

[20] Roger Lancelyn Green and Walter Hooper, *C.S. Lewis: A Biography* (Orlando: Harcourt Harvest, 1976, 1994), p. 89. Lewis describes this in his diary *All my Road Before Me: The Diary of C.S. Lewis, 1922–1927*. Walter Hooper, ed. (London: HarperCollins, 1991), pp. 410–414.

among academics at Oxford and Cambridge, who needed to compete against each other for highly-prized professorial chairs, found fuel for their fire in the fact that Lewis was better known for popular works than for his serious academic research.

Lewis's friend J.R.R. Tolkien explains:

> In Oxford, you are forgiven for writing only two kinds of books. You may write books on your own subject whatever that is, literature, or science, or history. And you may write detective stories because all dons at some time get the flu, and they have to have something to read in bed. But what you are not forgiven is writing popular works, such as Jack did on theology, and especially if they win international success as his did.[21]

In certain academic circles in Great Britain Lewis is still unpopular. Few doctoral dissertations on Lewis have been defended at British universities. Likewise, Lewis's popularity among evangelicals is certainly surprising considering his views on a number of hot button issues:

> There are in his work unlikely opinions that surprise even his most devoted readers: that young lovers should live together without marriage if the alternative is to break their marriage vows; that anti-abortion laws may be very ill-advised; that obscenity laws are useless at best, as are anti-sodomy laws; that a truly Christian economic order would have more than a small bit of socialism in it; that Darwin is useful ...; and that Freud has something to teach us, though a good deal less than he thought.[22]

Lewis was neither a professional theologian nor a philosopher. He was an autodidact – and amazingly well-read – within a vast range of disciplines. He wanted to write popular books and help normal people come to a deeper understanding of their faith. He thought that "real" theologians had done such a poor job of it that he felt challenged to have a go at it.

> What makes some theological works like sawdust to me is the way the authors can go on discussing how far certain positions are adjustable to contemporary thought, or beneficial in relation to social problems, or 'have a future' before them, but never

[21] Quoted in David Mills, *The Pilgrim's Guide: C.S. Lewis and the Art of Witness* (Grand Rapids: Eerdmans, 1998), p. 7.

[22] James Como, *Branches to Heaven: The Genuises of C.S. Lewis* (Dallas: Spence, 1998), p. 115.

> squarely ask what grounds we have for supposing them to be true accounts of any objective reality. As if we were trying to make rather than to learn.[23]

Paul Holmer comments on Lewis's attitude to books on theology.

> He saw that he did not need theories, second-level theologies, and general views, the sort of thing that the sophisticated world of letters and science mostly produces. He did not altogether disparage them, but he found that their role was severely limited. That recognition must have been momentous. It certainly gave his literature a different focus and power.[24]

Robert MacSwain reflects on the criticism directed against Lewis for not being a real theologian:

> Yes, of course it is ludicrous to compare Lewis's *Mere Christianity* to Barth's *Church Dogmatics* – but perhaps it is equally ludicrous to let Barth define the character of theology.[25]

> [It is] fair to ask whether the importance of a figure is best judged by their standing in the academy or by their influence outside of it. [A]cademic theology ignores Lewis at its peril. He is [...] almost certainly the most influential religious author of the twentieth century, in English or any other language. For good or ill, literally millions of people have had their understanding of Christianity decisively shaped by his writings... [F]or good or ill – he is too important to be ignored.[26]

MacSwain continues:

> [A]cademic theology can ill afford to disregard C.S. Lewis. If only because he is so influential, scholars and students need to be familiar with the specific content of his many books in order to know (and if necessary counter or correct) his impact on the masses. But, more positively, it is at least possible that Lewis – despite not being an academic theologian himself – might have

---

[23] *Malcolm*, ch. 19, p. 104.

[24] Holmer, p. 110.

[25] Robert MacSwain and Michael Ward, ed., *The Cambridge Companion to C.S. Lewis* (Cambridge: Cambridge University Press, 2010), p. 8.

[26] Ibid, pp. 2–3.

> something to teach academic theologians about their own subject.[27]
>
> In its commendable quest for disciplinary purity and intellectual integrity, academic theology is actually in great danger of sealing itself within a very small, self-enclosed echo chamber in which experts talk to other experts while losing all contact with the outside world. Meanwhile, Lewis continues to sell millions of books a year and to shape the religious faith of thousands.[28]

Pope Gregory the Great (c. 540 – 604) compared scripture to a "a river that is both shallow and deep, in which both a lamb can wade and an elephant can swim."[29] Gregory's point is that one can read the Bible on several levels, for both pious and academic purposes. The same can also be said of Lewis. Regardless of whether you are an academic theologian or just a person who loves a good story – whether you're a Christian, a seeker or something else – there's something in Lewis for you.

It is difficult to place Lewis in a box. No label succeeds in covering all the many facets of his personality and work. Holmer concludes: "He is a moralist without a definitive moral thesis, a theologian without being a schoolish type, a critic without having quite a critical theory."[30]

Overview

Through many years of public teaching and informal discussions with people about C.S. Lewis, it is my unscientific conclusion that most people never get beyond Narnia. *The Chronicles of Narnia* are naturally an outstanding introduction to Lewis, but what a shame if that's all a person ever reads of this genius. After all, Aslan only figures in seven out of more than 40 books Lewis wrote in his lifetime! It's true that many people I meet have also read *Mere Christianity*. The Lord has even used that book to lead some of the people I've met to faith in Christ. Some have read *The Screwtape Letters* or *Miracles* or *The Problem of Pain*, but very few have ever mined the riches that are to be found in Lewis's collected essays or had their longing for the numinous stirred by hauntingly brilliant *Dymer* and *The Pilgrim's Regress*. It is my desire in this book to show that Lewis is more

[27] Ibid, p. 4.

[28] Ibid, p. 4.

[29] Gregory the Great, *Moralia*, 4; *MPL* LXXV, 16.

[30] Holmer, p. 63.

than just Narnia. As such, the familiar tales of Aslan, Caspian and the Pevensie children are often present in what follows, albeit in supporting roles as imaginative illustrations of the theological and philosophical arguments Lewis lays out elsewhere in his considerable corpus.

In the next chapter I will present a short biographical sketch. The details of Lewis's life are well known to many readers.[31] In chapter three I begin to examine some of the important themes in Lewis's works with a look at his apologetic method. Here I will use two examples from his books: his version of the moral argument for the existence of God and the famous "Lord, liar, lunatic" defense of the divinity of Christ. In chapter four I will highlight what I believe to be the most important theme in Lewis's books – the sensation of joy or longing as a road marker pointing the way to God. I subsequently present in chapter five an analysis of Lewis's view of the Bible as the word of God – ideas which both surprise and annoy many readers. In chapter six I attempt to summarize and analyze Lewis's defense of miracles against Hume's famous critique. The focus in chapter seven is the problem of pain – both as an abstract question and as an issue of personal suffering which he processed in the book *A Grief Observed*. Lewis's thoughts on hell were groundbreaking for his day and have served as an inspiration for many theologians and philosophers of religion since then. I will analyze his contributions to this discussion in chapter eight. Finally, I will round out our examination of Lewis in chapter nine with some of his reflections on the Christian life, including his thoughts on doubt and faith, prayer, sanctification and calling.

There are certain risks with a book *about* C.S. Lewis such as this. First is the dual risk of relying too heavily on quotes from Lewis on the one hand or simply restating anecdotes with a mediocrity of language and imagery that leaves much to be desired on the other. This book is amply spiced with quotes from Lewis. And for good reason. Lewis was a genius of English prose and his communication is rich in clever and memorable images. But I also hope to contribute with my own analysis. A second risk is that people who have never read the primary sources will simply use a book like this to pick the best and leave the rest. The temptation is then to read this book and neglect Lewis. Naturally I hope that this book will serve as an appetizer – that readers would be filled with a hunger to read

[31] Readers who are already well acquainted with Lewis's life story may skip chapter two and move on to chapter three. Those who on the other hand wish to delve deeper have a wide range of biographies to choose from. See the annotated bibliography at the end of this book.

Lewis's own books and discover for themselves the wide variety of taste experiences: sweet and salty, fiction, apologetics, literary criticism and much more. As an aid to first-time Lewis readers, I have enclosed at the end of this book a suggested reading plan for sections from eight different Lewis books with questions for personal reflection or discussion in a small group setting.

I sometimes meet Christians who claim that we don't need theology. They say that we only need to read the Bible and let God speak to us directly. Theology is just human opinions (in their opinion). On occasions when I can be bothered to give an answer at all, I sometimes explain that theology is like a roadmap.[32] Imagine you come to a foreign city – let's say Tokyo. Certainly, you can just wander about at random and have many fascinating and memorable experiences. But if you have a map and understand where the most important sites are located, as well as the main streets and landmarks, then you can get so much more out of your visit in that foreign city. That's the way it is with theology. Of course, God can speak directly to us when we read the Bible, but it was written at a time and in a culture that are very foreign to us. With the help of theology we can understand more of how things relate to each other and get so much more out of our Bible reading. It is my hope that this book will also act as a roadmap to show how the various parts of Lewis's life and works relate to each other to form a whole. Just like studying a map of Tokyo is no substitute for visiting that living city, this book should not come as a surrogate for a personal encounter with Lewis's books.

---

[32] I developed this illustration on my own and discovered only later that Lewis also saw this similarity between theology and a personal relationship with the living God. *Great minds think alike*, I suppose ... *MC*, fourth book, ch. 1, p. 84.

"I can't abide the idea that a man's books should be 'set in their biographical context' and if I had some rare information about the private life of Shakespeare or Dante I'd throw it in the fire, tell no one, and re-read their works."[1]

[1] Personal letter to Roy W. Harrington dated January 19, 1948 in *Letters2*, p. 831.

The Most Dejected and Reluctant Convert: A Biographical Sketch

Lewis was born in 1898 in Belfast in Northern Ireland to a family that included a number of prominent clergymen and even a bishop. Lewis's parents Albert and Flora were nominal Christians – they were regular church attenders, but faith played no prominent role in their daily lives. Lewis's father Albert was a solicitor (lawyer) and his mother had studied mathematics at university. She died of cancer when Jack, as Lewis called himself, was only nine years old. He recounts how he had prayed for her recovery, but how she died all the same. Albert Lewis was a typical man of the British upper middle class of that time – he couldn't bring himself to show his feelings and didn't know how to communicate in any meaningful way with his sons Jack and older brother Warnie.

Not knowing how to raise the boys on his own, Albert sent the boys off to boarding schools in England. Jack went to four different schools between 1908 and 1914 and presented bleak pictures of these schools in his autobiography. He portrayed them as cruel places filled with bullying, hazing and sexual abuse. In fact he gave one school the code name "Belsen" after the Bergen-Belsen concentration camp.[2]

Lewis was a diligent student. According to one hagiographic biographer Jack could read both Greek and Latin by the time he turned six.[3] Before he turned ten he is said to have read Milton's *Paradise Lost.*

It is ironic that C.S. Lewis, a masterful communicator, and his father Albert, whose rhetorical skills were well known in court, had difficulty in communicating with each other. Jack didn't think his father ever fully recovered from the loss of his wife. Nor did Jack think he was ever quite good enough in his father's eyes, and recounted how even the most trivial offenses could lead his father to hold long, critical, impromptu lectures over the boys. Although he had the opportunity to visit Jack for what could have been the last time when Jack left to serve in the great war,

---

[2] *Surprised*, ch. 2.

[3] Walter Hooper, *Through Joy and Beyond: A Pictorial Biography of C.S. Lewis* (New York: Macmillan, 1982), p. 16. According to George Sayer, on the other hand, Lewis's grades in Greek and Latin were nothing special. George Sayer, *Jack: A Life of C.S. Lewis* (New York: Harper & Row, 1998; Wheaton: Crossway, 1994), p. 75.

Albert chose to stay at home. Their relationship continued to be strained until Albert's death in 1929.

Lewis the atheist

From 1914 to 1917 Jack studied under Albert's old tutor W.T. Kirkpatrick, who was called "The Great Knock" by his students. The young Lewis expected an emotionally distant man much like his father, but was pleasantly surprised when he met Kirkpatrick the first time. The Great Knock demanded a strict logical rigor even in the most trivial of questions. Lewis recounts how in his attempts at small talk with Kirkpatrick he made the off-handed comment that the landscape was much wilder than he had expected. Kirkpatrick challenged him and demanded to know how Lewis defined *wild* and what grounds he had to expect anything at all about the local landscape since Lewis had never been in that part of England and had never undertaken any study of the matter. Lewis was in heaven![4]

Three years with Kirkpatrick as an intellectual sparring partner made an enormous impact on the malleable young Lewis. By this time Lewis had studied so much classical literature that he says he was even *thinking* in Greek.[5] Kirkpatrick wrote in letters to Albert Lewis on September 16, 1915 that "He is the most brilliant translator of Greek plays I have ever met" and on March 28, 1915 that "He has read more classics than any boy I ever had – or indeed I might add than any I ever heard of."[6]

One of the many ways in which Kirkpatrick impacted Lewis was through his atheism. Jack had already begun to doubt the goodness of God after the death of his mother. Now he had a much-admired mentor who was an outspoken atheist. Jack wrote to his lifelong friend Arthur Greeves:

> I think that I believe in no religion. There is absolutely no proof for any of them, and from a philosophical standpoint Christianity is not even the best. All religions, that is, all mythologies to give them their proper name are merely man's own invention – Christ as much as Loki. ... Superstition of course in every age has held the common people, but in every

---

[4] Lewis relays this first meeting in chapter 9 of *Surprised by Joy.*

[5] *Surprised,* ch. 9.

[6] Green and Hooper, pp. 28, 46.

> age the educated and thinking ones have stood outside it, though usually outwardly conceding to it for convenience.[7]

Although Lewis wanted to embrace the strict empiricism that was growing in influence in English universities at that time, he discovered that it left him existentially unsatisfied. There was no room for beauty or imagination. He wrote: "Nearly all that I loved I believed to be imaginary; nearly all that I believed to be real I thought grim and meaningless."[8]

The road to faith

Jack's studies at Oxford were put on hold once he was called into the army during the great war. He was eventually wounded by shrapnel during a battle in northern France. Lewis had a friend and roommate at Oxford named Edward F.C. "Paddy" Moore. They had promised each other that Paddy would care for Albert Lewis if Jack were to die in battle, and that Lewis would care for Paddy's mother and younger sister in the event of Paddy's death.[9]

Paddy was killed in battle. His then 45-year-old mother Mrs. Moore moved in with the 18-year-old Jack Lewis. Her daughter Maureen Moore was then 11 years old. Biographers have different takes on the nature of Lewis's relationship with Mrs. Moore. Some view her as a tedious old woman who was a wearisome burden on Lewis and whose nagging was a constant source of irritation and distraction for Lewis's important studies and work.[10] They say that Lewis was only fulfilling his

---

[7] Personal letter to Arthur Greeves dated October 12, 1916 in *They Stand Together: The Letters of C.S. Lewis to Arthur Greeves (1914–1963)* (New York: Macmillan, 1979), p. 135. Also in *Letters1*, pp. 230–231.

[8] *Surprised*, ch. 11, p. 170.

[9] Some researchers have called into question this story. "The two-way promise would not have made any sense. C.S. Lewis's father Albert, a successful Belfast attorney, was a widower with two sons and many other relatives. He was moody, eccentric, and set in his ways. He certainly would not have wanted a young stranger with a dependent mother and sister in tow 'rescuing' him. The idea is ridiculous, and C.S. Lewis would not have entertained it for a moment." (Lindskoog 2001, p. 63). Lindskoog claims that the "myth" of the mutual promise was created by Walter Hooper (p. 64).

[10] Anne Arnot, *The Secret Country of C.S. Lewis* (London: Hodder & Stoughton, 1974) p. 78; William Griffin, *Clive Staples Lewis: A Dramatic Life* (San Francisco: Harper & Row, 1986), p. 11. Warnie wrote about Mrs. Moore: "She was a woman of very limited mind, and notably domineering and possessive by temperament. She cut down to a minimum his visits to his father, interfered constantly with his work, and imposed upon him a heavy burden of minor domestic tasks." (W.H. Lewis, "Memoir of C.S. Lewis" in *LettersWHL*, pp. 32–33).

commitment to his fallen comrade and Mrs. Moore. Other writers claim that Lewis was in love with Mrs. Moore and that they had a sexual relationship in spite of their 27-year age difference.[11] Jack never spoke to his father about this relationship – and only rarely to his friends.[12]

Jack and Warnie, along with Mrs. Moore and Maureen, bought the house known as The Kilns on the outskirts of Oxford, where they lived together for 30 years. For some reason only Mrs. Moore's name was registered as legal owner of the house in spite of the fact that the Lewis brothers had also contributed financially to the purchase. It was clear however that Jack and Warnie would be allowed to live in the house as long as they wished or as long as they lived. The house would subsequently go to Maureen as Mrs. Moore's only heir.

British universities at that time had a rigorous entrance exam. Lewis failed the mathematics section of the test twice before it was finally waived for former soldiers. Lewis studied at University College, the oldest of Oxford's thirty colleges, and graduated with highest marks in Greek and Latin classics, as well as English literature and philosophy.

During the period between the two world wars Oxford and Cambridge were still dominated by idealism, a philosophical direction with roots in nineteenth-century Hegelianism where ultimate reality was not the physical universe, but spirit. But logical positivism was gaining ground. When Lewis returned from the war and began his studies, he was in many ways a child of his times. Starting with a closed system where the laws of nature function consistently without any interference from external powers or agents, Lewis wanted to be strictly logical and apply positivism's narrow limitations to both what can be known and how knowledge could even possible at all.

---

[11] Among others Lindskoog 2001; Sayer 1999; David C. Downing, *Into the Wardrobe: C.S. Lewis and the Narnia Chronicles* (San Francisco: Wiley / Jossey-Bass, 2006), p. 14; A.N. Wilson, *C.S. Lewis: A Biography* (New York: W.W. Norton, 1990, 2002), p. 58; Alister McGrath, *C.S. Lewis – A Life: Eccentric Genius, Reluctant Prophet* (Wheaton: Tyndale House, 2013). Walter Hooper changed position from first believing that their relationship was that of mother and son (Green and Hooper, p. 62) to a later admission that their relationship was probably sexual.

[12] Jack's relationship with Mrs. Moore has almost Freudian and oedipal overtones. Lewis, who lost his mother at a young age found a replacement who eventually also became his mistress. This relationship led to further tensions between Jack and his father, who called the relationship an affair and expressed his displeasure over the fact that Mrs. Moore was old enough to be Jack's mother. Albert was afraid that she was even using him financially. Lindskoog 2001, p. 64.

One author whose books Lewis admired was George MacDonald, who was a Christian. Not only that, Lewis wrote: "All the books were beginning to turn against me".[13] Authors like Spenser, Milton and Samuel Johnson spoke to Lewis's imagination much more than writers like Shaw, Wells, Mill and Voltaire who shared Lewis's skeptical worldview. "The upshot of it all could nearly be expressed in a perversion of Roland's great line in the *Chanson – Christians are wrong, but all the rest are bores.*"[14] Lewis discovered to his great chagrin that not only were all his favorite writers Christians, many of his friends in Oxford were also believers. Nevill Coghill ("clearly the most intelligent and best-informed man in that class")[15] was a Christian. So was Hugo Dyson, an Anglican and J.R.R. Tolkien, who was a Roman Catholic. All his best friends and those he most admired were Christians. Lewis wrote that all this Christian influence made him feel like "a man of snow at long last beginning to melt."[16]

There were several steps to Lewis's conversion. He first abandoned his atheism in favor of a form of idealism with its belief in an absolute spirit or world soul as the ground of all being. In 1929 he later accepted the existence of God and became a theist. He wrote about this event in his diary: "I gave in, and admitted that God was God, and knelt and prayed: perhaps, that night, the most dejected and reluctant convert in all England,"[17] but at this stage his conversion was still only "to Theism, pure and simple, not to Christianity. I knew nothing yet about the Incarnation. The God to whom I surrendered was sheerly nonhuman."[18]

In his autobiography *Surprised by Joy* Lewis focused primarily on his initial conversion to theism and not on his subsequent conversion to Christian faith in 1931. His Christian commitment almost comes across like an anticlimax in the book.

He described the long process in several letters to his childhood friend Arthur Greeves. He wrote on January 9, 1930, "In spite of all my recent changes of view, I am still inclined to think that you can only get what *you* call 'Christ' out of the Gospels by picking & choosing, & slurring

---

[13] *Surprised*, ch. 14, p. 213.

[14] Ibid, ch. 14, p. 214.

[15] Ibid, ch. 14, p. 212.

[16] Ibid, ch. 14, p. 225.

[17] Ibid, ch. 14, p. 229.

[18] Ibid, ch. 15, p. 230.

over a good deal."[19] Several months later he wrote to A.K. Hamilton Jenkin that what he believed in "is not precisely Christianity, though it may turn out that way in the end."[20] At this time Lewis also began attending services at the college chapel.

The great change came during the fall of 1931. On September 19 Lewis went on a long walk with Tolkien and Hugo Dyson. They discussed until the wee hours of the morning how the stories of Jesus' incarnation and resurrection were similar or dissimilar to the mythological stories of other dying and rising gods. Dyson pointed out that "Christianity works for the believer. The believer is put at peace and freed from his sins."[21]

On September 28, 1931 the Lewis brothers rode to Whipsnade Zoo on Warnie's motorcycle with Jack in the sidecar. He writes, "When we set out I did not believe that Jesus Christ is the Son of God, and when we reached the zoo I did."[22] Several days later he wrote to Greeves, "I have just passed from believing in God to definitely believing in Christ – in Christianity. … My long night walk with Dyson and Tolkien had a good deal to do with it."[23]

In his acclaimed Lewis biography, Alister McGrath makes a case for a revised chronology of the events leading up to Lewis's conversion to Christian faith. Based on journals and letters that are now available to researchers, McGrath claims that Lewis became a theist in 1930, not 1929 as Lewis himself wrote in *Surprised by Joy*. McGrath does not call into question the process of Lewis's conversion, only its chronology.[24]

Lewis the Christian

Lewis had published two collections of poems before he embraced faith in Christ. His first book after his conversion was *The Pilgrim's Regress,* an allegory of his own journey to faith that is something of an homage to Bunyan's classic *Pilgrim's Progress.*

---

[19] Personal letter to Arthur Greeves dated January 9, 1930 in *They Stand Together*, pp. 330–331. Also in *Letters1*, p. 862.

[20] Personal letter to A.K. Hamilton Jenkin dated March 21, 1930 in *Letters1*, p. 887.

[21] Sayer, p. 226.

[22] *Surprised*, ch. 15, p. 237.

[23] Personal letter to Arthur Greeves dated October 1, 1931 in *They Stand Together*, p. 425. Also in *Letters1*, p. 974.

[24] Alister McGrath, "The Date of Lewis's Conversion: A Reconsideration" in McGrath 2013, ch. 6.

Lewis's literary breakthrough came with the publication of *The Screwtape Letters* in 1942. The book is a collection of clever letters from an older demon to his chthonic disciple on the art of tempting humans.

Lewis admitted much later in an interview with *Decision* magazine that he did not enjoy writing *The Screwtape Letters.*

> They were dry and gritty going. At the time, I was thinking of objections to the Christian life, and decided to put them into the form, 'That's what the devil would say.' But making goods 'bad' and bads 'good' gets to be fatiguing.[25]

Based on the popularity of *The Screwtape Letters,* Lewis was asked to give a series of talks about the Christian faith on BBC radio. The manuscripts for these broadcast talks were subsequently published as three short books that were eventually merged to form *Mere Christianity.* About this time Lewis also started the famous Oxford University Socratic Club – a forum where Christians, agnostics and atheists like A.J. Ayer could meet to discuss and debate various ideas. Lewis served as the club's chair for 22 years.

The 1940s were a prolific time in Lewis's life. In addition to *Mere Christianity* and *The Screwtape Letters,* he wrote some of his most important apologetic works during this decade, including *The Problem of Pain* (1940), *The Abolition of Man* (1943), *The Great Divorce* (1946) and *Miracles* (1947).

In the fall of 2015 news broke that Lewis had collaborated with the British MI6 during the second world war. Germany had invaded Denmark and Norway on April 9, 1940. At that time Iceland was still a Danish territory.[26] In order to prevent Germany from gaining control of Iceland as a potential launching pad for attacks against North America, Britain occupied Iceland on May 10, 1940. The British "Joint Broadcasting Committee," an unknown entity whose primary task seems to have been propaganda, recorded a lecture in which Lewis spoke on "The Norse Spirit in English Literature." The lecture, which was on two 78-RPM phonographs, was distributed in Iceland in order to create good will among the Icelanders towards the British occupation. Lewis never spoke of this, but mentioned in a letter to Arthur Greeves on May 25, 1940 that he had for the first time in his life heard a recording of his own voice. Until now Lewis researchers have assumed that Lewis was speaking of some test recordings for the broadcast talks that became *Mere Christianity.* At the

---

[25] C.S. Lewis, "Cross-Examination" in *Dock+,* p. 263. Also in *EC,* p. 555.

[26] Iceland gained its independence from Denmark on June 17, 1944.

moment of writing, only one copy of one of the original albums has surfaced. It was purchased from Iceland on eBay by an American Lewis researcher and collector.[27]

During the 1930s and 40s, an informal gathering of friends began to revolve around Lewis. They were authors and cultural profiles from Oxford, many of whom were also Christians. They were called "The Inklings." Group regulars included J.R.R. Tolkien and his son Christopher, C.S. Lewis and his brother Warnie, Owen Barfield, Charles Williams, Roger Lancelyn Green, Hugo Dyson, Nevill Coghill and others. They met every Tuesday for lunch at The Eagle and Child, a pub where they discussed books and authors, and where members could read drafts of their latest works for their friends – who sometimes responded with scathing critique. Among other famous works, parts of both *The Lord of the Rings* and *The Chronicles of Narnia* had their first public hearings here.

Joy at the end of the road

Joy Davidman Gresham was a secularized American Jew, a former atheist and communist who came to faith with the help of Lewis's books. She had a sharp intellect and was free-spoken. She had begun to study at university as a 14-year-old and had completed her master's degree by the age of 20. It is said that she had a photographic memory. She was also an author with several books to her credit.

During the fall of 1952 Davidman came to England for an extended visit. Lewis and Davidman met during this first visit. Joy later returned to England with her two sons in December 1953 once her divorce from an abusive husband was finalized.

Warnie wrote: "For Jack the attraction was at first undoubtedly intellectual. Joy was the only woman whom he had met … who had a brain which matched his own in suppleness, in width of interest, and in analytical grasp, and above all in humor and a sense of fun."[28] According to biographer Alister McGrath, no one in Jack's inner circle liked Joy. He portrays her as a scheming gold digger who sought to seduce Lewis and thereby secure a future for herself and her boys through Lewis's fame and fortune.[29]

---

[27] Harry Lee Poe, "C.S. Lewis was a Secret Government Agent" *Christianity Today* (December 10, 2015).

[28] W.H. Lewis, "Memoir of C.S. Lewis" in *LettersWHL*, p. 43.

[29] McGrath 2013, p. 330.

On April 23, 1956 Davidman wedded Lewis in a marriage of convenience so that Joy and her sons would have the right to remain in England. Their relationship continued to grow, but when Joy's diagnosis of cancer became clear, they decided to marry in the sight of God with a ceremony at Joy's hospital bed on March 27, 1957. The officiating minister, Reverend Peter Bide, also prayed for Joy's healing, and her cancer subsequently went into remission for several years. Joy and the boys moved in with Jack and Warnie at The Kilns.

The cancer eventually returned and Joy passed away on July 13, 1960 at the age of 45. Lewis was devastated and wrote *A Grief Observed*, which was originally published under the *nom de plume* N.W. Clerk. One of Lewis's friends is said to have read the book and thought that Jack might benefit from it and gave him a copy![30]

Not long after Joy's death, Lewis's own health began to fail. He suffered from kidney infection that led to blood poisoning. He missed the whole fall term 1962 at Cambridge due to poor health. Although he eventually rallied from this problem, his general condition continued to fail. On July 15, 1963 he once again fell sick and was hospitalized. The next day he suffered a heart attack and fell into a coma, but revived the day after that. In due course he was able to return home, but was far too weak to be able to work. In November he was diagnosed with terminal kidney failure. He passed away on November 23, 1963, but his death was overshadowed by the assassination of President John F. Kennedy that same day. Another famous person also passed away that day, Aldous Huxley, author of *Brave New World* (1932).[31]

---

[30] Lindsley 2005, p. 60.

[31] The American philosopher Peter Kreeft has written a clever book about an imaginary meeting "on the other side" between the Christian Lewis, the secular humanist Kennedy and Huxley, who was interested in Eastern mysticism. Peter Kreeft, *Between Heaven and Hell* (Downers Grove: InterVarsity Press, 1982, 2008).

"Unsatisfactory answers do not become satisfactory by being tentative."[1]

"I believe in Christianity as I believe that the Sun has risen, not only because I see it, but because by it I see everything else."[2]

"We know, in fact, that believers are not cut off from unbelievers by any portentous inferiority of intelligence or any perverse refusal to think."[3]

---

[1] C.S. Lewis, "The Pain of Animals" in *Dock+*, p. 166. Also in *EC*, p. 192.

[2] C.S. Lewis, "Is Theology Poetry?" in *EC*, p. 21.

[3] C.S. Lewis, "On Obstinacy in Belief" in *EC*, p. 209.

Proclaiming Christianity Because It's True: Lewis's Apologetic Method

Apologetics is a branch of Christian theology dedicated to defending the truth claims of the Christian faith. The word comes from the Greek word *apologia,* a defense speech, like Socrates' famous apologia before being forced to drink the cup of hemlock. The word occurs 18 times in the New Testament, including 1 Peter 3:15 – "But in your hearts revere Christ as Lord. Always be prepared to give an answer to everyone who asks you *to give the reason* for the hope that you have." Apologists make use of logical arguments, archaeological discoveries, scientific theories,[4] ancient documents and more to show that it is reasonable to be a Christian.

In this chapter I shall present an introduction to Lewis's apologetic method. I will begin with some reflections over Lewis's view of the tension between reason and imagination. I shall then show a model that Lewis commonly uses in developing a line of thought. I will conclude the chapter by illustrating how he follows this model in two arguments: one for the existence of God and one for the deity of Christ.

Reason and imagination

There are two sides to Lewis's apologetic: reason and imagination. The imagination helps us embrace and personalize a train of thought. We can identify with another person's experiences, thoughts and situations. Imagination can strengthen the impression made by the rational argument – not by making the argument more reasonable, but by applying it to our lives and making it existentially relevant. One could compare Lewis's rational apologetic with a foundation upon which one can build a house. The imaginative side of his apologetic, on the other hand, is more like the preparatory work one does in the garden before planting a tree.

---

[4] As a "humanities" guy, Lewis was critical of building an apologetic on scientific theories. "If we try to base our apologetic on some recent development in science, we shall usually find that just as we have put the finishing touches to our argument science has changed its mind and quietly withdrawn the theory we have been using as our foundation stone." (C.S. Lewis, "Christian Apologetics" in *Dock+,* p. 92. Also in *EC,* p. 150). This is illustrated in the current trend for scientists to steer away from the Big Bang theory in favor of multiverse theories because of the Big Bang theory's implications for the Kalam cosmological argument.

It would nevertheless be misleading to make a clear demarcation and say that fictional works like *The Great Divorce, The Screwtape Letters, Till We Have Faces* and *The Chronicles of Narnia* are examples of Lewis's imaginative apologetic while books like *The Problem of Pain, Mere Christianity* and *Miracles* are examples of his rational apologetic. There is certainly a lot of good logic and theology in the fictional works and many humorous, imaginative illustrations in his non-fiction works.

Lewis researcher Michael Ward lists the metaphors for salvation Lewis uses in *Mere Christianity*:

> [B]ecoming a Christian (passing over from death to life) is like joining a campaign of sabotage, like falling at someone's feet or putting yourself in someone's hands, like taking on board fuel or food, like laying down your rebel arms and surrendering, saying sorry, laying yourself open, turning full speed astern; it is like killing part of yourself, like learning to walk or to write, like buying God a present with his own money; it is like a drowning man clutching at a rescuer's hand, like a tin soldier or a statue becoming alive, like waking after a long sleep, like getting close to someone or becoming infected, like dressing up or pretending or playing; it is like emerging from the womb or hatching from an egg; it is like a compass needle swinging to north, or a cottage being made into a palace, or a field being plowed and resown, or a horse turning into Pegasus, or a greenhouse roof becoming bright in the sunlight; it is like coming around from anesthetic, like coming in out from the wind, like going home.[5]

The dichotomy between reason and imagination has its roots in the Enlightenment with its artificial demarcation between faith and knowledge, where one can only know that which can be proven empirically or analytically. One can believe other claims if one is so moved, but it is only a matter of faith. This Enlightenment-inspired dividing line lies behind the claims sometimes made by atheists like Richard Dawkins that if Christians have good reasons for their beliefs then it is not faith.

---

[5] Michael Ward, "Escape to Wallaby Wood: Lewis's Depiction of Conversion" in Angus J.L. Menuge, ed., *Lightbearer in the Shadowlands: The Evangelistic Vision of C.S. Lewis* (Wheaton: Crossway, 1997), p. 151.

For Lewis there was no opposition between reason and imagination. He insisted that "[g]ood philosophy must exist, if for no other reason, because bad philosophy needs to be answered."[6] At the same time he also stated that "[a]ll our truth, or all but a few fragments, is won by metaphor." Lewis continued: "For me, reason is the natural organ of truth; but imagination is the organ of meaning. Imagination … is not the cause of truth, but its condition."[7]

In other words, one cannot grasp a word or concept without a mental picture. For Lewis, this was the role of the imagination: identifying and creating meaning by internalizing what would otherwise be an abstract truth. He saw reason and imagination as two inalienable parts of an important collaboration. Without the imagination, reason can easily become boring and limited. Without reason, imagination can give birth to an illusory chimera. Ward explains that both parts must work together. "Imagination can work without reason, though. It can produce meanings that are simply 'imaginary.'"[8]

He continues:

> There is just as much imaginatively discerned meaning in *Miracles* as in *Perelandra*, but of a different kind, put to a different end. Not only is imagination as necessary as reason in Lewis's approach; in a sense, imagination is more important than reason, because it comes first. Reason depends on imagination in a way that imagination doesn't depend on reason. And certainly, in Lewis's own path to faith, imagination came first.[9]

At the risk of promulgating a false dichotomy, one could say that Lewis's rational apologetic speaks to people with a modernist worldview while his imaginative apologetic is more appealing to postmodern people. However life is very rarely so easily divided into neat little categories. Ward comments,

> Life is more like a story than like an argument. And so, all things being equal, a storied presentation of Christianity will always be

---

[6] "Learning in War Time" in *WoG*, p. 58. Also in *EC*, p. 584.

[7] C.S. Lewis, "Bluspels and Flalansferes: A Semantic Nightmare" in *SLE*, p. 265.

[8] Michael Ward, "How Lewis Lit the Way to Better Apologetics" *Christianity Today* 57/9 (October 22, 2013): 36.

[9] Ward 2013, p. 36.

> more effective than an argued one. But, of course, things are not always equal, and therefore the church needs both methods.[10]

Even Lewis's non-fiction contains a lot of imagination and many creative illustrations that sometimes lead the reader to an "a-ha" experience where they resonate on a deep level with something Lewis has written. At the same time, some characters in Lewis's fiction embody ideas and arguments he has laid out in his non-fictional works.

Lewis's apologetic method

Criticism is sometimes voiced that Lewis presented simple answers to complex questions. The American actress Debra Winger read many of Lewis's books in preparing for her role as Lewis's wife Joy Davidman in the film *Shadowlands* (1993). She gave a speech at the Marion E. Wade Center[11] in connection with the release of the film.

> He may make difficult questions accessible. I don't think he makes the answers easy. I don't think he answers questions. I think he discusses them. ... He's in that school of discourse where his statements are not like books that are written by experts ... He's saying 'think about this.' That's why I think he opened [Christianity] to so many people. He wasn't dogmatic.[12]

Lewis researcher James Como has attempted to systematize Lewis's apologetic method.[13]

Lewis generally begins by making an observation or by asking a question he hopes to analyze. He then goes on to define all the relevant terms. This is an important step for Lewis, since he often points out how a word may be used equivocally or where its meaning may have been somewhat distorted. It is not at all unusual for Lewis himself to redefine words or give them a new dimension, as he does with the word *myth*.

A third step is for Lewis to reflect over several interpretations of the situation or possible answers to the question at hand. These answers

---

[10] Ward 2013, p. 36.

[11] The Marion E. Wade Center is a specialized research library located in Wheaton, Illinois dedicated to the works of seven British Christian writers: C.S. Lewis, J.R.R. Tolkien, Owen Barfield, G.K. Chesterton, George MacDonald, Dorothy L. Sayers and Charles Williams. <http://www.wheaton.edu/wadecenter/Welcome>.

[12] Quoted in Como 1998, p. 150.

[13] Como 1998, pp. 153–154.

sometimes take the form of logical or psychological objections that one could raise against the answer or perspective Lewis will propose. Once he has shown the weaknesses of these potential objections he presents his own hypothesis or preliminary conclusion as a fourth step. He continues by showing how his theory presents a better explanation of all the relevant phenomena than any of the alternatives. A final step comes when Lewis presents these ideas in an imaginative way.

Lewis rarely goes systematically through all six steps in one context. His reflections on a topic may be spread through many texts written over an extended period of time. Sometimes he places the imaginative presentation in the mouth of one of his fictional characters while the analysis is found in a more academic text.

Lewis's arguments for Christian faith were rarely deductive. His reasoning is generally abductive in nature, much like the form of logic employed by Thomas Aquinas and other scholastics. One postulates a cause based on observable effects. That is, when an observable phenomenon doesn't have an obvious cause or explanation, one may posit a cause or explanation that if true would show the phenomenon to be self-evident. It would then be reasonable to conclude that the explanation or cause is correct. For example, you wake up a sunny summer morning and discover that the whole lawn is wet. Why? There are several possible explanations: maybe it rained during the night while you were asleep. Or maybe some kids from the neighborhood turned on the hose and sprayed the whole lawn. Or maybe it was a miracle? If any of these things really happened then the wet lawn would be a natural result. The challenge of an abductive argument is trying to discern which hypothesis is the most reasonable based on the information we have access to.

Abductive reasoning differs from both deduction and induction. In deductive reasoning the conclusion must necessarily follow from the premises of the argument. If all the premises are true, then the conclusion must necessarily also be true. With inductive reasoning one draws probable conclusions based on observations made in a number of similar circumstances. Every time all the lawns in the neighborhood are wet at the same time it is because of rain. While it is logically possible that the kids in the neighborhood have been playing pranks all night, or that God or aliens have been crying so much that all the lawns became wet, these explanations are less reasonable than the assumption that it has rained during the night.

Lewis's arguments are often abductive in nature. He directs our attention to a phenomenon and presents a number of possible explanations or causes. He then dismisses each of these alternatives with the help of other observations and information until he is left with one explanation he believes to be the most reasonable interpretation of the phenomenon.

Faith and reason

An appealing aspect of Christian faith is its ability to encompass both rigorous thought and imagination. Christian faith is reasonable without having to limit itself to what can be proven empirically. This was an insight that Lewis came to after the revolutionary late-night walk and talk with Tolkien and Dyson.

Even before he embraced the Christian faith, Lewis always had a sense that there must be something more than just that which could be empirically verified – something beyond the bounds of reason. It is not irrational, but it is something that is sensed more through intuition than through logic. Lewis called it *the Numinous,* a concept he borrowed from the German theologian Rudolf Otto. Experience of the numinous or numen happens when a person becomes aware of something transcendent or possibly even divine. Encounters with the numinous can instill a sense of fear, but also one of fascination that makes the experience all the more tantalizing.

A complete philosophy must be able to give account of reality. Lewis believed that reality is both logically consistent and systematic.[14] Based on this conviction about the nature of reality, Lewis believed there are two criteria for assessing the truth of a statement: correspondence and coherence. Correspondence is when a statement accurately reflects an external reality. It describes the world as it really is and does not start with a person's subjective interpretation of the world. Coherence is a criterion one applies to a set of statements; based on the information we have available; the set of statements must be both logically consistent and comprehensive. One can also use these criteria to assess religious experiences and claims of divine revelations – both within Christianity and in comparison with the experiences, ideas and putative revelations of other religious traditions.

---

[14] *Miracles*, ch. 8, p. 75.

The purpose is not to determine whether a religious idea satisfies or "works", but to uncover the truth. Lewis once explained the importance of Christianity's truth claims to a group of clergymen:

> The great difficulty is to get modern audiences to realize that you are preaching Christianity solely and simply because you happen to think it *true*; they always suppose you are preaching it because you like it or think it good for society or something of that sort.[15]

Lewis believed that faith should be based on three foundational ideas. In the first place, faith should be built on good reasons and good reasoning. Secondly, these truths about God should not remain abstract facts about God; one should apply them to one's life through a personal commitment to the God in whom one has good reason to place one's trust. Thirdly, Lewis believed that faith calls for a certain perseverance in spite of shifting emotions and situations.

A well-known Christian youth organization once illustrated this with a train in all its publications.

Facts is written on the locomotive. Facts are objectively true; one doesn't even need to be cognizant of them or believe in them for them to be true. For Lewis, however, it is important to have knowledge about these facts. *Faith*, or personal commitment, is written on the tender or coal wagon. It is the fuel that makes the engine run. Without personal commitment, statements about God are reduced to irrelevant tidbits on the same level as the questions on Jeopardy.

Many years ago, I led an evangelistic Bible study group for university students in another country where I lived. We studied Jesus' encounters with various people in the gospels. One of the regulars in our group was a young man from the People's Republic of China. He had no prior knowledge about the Christian faith but realized that it was important since Christianity has had played such a key role in the development of

[15] "Christian Apologetics" in *Dock+*, pp. 90–91. Also in *EC*, p. 148.

Western culture. After several months I asked him what he thought about Jesus Christ. He answered, "I believe that Jesus is the savior of the world." But for him, it was merely the recognition of a fact that doesn't really have any personal relevance, much like saying that you believe that Iceland is a republic.

At the end of the train comes a coach with the word *feeling*. The train will work even without this coach, but it will be more meaningful if the locomotive has something to pull. In the same way, our feelings do not determine the truth of Christianity, but it is certainly nice to *feel* that God loves me, or that God hears my prayers. Many believers can look back at times when God has felt especially close – maybe at a large Christian conference, or a church service with moving music and anointed teaching. Just as these positive religious experiences do not prove the truth of the Christian faith, the absence of such feelings does not mean that faith in Christ is misdirected. Members of the Church of Jesus Christ of Latter-day Saints (the Mormons), have subjective religious experience as the only support for the unique aspects of their faith. Based on a text from the last chapter in the *Book of Mormon*,[16] people are encouraged to read the *Book of Mormon* and pray that God would confirm the book's truth through a subjective, inner feeling.

Although Lewis never made any public comments on the Church of Jesus Christ of Latter-day Saints, this illustrates an important aspect of Lewis's views of faith and reason. Prioritizing one's religious experience – placing *feelings* on the locomotive – could lead to a subjective confirmation of an idea that lacks an objective foundation. Placing *faith* on the locomotive ultimately leads to fideism, the idea that one should believe for belief's sake – faith in spite of reason.[17]

Lewis did not think that mysticism in itself was a proof of the religious tradition in which the mystical experience has taken place. Truth

---

[16] Moroni 10:3–5 – "Behold, I would exhort you that when ye shall read these things, if it be wisdom in God that ye should read them, that ye would remember how merciful the Lord hath been unto the children of men, from the creation of Adam even down until the time that ye shall receive these things, and ponder it in your hearts. And when ye shall receive these things, I would exhort you that he would ask God, the Eternal Father, in the name of Christ, if these things are not true; and if ye shall ask with a sincere heart, with real intent, having faith in Christ, he will manifest the truth of it unto you, by the power of the Holy Ghost. And by the power of the Holy Ghost ye may know the truth of all things."

[17] *Credo quia absurdum* is a phrase that is often quoted in this context. "I believe because it is absurd." It is an idea that the church has historically rejected, but which has gained a firm foothold among some religious existentialists.

depends on facts, and true beliefs give justification for religious experiences, not the other way round. "The true religion gives value to its own mysticism; mysticism does not validate the religion in which it happens to occur."[18] Lewis argued that seafarers' common experiences of sea breezes, gulls, the horizon and the receding coastline are no argument for the worthiness or moral value of the sea journey. The seafarer may be going on vacation, seeking life in a new country, shipping freight, spreading the gospel to a mission field, going to war or undertaking acts of piracy. Likewise, the experiences common to mystics in all the world's religions is no proof in itself of the religion's truth claims, worthiness or morality.

Lewis saw both fideism and an emotional subjectivism as aberrant. One's will and emotions are both important, but they have validity only when grounded in fact. Lewis describes the importance of the factual basis in a discussion on doubt.

> Now Faith … is the art of holding on to things your reason has once accepted, in spite of your changing moods. For moods will change, whatever view your reason takes. I know that by experience. Now that I am a Christian I do have moods in which the whole thing looks very improbable: but when I was an atheist I had moods in which Christianity looked terribly probable. This rebellion of your moods against your real self is going to come anyway. That is why Faith is such a necessary virtue: unless you teach your moods "where they get off," you can never be either a sound Christian or even a sound atheist, but just a creature dithering to and fro, with its beliefs really dependent on the weather and the state of its digestion.[19]

If one has made the choice for Christian faith on reasonable grounds, one should not allow shifting feelings to trump reason. For Lewis there was no tension or contradiction between faith and reason. He believed that faith and reason stand together on one side of a balance scale over against feelings and fantasy on the other.

---

[18] *Malcolm,* ch. 12, p. 65.

[19] *MC,* book 3, ch. 11, p. 77.

Lord, Liar, Lunatic

In this section I shall examine one of Lewis's most well-known arguments for Christian faith, a line of reasoning that focuses on Jesus' identity and claims. I shall also show how the six steps of Lewis's apologetic method come to play in the development and presentation of this argument.

The trilemma, as it has been called, is no proof of the existence of God. It is rather to be understood as a challenge for people to examine Jesus' claims about himself and make a decision. Although it has often been criticized for leaving out other possible explanations, the argument continues to titillate and has a natural place in Christian apologetics. One example of the critique leveled against the argument comes from philosopher John Beversluis.

> We must therefore emphatically reject the Lord-or-lunatic dilemma. Once its high-voltage psychological charge has been neutralized, it will no longer be able to jolt us into supposing that we can remain unorthodox only by reviling a universally revered sage. It is perfectly legitimate to suggest that Jesus was a great moral teacher even though he was not God. Because of the manner in which it denies this obvious fact, the Lord-or-lunatic dilemma is the most objectionable of Lewis's many attempts to confront us with false dilemmas and to formulate non-exhaustive sets of options in emotionally inflammatory ways.[20]

Lewis raises the question of Jesus' claims and identity in a number of texts, including this personal letter:

> Now the truth is, I think, that the sweetly-attractive-human-Jesus is a product of 19th century scepticism, produced by people who were ceasing to believe in his divinity but wanted to keep as much of Christianity as they could. It is not what an unbeliever coming to the records with an open mind will (at first) find there. The first thing you really find is that we are simply not *invited*, so to speak, to pass any moral judgement on him ... *He* is going to do whatever judging there is: it is we who are *being* judged, sometimes tenderly, sometimes with stunning

[20] John Beversluis, *C.S. Lewis and the Search for Rational Religion* (Grand Rapids: Eerdmans, 1985), p. 57.

> severity … The first real work of the Gospels on a fresh reader is, and ought to be, to raise very acutely the question, 'Who – or – What is This?' For there is a good deal in the character which, *unless* He really is what He says He is – is not lovable or even tolerable.[21]

The question of who – or what – Jesus is has roots in the patristic era. The alternatives there were that Jesus was either God or an evil man – *aut deus aut malus homo*. This line of thought was developed by Christian thinkers like Gaius Marius Victorinus, Pope Innocent III, Thomas More and Lewis's muse G K Chesterton. When Lewis first began to reflect on this theme he followed the church fathers' simple dichotomy.

> The claim is so shocking – a paradox, and even a horror, which we may easily be lulled into taking too lightly – that only two views of this man are possible. Either he was a raving lunatic of an unusually abominable type, or else He was; and is; precisely what He said. There is no middle way. If the records make the first hypothesis unacceptable, you must submit to the second. … Christianity is not the conclusion of a philosophical debate on the origins of the universe: it is a catastrophic historical event following on the long spiritual preparation of humanity which I have described.[22]

He added a third alternative in the BBC radio broadcasts.

> I am trying here to prevent anyone saying the really foolish thing that people often say about Him: 'I'm ready to accept Jesus as a great moral teacher, but I don't accept His claim to be God.' That is the one thing we must not say. A man who was merely a man and said the sort of things Jesus said would not be a great moral teacher. He would either be a lunatic – on a level with the man who says he is a poached egg – or else he would be the Devil of Hell. You must make your choice. Either this man was, and is, the Son of God: or else a madman or something worse. You can shut Him up for a fool, you can spit at Him and kill Him as a demon; or you can fall at His feet and call Him Lord and God. But let us not come with any patronising nonsense about

---

[21] Personal letter to Mary Neylan dated March 26, 1940 in *Letters2*, pp. 374–375.

[22] *ProbPain*, ch. 1, p. 13.

> His being a great human teacher. He has not le that open to us. He did not intend to.[23]

Lewis understood that a person could reject the fact that Jesus made divine claims – many people have done that – but one cannot come to this conclusion on the basis of a rational examination of the evidence.

Although the most popular expression of this argument is found in *Broadcast Talks / Mere Christianity*, the most thorough presentation is found in a philosophical theological essay from 1950 – "What Are We to Make of Jesus Christ?"[24] In this section I will show how Lewis applies his apologetic method to this argument.

In the first step Lewis poses a question. The question in the title reminds readers of a question that Jesus himself asked his disciples in Matthew 16:15 – "Who do you say that I am?"

The second stage of James Como's structuring of Lewis's apologetic method is the definition of key terms. It is not as clear here in the Lord-Liar-Lunatic argument, but Lewis reflects on what it means to be a good moral teacher. If one accepts the gospels' biographical information as reliable then one must conclude that Jesus made surprising and even shocking claims that bordered on megalomania. He thought he had the right to forgive people for their sins against God and believed that his very presence was a sufficient reason to repeal many religious traditions and duties like fasting. Lewis states that a person with putative signs of megalomania cannot be a good moral teacher.

In the third place Lewis mulls over several possible explanations of the phenomenon. One possible explanation is that Jesus never claimed to be God. Lewis responded that it was highly unlikely that the Jewish people of that time would lie about something like that. Likewise, Chesterton comments on the improbability that the church would have misunderstood Jesus' claims:

> Even if the Church had mistaken his meaning, it would still be true that no other historical tradition except the Church had ever even made the same mistake. Muslims did not misunderstand Muhammad and suppose he was Allah. Jews did not misinterpret Moses and identify him with Jehovah. Why was this claim alone exaggerated unless this alone was made? Even

[23] *MC*, book 2, ch. 3, p. 32.

[24] C.S. Lewis, "What Are We to Make of Jesus Christ?" in *EC*, pp. 38–41. Also in *Dock+*, pp. 156–160.

> if Christianity was one vast universal blunder, it is still a blunder as solitary as the incarnation.[25]

If the Christian church really has misunderstood its master, then it was a mistake that no other group of devotees made. Stefan Gustavsson points out the absurdity of an interpretation on the grounds that the Jewish leaders wanted to execute Jesus precisely because of what they understood to be Jesus' claims to be God.

> Those who attempt to undermine Jesus' words about himself by maintaining that they were never meant to be taken as claims of divine sanction have a real problem here. In part in relation to the claims in and of themselves which can hardly be interpreted as anything other than claims to be more than human, and partly in relation to his execution. Remember that his trial was all about who he claimed to be. The accusation was that of blasphemy; he had said things about himself that it was simply not right to say. His sentence was death.[26]

Another possible explanation of Jesus' claims is that they were the results of a gradual development in the church's proclamation and tradition. The criticism has been raised against the Lord-Liar-Lunatic argument that Lewis left out an L – *legend*. Bart Ehrman writes in *Jesus, Interrupted*:

> I suggested that in fact there were not three options but four: liar, lunatic, Lord, or legend. ... What I meant was that the idea that he called himself God was a legend, which I believe it is. This means that he doesn't have to be either a liar, a lunatic, or the Lord. He could be a first-century Palestinian Jew who had a message to proclaim other than his own divinity.[27]

In this way Ehrman combines the first objection – that Jesus never made such claims – with the second, that the claims are legends that were ascribed to him much later by his followers. Yet Lewis was aware of this alternative and addressed it in "What Are We to Make of Jesus Christ?". Even so, Lewis's answer differs somewhat from what most apologists would give today. He claims that the gospels' literary style has little in

---

[25] G.K. Chesterton, *The Everlasting Man* (London: Hodder & Stoughton, 1947), p. 168.

[26] Stefan Gustavsson, *Skeptikerns guide till Jesus, vol. 2: Om Jesu identitet och uppståndelse* (Stockholm: CredoAkademin, 2015), p. 115. My translation.

[27] Bart D. Ehrman, *Jesus, Interrupted: Revealing the Hidden Contradictions in the Bible (and Why We Don't Know About Them)* (New York: HarperCollins, 2009), p. 141.

common with the legend genre. He wonders aloud whether the people who say that the divine claims were legends have ever actually read any real legends.

> If he tells me that something in a Gospel is legend or romance, I want to know how many legends and romances he has read, how well his palate is trained in detecting them by the flavour; not how many years he has spent on that Gospel. … I have been reading poems, romances, vision-literature, legends, myths all my life. I know what they are like. I know that not one of them is like this. Of this text there are only two possible views. Either this is reportage – though it may no doubt contain errors – pretty close up to the facts; nearly as close as Boswell. Or else, some unknown writer in the second century, without known predecessors or successors, suddenly anticipated the whole technique of modern, novelistic, realistic narrative. If it is untrue, it must be narrative of that kind. The reader who doesn't see this has simply not learned to read.[28]

Apologists today would answer differently and focus on the chronology behind the composition of the New Testament texts in order to show that not enough time had passed between the events and the origin of the texts for legends to be able to develop.[29]

Lewis addresses a third objection to the idea that Jesus was Lord: that his disciples' supposed encounters with the risen Christ were subjective religious experiences. Lewis dismisses the idea that the disciples' experiences of the risen Jesus were merely ghost stories or a general assertion that the soul survives the death of the body. The disciples were very aware that what they had seen – an encounter with someone whom they knew had been brutally executed only a few days earlier – was something new. It did not belong to the same category as stories about ghosts and haunted houses. In the course of just a few years they had given the event the theological interpretation that Jesus was victorious over death – a conviction for which they were willing to die as martyrs.

Critics have sometimes presented a fourth objection to the Lord-Liar-Lunatic argument. They admit that Jesus actually made divine claims, but that he was simply mistaken. There are two possible answers to this

---

[28] C.S. Lewis, "Modern Theology and Biblical Criticism" in *CR*, pp. 154, 155.

[29] See for example Richard Bauckham, *Jesus and the Eyewitnesses* (Grand Rapids: Eerdmans, 2008).

objection. First, one could take an agnostic position whereby one does not know whether or to what extent Jesus was mistaken. Yet agnosticism in this question does not preclude the possibility that Jesus was correct in his claims. There is nothing in this objection that makes it logically more probable that Jesus was mistaken than that he was correct in his claims to be God. The resurrection is another possible answer to this objection. If Jesus made erroneous assertions about himself then why would God raise such a person from the dead?

Once Lewis has dismissed every alternative explanation for Jesus' divine assertions, he proceeds to the fourth step in his apologetic method and presents his own hypothesis as the most reasonable explanation. "The question is, I suppose, whether any hypothesis covers the facts so well as the Christian hypothesis."[30] A little earlier in the same context Lewis writes: "In my opinion, the only person who can say that sort of thing is either God or a complete lunatic suffering from that form of delusion which undermines the whole mind of man."[31]

In the fifth step of his apologetic method, Lewis attempts to show that his hypothesis is a more reasonable interpretation of all the relevant facts than any of the alternatives he has examined. The idea that Jesus was simply a good moral teacher is untenable in light of the facts: only God or a megalomaniac would say the things Jesus said. People who had actually met him did not consider him to be merely a good moral teacher.

> We may note in passing that He was never regarded as a mere moral teacher. He did not produce that effect on any of the people who actually met Him. He produced mainly three effects – Hatred – Terror – Adoration. There was no trace of people expressing mild approval.[32]

The last step in Como's schematic of Lewis's apologetic method is that Lewis presents his argument in a creative way that both speaks to the imagination and is existentially satisfactory. An example of how Lewis presents the Lord-Liar-Lunatic argument in a work of fiction is found in chapter five "Back on This Side of the Door" in *The Lion, the Witch, and the Wardrobe*. In this passage Lucy and her brother Edmund have been in the magical land of Narnia. When Lucy recounts her adventures to her skeptical siblings Susan and Peter, they refuse to believe her. Not only

---

30 "What Are We to Make of Jesus Christ?" in *Dock+*, p. 159. Also in *EC*, p. 41.

31 Ibid in *Dock+*, p. 158. Also in *EC*, p. 39.

32 Ibid in *Dock+*, p. 158. Also in *EC*, p. 40.

that, Edmund lies and denies having been in Narnia. The children go to ask advice from the kindly professor with whom they live.

> "That is a point," said the Professor, "which certainly deserves consideration; very careful consideration. For instance – if you will excuse me for asking the question – does your experience lead you to regard your brother or your sister as the more reliable? I mean, which is the more truthful?"
>
> "That's just the funny thing about it, sir," said Peter. "Up till now, I'd have said Lucy every time."
>
> "And what do you think, my dear?" said the Professor, turning to Susan.
>
> "Well," said Susan, "in general, I'd say the same as Peter, but this couldn't be true – all this about the wood and the Faun."
>
> "That is more than I know," said the Professor, "and a charge of lying against someone whom you have always found truthful is a very serious thing; a very serious thing indeed."
>
> "We were afraid it mightn't even be lying," said Susan; "we thought there might be something wrong with Lucy."
>
> "Madness, you mean?" said the Professor quite coolly. "Oh, you can make your minds easy about that. One has only to look at her and talk to her to see that she is not mad."
>
> "But then," said Susan, and stopped. She had never dreamed that a grown-up would talk like the Professor and didn't know what to think.
>
> "Logic!" said the Professor half to himself. "Why don't they teach logic at these schools? There are only three possibilities. Either your sister is telling lies, or she is mad, or she is telling the truth. You know she doesn't tell lies and it is obvious that she is not mad. For the moment then and unless any further evidence turns up, we must assume that she is telling the truth."[33]

Peter and Susan are unable to judge the truth claims of Lucy's story about the faun and Narnia. They think her story is false, but the professor challenges them to judge her tale on the basis of her trustworthiness. Her

---

[33] C.S. Lewis, "Back on This Side of the Door" in *Lion*, pp. 51–52.

fantastic story is not *against* reason, but *beyond* it. One cannot assess Jesus' divine claims based on our limited personal experience. Therefore, we must – just like Peter and Susan – ground our assessment on what we believe about the trustworthiness of Jesus and those who wrote of his life and teaching. No other prophet or religious teacher of Jesus' status has made comparable claims. Historical facts surrounding Jesus of Nazareth make it highly unlikely that his disciples would have ascribed such claims to Jesus if he had not actually made them. Lewis's Lord-Liar-Lunatic argument is not a strict logical syllogism that proves Jesus was God, but it does succeed in presenting and evaluating some of the most common explanations and leaves it up to the reader to make her own decision.

Summary of the Lord-Liar-Lunatic Argument

Here are the six major steps of Lewis's line of reasoning:

I. Question: What are we to make of Jesus Christ?

II. Definitions: How do we understand key words like *good* and *moral*? Our understanding of these terms gives us reason to dismiss the possibility that Jesus was a liar or a lunatic.

III. Lewis presents and rejects various objections.
  - A. Jesus never claimed to be God.
    1. Lewis's answer to the objection: No other religious group has misunderstood their leader in this way.
    2. Another answer to this objection: It is precisely because of Jesus' claim to be God that people wanted to kill him.
  - B. Jesus (or at least his claims to divinity) were a legend.
    1. Lewis's answer to the objection: The gospels do not fit the literary character of the legend genre.
    2. Another answer to this objection: The early dating of the composition of the New Testament texts do not allow for the development of this type of legend.
  - C. The disciples had subjective religious experiences of having met the risen Jesus.
    1. Lewis's answer to the objection: The disciples were not stupid; they did not interpret their encounters with the risen Jesus as a kind of ghost story.
  - D. Jesus claimed to be God, but he was mistaken.
    1. Lewis's answer to the objection: One could remain agnostic as to whether Jesus was mistaken, but that

leaves open the possibility that Jesus was correct in his claims.

2. Another answer to this objection: Jesus' resurrection as a historical event serves as confirmation that he was not mistaken.

IV. Lewis presents his hypothesis or explanation. Jesus claimed to be God and was correct in his claims.

V. Lewis shows why his explanation is better than the alternatives he has rejected.

A. Only a liar or a lunatic would make such claims if they were not true.

B. People who knew Jesus understood that he was not a lunatic.

C. Our understanding of goodness leads us to the conclusion that Jesus was a good person.

IV. Lewis presents his line of reasoning in a creative manner. The example from *The Lion, the Witch, and the Wardrobe,* where people are encouraged to use their faculties of reason to judge the credibility of someone who makes claims when our limited personal experience prevents us from knowing the truth of the claims first hand.

The moral argument

The six steps of Lewis's apologetic method are also clear in his argument for the existence of God based on human perceptions of morality. The most complete presentation of this argument is in the opening chapters of *Mere Christianity.*

Lewis first shows that all people have an implicit belief in an objective moral law even if they don't have any clear ideas about the origins of this moral law. His argument is a defense of moral realism – the idea that there is an objective moral law, and a critique of moral relativism, the idea that conceptions of right and wrong are subjective. Thomas Carson and Paul Moser define moral relativism: "Moral judgements are not objectively true or false and thus … different individuals or societies can hold conflicting moral judgements without any of them being mistaken."[34]

[34] Thomas L. Carson and Paul K. Moser, *Moral Relativism: A Reader* (Oxford: Oxford University Press, 2001), p. 2.

Moral realism, on the other hand, is the idea that moral claims can be genuine reflections of objective facts. That is, moral statements have their basis in objective moral values that are not the product of subjective human conceptions.

Lewis begins with an observation. People argue about what they think other people should or should not do. Sooner or later everyone experiences frustration or anger at other people's behavior. They simply don't behave the way we want or expect them to. The question is then why this is so.

The second step in the apologetic method is the definition of terms. At this point Lewis makes an important distinction between the laws of nature on one hand and the natural law on the other.[35] The laws of nature are human descriptions of observations about how the physical world normally operates. We perceive regular patterns in nature, such as the 24-hour rhythm of day and night, the seasons and the tendency of objects to fall to the ground, and infer certain conclusions that we call laws of nature.

The laws of nature have a descriptive function. The natural law, on the other hand, has a prescriptive function. It tells us how a person *ought* to behave without necessarily describing how a person actually behaves.

An important distinction between the laws of nature and the natural law is that it is impossible for a person to break a law of nature. When a person sees something that appears to violate a law of nature, there are generally other laws of nature that can explain the anomaly. One may throw a one-pound stone into the air and see it fall to the ground again, but a hot air balloon that weighs a ton or more can float through the air for hours. The stone falls because it weighs more than the air with the same volume that the stone displaces. The hot air balloon flies because hot air weighs less than cold air. If the combined weight of the balloon (including its basket, passengers, etc.) is lighter than the same volume of cold air, then the balloon should fly. It does not violate a law of nature; other laws come into play.

On the other hand, it is possible to violate the natural law; in fact, we do it quite often. We have a belief that people should tell the truth or keep a promise, but then situations come along where we tell a lie or break a promise. Lewis believed that people's tendency to come up with excuses when they violate a moral law is an indicator that there is an objective moral law or natural law that everyone implicitly acknowledges. If one

---

[35] Lewis also (somewhat confusingly) uses the terms "the law of human nature" and "the Law of Nature" for the natural law in *Mere Christianity*.

did not believe in any binding moral duty, then one would not need to defend or excuse oneself at all. The exception confirms the rule.

One could summarize Lewis's thought thus: he believed there must be a natural law, otherwise all disputes and arguments would be meaningless (in spite of the fact that we act as though they are meaningful). Moreover, all critique would be meaningless. Statements like *meat is murder* or *it is wrong to discriminate against a person because of the color of her skin* would not be based on anything more than my subjective feelings and tastes. Lewis believed that it would also be unnecessary to keep a promise or treaty if there were no objective natural law. Nor would we present excuses or justifications for breaking the moral law.

In chapter 2 of *Mere Christianity* Lewis presents a number of possible alternatives to belief in an objective natural law. This is the third step in Lewis's apologetic method – presenting and dismissing various forms of moral relativism and subjectivism.

The first alternative to belief in an objective moral law is the idea that morality is merely an expression of herd instinct. Humans are highly evolved animals who have learned that certain types of behavior favor the survival of the species. Altruism and care for the weak may at first seem to go contrary to the survival of the fittest, but upon closer examination one may argue that a larger gene pool may be better from an evolutionary perspective than inbreeding among the strongest.

Lewis rejects this explanation on the grounds that if our conceptions of morality and ethics were merely expressions of our herd instinct, then the stronger impulse would always win, which it does not always do. Lewis believed that the natural law sometimes demands that we follow a weaker impulse, such as when our moral "duty" calls us to save people (including sick people or people past their child-bearing years) from a burning building even at the risk of our own life.

Lewis also believed that if our ideas of morality were nothing more than herd instinct, then some instinct or instincts would always be right, which we do not believe. Even a mother's love and patriotism can be misguided at times.

The responses that Lewis presents to the belief that morality is nothing more than herd instinct are singularly weak. It would be reasonable for a naturalist to conclude that a person's choice to take potentially mortal risks in order to save someone is in fact a stronger impulse than the drive to self-preservation. However, Lewis does present a stronger argument against the idea of morality as herd instinct by pointing to Hume's law, as he does in chapter 3 – "The Reality of the Law."[36] Hume correctly argued that it is not possible to go from a description of how people *actually* behave to a prescription of how people *should* behave.

Lewis goes on to analyze another alternative to the idea of an objective natural law. It is possible that our ideas of morality are nothing more than social conventions. The collective experience of humanity has shown us that certain ways of living lead to better results than others. This has gradually been systematized into a number of written and unwritten rules about how we should live our lives. These rules are passed from one generation to the next by parents, schools, media, culture, religious institutions, etc.

Lewis rejected the idea that the natural law was only a matter of social convention because not everything that is passed on by our culture is a subjective social convention. For example, we learn mathematics from our parents and schools, but the validity of math is not dependent on society. A moral relativist may nonetheless object and say that there is an important distinction between math and the natural sciences, which are empirically verifiable, and ideas of morality that do not have a foundation in empirical observation.

Lewis gives two rejoinders to this objection. The first one is rather weak. He writes that the geographic and historical differences between human understandings of morality are not so great as one might at first suppose. He names witch hunts as a case in point and explains, "But surely the reason we do not execute witches is that we do not believe there are such things."[37] This example misses the mark. A better example from our day and age would be to say that abortions are legal – not because we now believe that it is morally acceptable to kill an innocent person (which would reflect a change in our culture's understanding of morality) but because our culture does not consider a fetus to be a person (which reflects an interpretation of factual conditions).

Yet even this illustration is unsatisfactory. Lewis sees changes in laws or comparisons between cultures as a sign that there are objective moral laws. In *Mere Christianity* Lewis presents no strong arguments for why the natural law must be objective or for why it cannot be an expression of a

---

[36] Lewis also makes use of Hume's law as part of his argument in *Miracles* that morality is a good indicator that supernaturalism provides a better explanation of our world than naturalism. See the chapter on miracles below.

[37] *MC*, book 1, ch. 2, p. 14.

culture's values at a particular point in its history. As a culture we have decided that a woman's right to choose in matters related to reproduction is a more important value than the right to life of a potential person, and that a democratic society with equality is better than an oligarchy led by an elite who has inherited its position. However Lewis gives a better answer in *The Abolition of Man* where he points to Hume's law.

> From propositions about fact alone no *practical* conclusion can ever be drawn. *This will preserve society* cannot lead to do *this* except by the mediation of *society ought to be preserved. This will cost you your life* cannot lead directly to *do not do this*: it can lead to it only through a felt desire or an acknowledged duty of self-preservation. The Innovator is trying to get a conclusion in the imperative mood out of premises in the indicative mood: and though he continues trying to all eternity he cannot succeed, for the thing is impossible.[38]

Ideas that culture *ought* to be preserved or that a certain legislative proposal would be *better* for society reveal an implicit belief in an objective moral law against which our culture and its laws can be assessed. If moral relativism were true, it would be impossible to speak in any meaningful way about a culture's progress – only of its change.

The fact that different cultures have different ideas about morality is often presented as a reason for rejecting belief in an objective natural law. Lewis responded that the differences are not as great as one may at first think, and stated that the differences in application often stem from differences in interpretation of facts more than differing moral values. It is not difficult to claim the opposite, even if it is difficult to think of good examples of cultures whose foundational moral values differ so much from ours that they would consider cowardice, murder of innocent people and betrayal of one's friends as positive moral values.

This objection from cultural relativism appears to assume a premise where objective moral norms must be so self-evident that no thinking person could deny them. If thinkers are in disagreement over moral values, then the values cannot be objectively true. The weakness of this idea is evident if one were to apply it to other fields of knowledge. Some scientific studies have shown that homosexuality has genetic causes. Other studies have come to other conclusions. According to the cultural relativist principle, one would have to reject the possibility of there being

[38] *Abolition*, ch. 2, p. 33.

a correct answer to the question since there is no consensus among researchers. Even the cultural relativist objection itself is self-refuting since there is no consensus among philosophers on the question of the objective or subjective nature of moral values.

One response that Lewis missed is that if morality is nothing more than a social convention, then there would be no place for social critics and reformers. If morality is only a systematization of the values a society implicitly affirms or rejects, then how should we evaluate the suffragettes or the prophetic voice of people like Nelson Mandela and Martin Luther King Jr who called their contemporaries to a radical change? Were they "wrong" until they succeeded in creating enough public opinion to push law changes through legislation?

A third alternative explanation of people's perceptions of morality is that they are laws of nature. Lewis also dismisses this interpretation on the grounds that the natural law is not a description of how people actually behave but a prescription of how people *should* behave. Moreover, we sometimes evaluate two factually identical situations differently ethically. If I step on a packed bus in rush-hour traffic, I don't believe that the other passengers have a moral responsibility towards me if I have to stand the whole way to work. On the other hand, I do believe that the chav with his baseball cap on backwards who pushes me aside so he can take the last seat on the bus does something morally wrong.[39]

Lewis also stated that a factually more convenient situation for me may be morally worse than one that is existentially less desirable. "I am not angry ... with a man who trips me up by accident; I am angry with a man who tries to trip me up even if he does not succeed.[40]

The final objection to the idea of an objective natural law is that it is simply a "mere fancy" or figment of the imagination. Lewis says that it cannot be imagination because we cannot escape even when we would like to. We are not the ones who created it; it comes to us from outside ourselves. Finally, Lewis says that all value judgments would be meaningless without it.

Once Lewis has considered and rejected a number of theories about morality as herd instinct, social convention, natural law and figment of the imagination, he is ready to move to the fourth step of his process – presenting what he believes to be the best explanation of the phenomenon.

---

39 Not only that – he is also committing a sartorial sin by wearing his baseball cap backwards.

40 *MC*, book 1, ch. 3, p. 18.

Lewis claims that we humans are the key to understanding the moral law because we have "inside information" that is more than a factual description. In some way we know more about what it means to be human than the natural sciences can describe. On this basis he wonders whether the source of the moral law might not be more like a person (with a soul or consciousness) than like the rest of the natural world (matter and laws of nature). He gives the analogy that the source of the moral law cannot be part of the descriptive, scientific world any more than an architect can be part of the building she designs.

Lewis's conclusion is that there must be an absolutely perfect power beyond humanity that is more like soul or consciousness than anything else we know about, because it gives us moral commands and is quite interested in our behavior. That is to say, how we obey those commandments. The personal moral-law giver must also be absolutely good, otherwise all moral effort would be pointless. It would be futile to sacrifice oneself for "the good" if there is no such thing as an absolute "good".

Lewis admits that this argument does not prove the existence of God as God is conceived in theistic religions, only to "a Somebody or Something behind the Moral Law."[41]

Much can be said by way of evaluation and critique of this argument. Lewis seems to assume that the moral lawgiver also is the one who created the universe. Even if this is not a necessary premise in his argument, it does represent a leap in logic. This version of the moral argument also appears to borrow the idea that anything that begins to exist must have a cause from the cosmological argument. Lewis believes that God is the cause of the natural law, but does not believe that it has a beginning.

Lewis has not proven that there is a God or moral lawgiver. Yet the goal of an abductive argument like this is much more modest; Lewis is only attempting to give a more plausible explanation to the phenomenon that people act in a way that seems to presume belief in an absolute moral law than any of the morally relativistic explanations he has rejected.

The last step in Lewis's apologetic method is to present his findings in an imaginative manner. In *The Abolition of Man* he creates the evocative image of men without chests as a symbol of people who reject the natural law. *The Abolition of Man,* which is a rather heavy academic text, has its creative counterpart in the novel *That Hideous Strength,* where we meet the

---

[41] *MC*, book 1, ch. 5, p. 29.

horrific consequences of a dark world ruled by men without chests, who live as if the natural law did not exist.

Lewis also penned several poems that illustrate a world without an objective ground for morality. In the poem "The Country of the Blind" (1951)[42] he presents the image of a seeing person in a country where people are not only blind, but where they have also lost belief that anyone ever could see.

The Country of the Blind

Hard light bathed them – a whole nation of eyeless men,
Dark bipeds not aware how they were maimed. A long
Process, clearly, a slow curse,
Drained through centuries, left them thus.
At some transitional stage, then, a luckless few,
No doubt, must have had eyes after the up-to-date,
Normal type had achieved snug
Darkness, safe from the guns of heavn;
Whose blind mouths would abuse words that belonged to their
Great-grandsires, unabashed, talking of light in some
Eunuch'd, etiolated,
Fungoid sense, as a symbol of
Abstract thoughts. If a man, one that had eyes, a poor
Misfit, spoke of the grey dawn or the stars or green-
Sloped sea waves, or admired how
Warm tints change in a lady's cheek,
None complained he had used words from an alien tongue,
None question'd. It was worse. All would agree 'Of course,'
Came their answer. "We've all felt
Just like that." They were wrong. And he
Knew too much to be clear, could not explain. The words –
Sold, raped flung to the dogs – now could avail no more;
Hence silence. But the mouldwarps,
With glib confidence, easily
Showed how tricks of the phrase, sheer metaphors could set
Fools concocting a myth, taking the worlds for things.
Do you think this a far-fetched
Picture? Go then about among

[42] C.S. Lewis, "The Country of the Blind" in *Poems*, p. 53.

Men now famous; attempt speech on the truths that once,
Opaque, carved in divine forms, irremovable,
Dear but dear as a mountain –
Mass, stood plain to the inward eye.

Since this disability developed over time, most people are not even aware that they are lacking something. As a kind of vestigial ability people still speak of light and color, but they are abstractions that become less and less meaningful as time goes on. Even if a person with sight would attempt to describe what she sees to her friends, they would only mock her for taking metaphors too literally and for creating a myth about a sense that no one else has ever had.

In the poem "Evolutionary Hymn" (1957)[43] Lewis ridicules our culture's ideas of progress without a moral foundation.

Evolutionary Hymn

Lead us, Evolution, lead us
Up the future's endless stair;
Chop us, change us, prod us, weed us.
For stagnation is despair:
Groping, guessing, yet progressing,
Lead us nobody knows where.
Wrong or justice, joy or sorrow,
In the present what are they
while there's always jam tomorrow,
While we tread the onward way?
Never knowing where we're going,
We can never go astray.
To whatever variation
Our posterity may turn
Hairy, squashy, or crustacean,
Bulbous-eyed or square of stern,
Tusked or toothless, mild or ruthless,
Towards that unknown god we yearn.
Ask not if it's god or devil,
Brethren, lest your words imply
Static norms of good and evil
(As in Plato) throned on high;

[43] *Poems*, p. 55.

Such scholastic, inelastic,
Abstract yardsticks we deny.
Far too long have sages vainly
Glossed great Nature's simple text;
He who runs can read it plainly,
'Goodness = what comes next.'
By evolving, Life is solving
All the questions we perplexed.
On then! Value means survival –
Value. If our progeny
Spreads and spawns and licks each rival,
That will prove its deity
(Far from pleasant, by our present,
Standards, though it may well be).

He asks why we care about justice, joy or sorrow when the main point is the survival of our offspring. Old ideas about good and evil are obsolete. It doesn't matter if a future humanity is hairy, squashy or crustacean. It makes no difference whether they have tusks or no teeth at all, whether they are gentle or cruel. "Goodness = what comes next." The poem ends with the possibility that our offspring may be far from nice by our current standards, but that it makes no difference as long as they survive.

Summary of Lewis's Moral Argument:

I. Question: Based on our observations of how people behave, where do we get our concepts about morality?

II. Definitions: The laws of nature and the natural law. The natural law has a fundamentally different character than the laws of nature. The natural law must also be universal because:
   A. Disputes and quarrels would otherwise be meaningless (but we assume that they are meaningful);
   B. All critique would be otherwise be meaningless;
   C. It would otherwise have undesirable consequences for society (for instance, it would be unnecessary to keep one's promises);
   D. People would not otherwise feel obligated to make excuses when they break the moral law.

III. Lewis presents and rejects various objections to moral realism.

A. *Herd instinct.* Morality is a by-product of biological evolution and contributes to the survival of the human species.

1. Lewis's answers to the objection that morality is only an expression of humanity's herd instinct:
   a. If morality were merely an expression of a herd instinct, then the stronger impulse would always win, which it does not.
   b. If morality were merely an expression of a herd instinct, then we would always act according to our instincts, which we do not always do.
   c. If morality were merely an expression of a herd instinct, then some instincts would always be right, which they are not.
   d. If morality were merely an expression of a herd instinct, then it would be impossible to maintain that an instinct is "right"– it just "is." This relates to Hume's law: it is not logically possible to bridge the gap between a factual description of how people *actually* behave to a prescription of how they *should* behave.

B. *Social convention.* Ideas about morality differ greatly between cultures and periods of time. Morality must therefore be culturally relative and not universal or absolute.

1. Lewis's answers to the objection that morality is only a social convention:
   a. Not everything that we learn from our culture is a social convention (such as mathematics).
      i. Rejoinder to Lewis's answer that mathematics is objectively true in spite of it being handed down through our culture: Math is empirically verifiable, which morality is not.
      ii. Lewis's answer to the rejoinder that morality is not verifiable: Differences in morality are not as great as they may at first appear.
      iii. Lewis's second answer to the rejoinder that morality is not verifiable: Hume's law. It is not logically possible to bridge the gap between a factual description of how people *actually*

behave to a prescription of how they *should* behave.

b. Differences in conceptions of morality between differing cultures and time periods reflect differences in applying facts to moral values, not differences in moral values.

2. Another answer to the objection that morality is only a social convention: There would otherwise be no place for a social critic or reformer who calls his/her culture to reform and change in ethical questions.

C. *Laws of nature*

1. Lewis's answers to the objection that morality is another type of law of nature:

a. The natural law is not a description of the workings of the physical world; it is a prescription for how people should behave.

b. We may arrive at differing moral evaluations of two nearly identical and equally undesirable situations.

c. We may evaluate a subjectively unpleasant situation as morally better than a subjectively more pleasant situation.

d. We cannot break a law of nature, but we can violate the natural law.

D. *Figment of the imagination*. Morality is a completely subjective idea within a person; it has nothing to do with any external reality.

1. Lewis's answers to the objection that morality is a figment of the imagination:

a. We cannot escape from our conceptions of morality even though we would sometimes like to do so.

b. Value judgments would be meaningless if they were merely subjective figments of the imagination.

IV. Lewis presents his hypothesis or explanation. There is a universal moral law or natural law that lies outside human conceptions.

V. Lewis shows why his explanation is better than the alternatives he has rejected. An immaterial cause for the natural law is better than any naturalistic explanation because:

A. People have inside information about morality that they have not gained from empirical observation.

B. The source for the natural law must be like humans in having an immaterial dimension like soul or consciousness.

VI. Lewis presents his line of reasoning in a creative manner.
   A. Men without chests in *The Abolition of Man.*
   B. *That Hideous Strength.*
   C. "The Country of the Blind"
   D. "Evolutionary Hymn"

Conclusion

C.S. Lewis's apologetics continue to engage and challenge people today. His Lord-Liar-Lunatic argument figures in the popular Alpha course, and Charles Colson, former advisor to President Richard Nixon, recounts that it made a strong impression on him and that it was a major road marker on his way to faith.[44] Researchers of greatly varying perspectives have both defended and dismissed the argument.[45]

Christians have a calling to always be "prepared to make a defense to anyone who asks you for a reason for the hope that is in you" (1 Peter 3:15). Believers today should seek to give good reasons for their Christian faith – using both good logic and creativity. Not to show how smart they are or to win an argument, but because people have a natural sense for reason and an innate longing for the truth. It is to this longing we will turn in the next chapter.

---

[44] Jonathan Aitken, *Charles Colson: A Life Redeemed* (Colorado Springs: Waterbrook Press, 2005), pp. 210–211.

[45] Stephen T. Davis, "Was Jesus Mad, Bad or God?" ch. 9 in *Christian Philosophical Theology* (Oxford: Oxford University Press, 2006), pp. 149–171. Daniel Howard-Snyder, "Was Jesus Mad, Bad, or God … or Just Plain Mistaken?" *Faith and Philosophy* 21/4 (2004): 456–479. Stephen T. Davis, "The Mad/Bad/God Trilemma: A Reply to Daniel Howard-Snyder" *Faith and Philosophy* 21/4 (2004): 480–492. N.T. Wright. "Simply Lewis: Reflections on a Master Apologist After 60 Years" *Touchstone Magazine* 20/2 (2007) <http://www.touchstonemag.com/archives/article.php?id=20-02-028-f>. Beversluis, p. 56. William Lane Craig, *Reasonable Faith: Christian Truth and Apologetics* (Wheaton: Crossway, 1994), pp. 38–39. Peter Kreeft and Ronald Tacelli, *Handbook of Christian Apologetics* (Downers Grove: InterVarsity Press, 1994), pp. 161–174. Christopher Hitchens, "In the Name of the Father, the Sons…" *The New York Times*. July 9, 2010. <http://www.nytimes.com/2010/07/11/books/review/Hitchens-t.html?_r=0>.

"and the longing, not now for the Island itself,
but for that moment when he had so sweetly longed for it,
began to swell up in a warm wave, sweeter, sweeter,
till he thought he could bear no more"[1]

"Joy is the serious business of Heaven."[2]

---

[1] *PRegress*, first book, ch. 6, p. 20.

[2] *Malcolm*, ch. 17, p. 93.

Ray Baker

The Serious Business of Heaven: The Problem of Longing

Maybe you remember a time when cameras had a little door on the back. You opened the door and inserted a small metal canister and hooked the film on some sort of sprocket. Once the little door was closed, you were ready to take pictures: all 24 – or 36 – of them. You couldn't check the pictures right away. *No no no* – once you've taken all the pictures, you have to remove the film from the camera and take it somewhere to be developed. This could normally take a couple days – or if you were really impatient, you could probably pay a little extra and pick up your pictures an hour later.

The moment of truth came when you returned to pick up your pictures. The clerk would hand over the envelope with your prints and ask you to check them. I don't know about you, but I always held the photos close to my chest when I looked so no one else would see. And then came the disappointment. Not because I'm a bad photographer (although that may certainly be a factor), but because the undeveloped photos somehow represented an unspoken longing. Deep down inside we mistakenly believed that we could recreate and relive all those happy moments – a wonderful vacation, your brother's graduation, your sister's wedding, the first picture of your newborn son. It was never realistic to hope that you could capture these joyful moments on a 4X6 inch piece of paper. What we really longed for was something else.

Joy is a word Lewis uses for a religious experience with a close connection to both pleasure and grief, longing and loss. He describes this experience in a lot of detail in his autobiography *Surprised by Joy*. The title is taken from a poem by the English romantic poet William Wordsworth (1770–1850), who believed that a sudden experience of joy in this sense is an insight into the very fabric of existence that rouses something in our soul – in clear contrast to the mechanistic worldview that was becoming more common at that time.

There are two ways of experiencing this type of joy: as a chronic feeling that there must be something more in life and as an acute sensation that strikes when one least expects it – often in connection with aesthetic experiences. Lewis describes this acute feeling as a beautiful but painful moment: "Joy flickers on the razor-edge of the present and is gone."[3]

Lewis also uses the German word *Sehnsucht* to designate these experiences. The word is often used within literary studies and philosophy of religion to describe a specially strong or intense, unfulfilled longing that is common to every person. Lewis defines "joy" in *Surprised by Joy* as "an unsatisfied desire which in itself is more desirable than any other satisfaction ... a technical term [that] must be distinguished both from Happiness and from Pleasure."[4]

In *Surprised by Joy* he also calls his experiences of *Sehnsucht* "the central story of my life"[5] and recounts several incidents from early childhood. As a young student at Oxford, the atheist Lewis published his first book – a collection of poems called *Spirits in Bondage*. In it, and in his second book *Dymer*, there is a clear sense of *Sehnsucht*. Lewis admitted that his attempts to satisfy these feelings of *Sehnsucht* took the shape of desiring to become a famous poet. Its effects on him were so persistent that they continued to haunt him until he became a Christian. Their fingerprints can clearly be seen even in Lewis's subsequent works as a Christian.

However, it was not Lewis who invented the idea. If joy is an experience common to all humanity, as he maintained, then it must be as old as humanity itself.

Pothos

As early as the fifth century BCE Plato described the experience Lewis would later call joy. The term *pothos* means a strong longing for something unattainable. There's also a real sense of grief or loss in the word. It figures in Greek mythology, where Pothos was the name of the god of longing. He is sometimes said to be the brother of Himeros, the god of desire. Pothos was also the lover of Aphrodite, the goddess of beauty and goodness. According to Plato, Pothos was son of Eros, the god of love.[6]

---

[3] *Dymer*, 5:10. A similar description is found in the essay "Different Tastes in Literature" in *EC*, p. 467: "an experience with a razor's edge which re-makes the whole mind, which produces 'the holy spectral shiver', which can make a man ... feel really sick..."

[4] *Surprised*, ch. 1, p. 18.

[5] Ibid, ch. 1, p. 19.

[6] Plato, *Symposium* in Louise Ropes Loomis, ed. and B. Jowett, trans. *Plato: Apology, Crito, Phaedo, Symposium, Republic* (Roslyn, NY: Classics Club, 1942), pp. 197, 48.

The Greek concept of longing was closely related to ideas of beauty, goodness, desire and love.

Plato describes *pothos* in the dialogues *Cratylus* and *Symposium*. The human soul existed in the world of ideas before a person's birth here on earth. There the soul had the ability to see the true nature of things. Once it is born into the world, it longs to return to the beauty and perfection of the world of ideas. The feeling of *pothos* is an unfulfilled longing for this lost beauty and perfection. In *Symposium* Aristophanes describes how Zeus split the original, androgynous human into two parts: man and woman. The two halves missed each other and longed for their lost intimacy.

> After the division the two parts of man, each desiring his other half, came together, and throwing their arms about one another, entwined in mutual embraces, longing [*pothos*] to grow into one; they were on the point of dying from hunger and self-neglect, because they did not like to do anything apart.[7]

In order to ease this unbearable longing for this lost unity, the gods created human sexuality. That's where Eros comes in as a personification of this longing. Since the eternal forms of the world of ideas are the true objects of our longing, immortality and a longing for eternity are also part of *pothos*.

Compunctio

The idea of *pothos* continued to develop throughout the Middle Ages. Augustine, Gregory of Nyssa and others who described the experience saw a clear connection between a person's tears of remorse over sin and her tears of joy over God's love and grace. It was interpreted as a signpost pointing the way to God.

At the end of the sixth century, Gregory the Great explained that *compunctio* is a foundational human experience. *Compunctio* was originally a medical term for intense physical pain. But beyond the physical pain, Gregory gave the word a more spiritual or existential meaning that lies somewhere between grief and joy. When reading the Bible or devotional literature, one should let it speak straight to the heart – not just to the intellect.

---

[7] Ibid, p. 180.

Gregory wrote that *compunctio* has two causes: a longing back to the Paradise that was lost with Adam and Eve's sin and a longing forward to the eternal life that is the destiny of every believer.

The Swedish professor of psychotherapy Reverend Owe Wikström explains:

> According to the doctrine of *compunctio*, the sense of beauty is caused by humanity's experiences this side of Eden that something is missing, even if we don't really know what it is. All of life plays itself out against a backdrop of latent grief. The cause of the tears is our human inkling that we are pilgrims – we are on a journey. We live in exile, but we are on the road to our true homeland. The bittersweet melancholy of music is therefore to be seen as God's working in us. Through it he rouses us to an awareness of our origins.[8]

Compunctio was a common theme among medieval Christian mystics. In a text that was typical for that era, St Teresa of Ávila wrote:

> Though I often have visions of angels, I do not see them ... In [one angel's] hands I saw a great golden spear, and at the iron tip there appeared to be a point of fire. This he plunged into my heart several times so that it penetrated my entrails. When he pulled it out, I felt that he took them with it, and left me utterly consumed by the great love of God. The pain was so severe that it made me utter several moans. The sweetness caused by this intense pain is so extreme that one cannot possibly wish it to cease, nor is one's soul then content with anything but God.[9]

Umberto Eco writes: "There was not a single medieval writer who did not turn to this theme ... and we find often ... that along with the calm and control of philosophical language there sounded a cry of ecstatic joy."[10]

Wikström sees a clear bond between aesthetic experiences and *compunctio*. He describes it as something that "overwhelms a person in the midst of this compelling moment of beauty. People are sometimes moved

---

[8] <http://www.owewikstrom.se/2011/03/mannen-som-bugade-%E2%80%93-om-skonheten-som-tilltal/>. My translation.

[9] Quoted in Geoffrey Parrinder, *Mysticism in the World's Religions* (Oxford: Oxford University Press, 1976), p. 169.

[10] Umberto Eco, *Art and Beauty in the Middle Ages* (New Haven: Yale, 1986), p. 18.

when they're at a concert; the throat tightens with the frisson of listening to the music of Scarlatti or Arvo Pärt."[11]

Sehnsucht

Pothos and *compunctio* were first called by the German name *Sehnsucht* by the romanticists. The longing mentality that characterized German romanticism was built upon a criticism of society. This displeasure was reflected among other things in the views of society, history and nature that were current at that time. The romanticists reacted to the way industrialization was impacting society. There was a real sense that an unprecedented gap was dividing people in the new society. Fellowship and community seemed to be threatened by a greater division of labor and tougher competition in the marketplace.[12] The result was alienation and humanity's sense of lostness in the world.

Sehnsucht was a common idea among German romanticists. F.W. Schelling, Friedrich Schleiermacher and Novalis claimed that *Sehnsucht* pointed towards something out of reach. Jacob Böhme, who was a major influence on German romanticism, wrote, "the longing appeared to be incapable of ever finding satisfaction."[13] Friedrich Schiller wrote a poem called "*Sehnsucht*" and Johann Gottlieb Fichte called *Sehnsucht* a compulsion to be "united and merged with the eternal" which is inherent in every finite being.[14] This longing was a distinctive feature of the universal romanticism that spread from the German university city of Jena. *Sehnsucht* was often associated with the idea that there lay just beyond the visible world a higher and more true reality.

Schleiermacher claimed that *Sehnsucht* was the fountain of every religion and called it "a feeling of unsatisfied longing for the infinite."[15]

---

[11] <http://www.owewikstrom.se/2011/03/mannen-som-bugade-%E2%80%93-om-skonheten-som-tilltal/>. My translation.

[12] Frederick Beisner, "Romanticism, German" in Edward Craig, ed., *Routledge Encyclopedia of Philosophy*, vol. 8. (London: Routledge 1998), pp. 348–352.

[13] <www.2web.erols.net/nbeach/boehme.html>.

[14] A. Corbineau-Hoffman, "Sehnsucht" in Joachim Ritter & Karlfried Grunder, ed., *Historisches Wörterbuch der Philosophie*, vol. 9. (Basel, 1971–1998), p. 166.

[15] Ibid, p. 167.

Sehnsucht in modern fiction

A number of twentieth-century writers like W.H. Auden, Simone Weil, Tennessee Williams, Dylan Thomas and Saul Bellow have either described *Sehnsucht* or created characters who experience *Sehnsucht*. This quote from John Steinbeck's *East of Eden* richly illustrates all the key elements of *Sehnsucht*: beauty, love, ecstasy, pain, longing and religiosity.

> He felt his heart smack up against his throat when he saw Cathy sitting in the sun, quiet, her baby growing, and a transparency to her skin that made him think of the angels on Sunday school cards. Then a breeze would mover her bright hair, or she would raise her eyes, and Adam would swell out in his stomach with a pleasure of ecstasy that was a close kin to grief.[16]

Malcolm Muggeridge was a British journalist and social commentator who was a contemporary of C.S. Lewis, and who also made an intellectual journey from communism and agnosticism to Christian faith.

> I had a sense, sometimes enormously vivid, that I was a stranger in a strange land; a visitor, not a native ... a displaced person. ... The feeling, I was surprised to find, gave me a great sense of satisfaction, almost of ecstasy. ... Days or weeks or months might pass. Would it ever return – the lostness? I strain my ears to hear it, like distant music; my eyes to see it, a very bright light very far away. Has it gone forever? And then – ah! the relief. Like slipping away from a sleeping embrace, silently shutting a door behind one, tiptoeing off in the grey light of dawn – a stranger again. The only ultimate disaster that can befall us, I have come to realize, is to feel ourselves to be at home here on earth. As long as we are aliens, we cannot forget our true homeland.[17]

The Romanian author Emil Cioran illustrates the transcendental nature of this experience where memories and longing merge into the eternal present.

> It would be a torture merely to breathe were it not for the remembrance or the presentiment of Paradise, the supreme

[16] John Steinbeck, *East of Eden,* ch. 15, p. 159.

[17] Malcolm Muggeridge, *Jesus Rediscovered* (New York: Doubleday, 1979), pp. 47–48.

object – although unconsciously – of our desires, the unexpressed essence of our memory and of our expectation.[18]

What do we really want?

> Before I knew what I desired, the desire itself was gone, the whole glimpse withdrawn, the world turned commonplace again, or only stirred by a longing for the longing that had just ceased. It had taken only a moment of time; and in a certain sense everything else that had ever happened to me was insignificant in comparison.[19]

This longing cannot be satisfied by aesthetic experiences, sex, or any other human emotion or experience. *Sehnsucht* has similarities to the attraction we experience towards exotic, far-away places, mountains, fantasy, magic and the occult. This led Lewis to conclude that there were certain dangers to the romantic interpretation of *Sehnsucht,* namely eroticism and occultism.[20] While the English poet Wordsworth and the French novelist Marcel Proust theorized that *Sehnsucht* really was all about a nostalgic longing for our lost childhood, Lewis says he was at first deceived by all these false explanations, but that he examined each one and was able to uncover their deceptions.[21]

It is a longing for something that we do not normally encounter as part of our everyday experience. Joy ambushes us when we go about our business, focusing on something completely different. Lewis writes, "All Joy reminds. It is never a possession..."[22]

When I was a kid, I could break the Guinness World Record for opening Christmas presents. Wiping sleepy sand from my eyes, I would make my way to the living room in the wee hours of Christmas morning and behold the wonders and unspoken longings that lay incarnate under the tree. At 7:00 I was finally able to wake my parents and start opening presents. *Rip!* A game – good. *Rip!* Underwear – meh. *Rip!* A book – good. *Rip!* A football – What were they thinking? It's *obvious* that my parents don't even know me! But what do you do when all the presents are

---

[18] Emil Cioran, *Histoire et utopie* (Paris: Gallimard, 1987), p. 13.

[19] *Surprised,* ch. 1, p. 16.

[20] C.S. Lewis, "Christianity and Culture" in *CR,* p. 22. Also in *EC,* p. 80.

[21] *PRegress,* preface to third edition, p. xxv.

[22] *Surprised,* ch. 5, p. 78.

opened? You look around of course. To make sure you haven't missed anything. There was almost always a sense of "Is that *all*?!" Not that we're unhappy with all the presents (we'll save the discussion of the underwear and the football for another occasion), but rather because for the whole month of December we had built up a false hope that our deepest longing could be satisfied with something that someone bought at the mall.

Our experiences of longing point to something beyond itself and beyond ourselves. Lewis writes towards the end of *Surprised by Joy* that

> I smuggled in the assumption that what I wanted was a "thrill," a state of my own mind. And there lies the deadly error. Only when your whole attention and desire are fixed upon something else ... does the "thrill" arise. It is a by-product. Its very existence presupposes that you desire not it but something other and outer.[23]

The object for our longing is nothing we encounter in this world, even though we can easily be deceived by things this world has to offer.

> The experience is one of intense longing. It is distinguished from other longings by two things. In the first place, though the sense of want is acute and even painful, yet the mere wanting is felt to be somehow a delight. ... This hunger is better than any other fullness; this poverty better than all other wealth. ... In the second place, there is a peculiar mystery about the *object* of this Desire.[24]

Lewis goes on to explain that we can all too easily be distracted by whatever is the focus of our attention at any particular moment. If we experience *Sehnsucht* while reading a romantic novel, we think that romantic love is what we desire.

In *The Lion, the Witch and the Wardrobe,* Edmund meets the White Witch who gives him Turkish Delight to eat. The more he eats, the more he wants. This is a key to a theme that runs through much of Lewis's work: humankind's longing for the Eternal can be distracted by temporal things.

This is a theme we also find in the biblical book of Ecclesiastes. The author seeks satisfaction in hedonism, wisdom, women, power, money, possessions and work. Time and again he arrives at the same conclusion: It's meaningless. Vanity of vanities. A chasing after the wind. Even though

---

[23] Ibid, ch. 8, p. 168.

[24] *PRegress*, preface to third edition, p. xxvi.

these things are all good and have their rightful place in a person's life, they can never satisfy our deepest longing or take the place of a relationship with the living God.

Edmund eats so much Turkish Delight that he has no appetite for the truly good food that the beavers have prepared. "There's nothing that spoils the taste of good ordinary food half so much as the memory of bad magic food."[25] As Aslan's creations, the Narnians should enjoy creation. As fallen creatures, they will always face the temptation to replace the eternal God with something God created. This is a temptation we all face. We can read about this in Romans 1:25 – "They exchanged the truth of God for a lie and worshiped and served created things rather than the Creator."

People must have a right relation to creation, and thereby also to God, the Eternal One who created everything, if we are ever to find satisfaction and cure the alienation we experience in a hostile world.

Longing as a clue to the existence of God

Lewis saw his experiences of joy or *Sehnsucht* as road signs that directed him to faith in God. Typically for Lewis, he doesn't develop his thoughts in the form of a strictly structured logical argument. His reflections on joy's role in his journey toward faith are peppered throughout his writings. Other Christian scholars like philosophers Peter Kreeft[26] and Robert Holyer[27] have attempted to formulate an abductive argument from Lewis's raw material. Kreeft structures the argument like this:

1) *Every natural, inherent longing in us relates to some real object which can satisfy that longing.*

There are two kinds of longing: an inherent, natural longing and an artificial longing. We have a natural longing for food and drink, sex, love, friendship and beauty, and abhor things like starvation, ignorance and loneliness. But we can also long for a cool car, a luxury vacation in the Caribbean, to be able to fly like a bird or for a fantasyland like Narnia. We can make two important distinctions between a natural longing and an artificial one: In the first place, we don't notice if our artificial longings are

[25] C.S. Lewis, "In the Witch's House" in *Lion*, p. 95.

[26] Peter Kreeft, "C.S. Lewis's Argument from Desire" in *The Riddle of Joy*. M.H. Macdonald and A.A. Tadie, ed. (London: Collins, 1989).

[27] Robert Holyer, "The Argument from Desire" *Faith and Philosophy* 5/1 (1988): 61–70.

not fulfilled in the same way as we notice if our true longings are not satisfied. A person who never drives a cool car or never takes a luxury vacation abroad does not suffer in the same way as the person who never experiences love or intimacy with another person, or whose needs for food and shelter are never met.

The second distinction between a natural longing and an artificial one is that our natural longings come from within, from our human nature. An artificial longing comes to us from the outside, from society, advertising, etc.[28]

Besides the distinction between natural and artificial forms of longing, Lewis believed that all natural, inherent forms of longing have an object that can satisfy that longing.

> Creatures are not born with desires unless satisfaction for those desires exists. A baby feels hunger well, there is such a thing as food. A duckling wants to swim: well, there is such a thing as water. Men feel sexual desire: well, there is such a thing as sex. If I find in myself a desire which no experience in this world can satisfy, the most probable explanation is that I was made for another world.[29]

2) *There is within us a longing which nothing temporal, nothing on earth, no created thing can satisfy.*

The argument is built partly on humanity's collective experience. If one has never reflected over what the object to this longing could be, or if one suppresses this longing, then there's no point in continuing the discussion. It would be as pointless as trying to discuss colors with the blind. They simply lack the necessary experience to be able to contribute something to the discussion. But just because some people suppress or deny their

---

[28] Besides professions that directly entail sin, Lewis dismissed two apparently innocent professions as unfit for a Christian: advertising and the insurance industry. Both professions capitalize on people's insecurities and try to sell them things they really don't need. Lewis placed these unworthy lines of work in the same category as prostitution – work you only do for money's sake. Advertising is "still worthless to him unless it persuades someone else to buy his goods; which themselves may well be ugly, useless, and pernicious luxuries that no mortal would have bought unless the advertisement, by its sexy or snobbish incantations, had conjured up in him a factitious desire for them." Honorable work is that which one would do even if one were not paid to do it – simply because it needs to be done, or because one *wants* to do it. C.S. Lewis, "Good work and good works" in *WLN*, pp. 74–76. Also in *EC*, pp. 380–381.

[29] *MC*, third book, ch. 10, p. 75.

longing doesn't mean that the argument is not valid.[30] Someone can claim that he personally hasn't had this longing, but not that no one has had it. "The dialectic of Desire, faithfully followed, would retrieve all mistakes, head you off from all false paths, and force you not to propound, but to live through, a sort of ontological proof."[31]

Through some kind of process of elimination, a thinking person could arrive at the insight that nothing in this world can satisfy this longing for the numinous.

> 3) *Therefore, there must be something more than time, the world and creation which can satisfy this longing.*

Lewis comments:

> It appeared to me therefore that if a man diligently followed this desire, pursuing the false objects until their falsity appeared and then resolutely abandoning them, he must come out at last into the clear knowledge that the human soul was made to enjoy some object that is never fully given – nay, cannot even be imagined as given – in our present mode of subjective and spatio-temporal experience.[32]

This insight comes as a result of diligent searching.

> 4) *We call this "God" and "eternal life with God."*

It does not automatically mean that everything that the Bible or our imagination tells us about God or heaven must be true – just that there is something which can satisfy our longing and which we call God or heaven.

Lewis does not argue for absolute certainty in this matter. He is only saying that his conclusion is at least as plausible as any other, and maybe even better than most. He does not claim that the conclusion is proven.[33]

---

30 The critic John Beversluis writes: "Joy leads nowhere, and *Surprised by Joy* is wholly unconvincing as an attempt to demonstrate that there is a 'road right out of the self!' that leads straight to God." (Beversluis 1985), p. 16.

31 *PRegress*, preface to third edition, p. xiii.

32 Ibid, preface to third edition, p. xvi.

33 The critical scholar John Beversluis does not think that Lewis even succeeds in showing this much. He calls into question the premise that there must be an object that can satisfy every natural, inherent longing. "Just as we cannot prove that we inhabit a world in which food exists simply on the ground that we get hungry, so we cannot prove that an infinite Object of desire exists simply on the ground that we desire it. The desire in and of itself proves nothing, points to nothing. For all we know, perhaps some desires *are* in vain.

> A man's physical hunger does not prove that man will get any bread; he may die of starvation on a raft in the Atlantic. But surely a man's hunger does prove that he comes of a race which repairs its body by eating and inhabits a world where eatable substances exist. In the same way, though I do not believe (I wish I did) that my desire for Paradise proves that I shall enjoy it, I think it a pretty good indication that such a thing exists and that some men will.[34]

Literary symbols for longing

These experiences of joy, longing or *Sehnsucht* are a recurring theme in Lewis's books. His fictional works are filled with people and things who represent the human longing for "something more."

A common symbol for *Sehnsucht* is *hills* and *mountains* in the distance. This can probably be traced to Lewis's childhood and the Castlereigh Hills the young Jack could see from his bedroom window in Belfast.

In the epic *Dymer*, it is precisely this kind of longing that compels the main character Dymer to leave the ironically named "perfect city." Like the German romanticists, Dymer begins by rejecting social conventions and seeking to return to a more natural state of being (1:16). He then seeks fulfillment in nostalgia (2:21), sensuality (2:33) and the intellect (6:13). Although there is nothing wrong with sex, enjoyment of nature, intellectual activity and nostalgia, they were never intended to satisfy a person's deepest sense of longing.

In an encounter with the Master, Dymer hears how some distant mountains are a constant reminder of this unsatisfied longing (6:11–12). The Master decides to plant some trees that will block the view so that he won't have to be badgered by this persistent reminder. But the trees refuse to grow.

In *Till We Have Faces* Psyche senses a constant, gnawing longing for something she associates with a mystical mountain. She dreams that she will marry a powerful king who will build a castle of gold and amber for her high on the mountain. She later explains what she experienced.

Inferences from our own psychological makeup to what actually exists, much less to what *must* exist, are fallacious." (Beversluis 1985, p. 19). However it is difficult, if not impossible, to imagine a natural, inherent longing that does not have an external object that can satisfy that longing.

[34] C.S. Lewis, "The Weight of Glory" in *WoG*, p. 32. Also in *EC*, p. 99.

> The colour and the smell, and looking across at the Grey Mountain in the distance? And because it was so beautiful, it set me longing, always longing. Somewhere else there must be more of it. Everything seemed to be saying, Psyche come! But I couldn't (not yet) come and I didn't know where I was to come to. It almost hurt me.[35]

Another common symbol for *Sehnsucht* in Lewis's fiction is that of *gardens,* especially exotic gardens. Even this symbol can be traced to Lewis's childhood. In *Surprised by Joy,* he recounts his experiences of *Sehnsucht* when he saw the toy garden his brother Warnie had made of moss, twigs and flowers in the metal lid of a biscuit tin. "As long as I live my imagination of Paradise will retain something of my brother's toy garden."[36]

Exotic gardens figure in many of Lewis's early poems in *Spirits in Bondage* and in *Dymer* (1:28). In *Till We Have Faces* the protagonist Orual departs on a journey to the mystical mountain on a mission to find her sister Psyche. There she discovers beauty in a garden.

> It was like looking down into a new world. At our feet, cradled amid a vast confusion of mountains, lay a small valley bright as a gem, but opening southward on our right. Through that opening there was a glimpse of warm, blue lands, hills and forests, far below us. ... I never saw greener turf. There was gorse in bloom, and wild vines, and many groves of flourishing trees, and great plenty of bright water – pools, streams, and little cataracts. And when, after casting about a little to find where the slope would be easiest for the horse, we began descending, the air came up to us warmer and sweeter every minute.[37]

Another example of a garden that symbolizes a person's longing is found in the otherworldly *Perelandra.*

> At long last he reached the wooded part. There was an undergrowth of feathery vegetation, about the height of gooseberry bushes, coloured like sea anemones. Above this were the taller growths – strange trees with tube-like trunks of grey and purple spreading rich canopies above his head, in which orange, silver,

[35] *Faces,* ch. 7, p. 74.

[36] *Surprised,* ch. 1, p. 7.

[37] *Faces,* ch. 9, pp. 100–101.

> and blue were the predominant colours. Here, with the aid of the tree trunks, he could keep his feet more easily. The smells in the forest were beyond all that he had ever conceived. To say that they made him feel hungry and thirsty would be misleading; almost, they created a new kind of hunger and thirst, a longing that seemed to flow over from the body into the soul and which was a heaven to feel.[38]

Here we see the close connection between aesthetic experiences and the deep longing that is the common experience of every person.

A third motif that Lewis often uses to symbolize the experience of *Sehnsucht* is *islands*. These islands are often found in combination with both mountains and exotic gardens. A long series of islands compels the brave mouse Reepicheep in his mission to find that which would fulfill his longing in *The Voyage of the Dawn Treader*.

Just as Dymer left the dystopian perfect city to seek satisfaction for his longing, John, the protagonist in *The Pilgrim's Regress*, leaves Puritania with its oppressive rules and prohibitions in order to follow his longing.

> Then came the sound of a musical instrument, from behind it seemed, very sweet and very short, as it were one plucking of a string or one note of a bell, and after it a full, clear voice – and it sounded so high and strange that he thought it was very far away, further than a star. The voice said, Come. Then John saw that there was a stone wall beside the road in that part: but it had (what he had never seen in a garden wall before) a window. There was no glass in the window and no bars; it was just a square hole in the wall. Through it he saw a green wood full of primroses: and he remembered suddenly how he had gone into another wood to pull primroses, as a child, very long ago – so long that even in the moment of remembering the memory seemed still out of reach. While he strained to grasp it, there came to him from beyond the wood a sweetness and a pang so piercing that instantly he forgot his father's house, and his mother, and the fear of the landlord, and the burden of the rules. All the furniture of his mind was taken away. A moment later he found that he was sobbing, and the sun had gone in: and what it was that had happened to him he could not quite remember, nor whether it had happened in this wood, or in the other wood

---

[38] *Perelandra*, ch. 3, p. 41.

> when he was a child. It seemed to him that a mist which hung at the far end of the wood had parted for a moment, and through the rift he had seen a calm sea, and in the sea an island, where the smooth turf sloped down unbroken to the bays, and out of the thickets peeped the pale, small-breasted Oreads, wise like gods, unconscious of themselves like beasts, and tall enchanters, bearded to their feet, sat in green chairs among the forests. But even while he pictured these things he knew, with one part of his mind, that they were not like the things he had seen – nay, that what had befallen him was not seeing at all. But he was too young to heed the distinction: and too empty, now that the unbounded sweetness passed away, not to seize greedily whatever it had left behind. He had no inclination yet to go into the wood: and presently he went home, with a sad excitement upon him, repeating to himself a thousand times, "I know now what I want."[39]

John eventually hears an explanation that what he was seeking was not really the island, but something else for which the island was merely a symbol.

> It does not always take the form of an Island, as I have said. The Landlord sends pictures of many different kinds. What is universal is not the particular picture, but the arrival of some message, not perfectly intelligible, which wakes this desire and sets men longing for something East or West of the world; something possessed, if at all, only in the act of desiring it, and lost so quickly that the craving itself becomes craved; something that tends inevitably to be confused with common or even with vile satisfactions lying close to hand, yet which is able, if any man faithfully live through the dialectic of its successive births and deaths, to lead him at last where true joys are to be found.[40]

In the quote above from chapter two in *The Pilgrim's Regress* Lewis combines not only mountains, gardens and islands, but even a fourth symbol for our human experience of *Sehnsucht, music.* Since *Sehnsucht* is closely associated with aesthetic experience, it is not so unusual that many

---

[39] *PRegress*, book 1, ch. 2, p. 12.

[40] Ibid, book 8, ch. 9, p. 158.

people report that their clearest experiences of *Sehnsucht* as acute pain are triggered by music.

Another book where all four symbols appear is *The Voyage of the Dawn Treader*. The voyagers hear a melody that is so melancholy that "It would break your heart." Yet the music, which comes from Aslan's country, was not sad.[41]

Music acts as a siren that calls people to follow their longing in Lewis's early books *Dymer* and *The Pilgrim's Regress*. In *Dymer* the protagonist hears music that comes from a garden. It entices him and fills him with a longing for something more than his quotidian experiences in the perfect city have to offer.

> A like thing fell to Dymer. Bending low,
> Feeling his way he went. The curtained air
> Sighed into sound above his head, as though
> Stringed instruments and horns were riding there.
> It passed and at its passing stirred his hair.
> He stood intent to hear. He heard again
> And checked his breath half-drawn, as if with pain.
> That music could have crumbled proud belief
> With doubt, or in the bosom of the sage
> Madden the heart that had outmastered grief,
> And flood with tears the eyes of frozen age
> And turn the young man's feet to pilgrimage –
> So sharp it was, so sure a path it found,
> Soulward with stabbing wounds of bitter sound.[42]

In *The Pilgrim's Regress* John hears music and a voice that calls from "very far away, further than a star."[43] John later meets a man who sings a melancholy song that induces a strong vision of the island John believes to be the object of his desire. When the song is over even the feelings of *Sehnsucht* disappear. John begs him to sing it again.

> "Now I shall sing you something else," said Mr. Halfways.
>
> "Oh, no," cried John, who was sobbing. "Sing the same again. Please sing it again."

---

[41] C.S. Lewis, "The Very End of the World" in *Dawntreader*, p. 243.

[42] *Dymer* 1:23–24.

[43] *PRegress*, book 1, ch. 2, p. 12.

"You had better not hear it twice in the same evening. I have plenty of other songs."

"I would die to hear the first one again," said John.[44]

But when the song is repeated John discovers that it doesn't have the same effect on him. The pangs of *Sehnsucht* come as a surprise; you can't induce them.

Where does all this lead?

According to Lewis there are three possible responses to our experiences of *Sehnsucht*.[45] One wrong way is what Lewis calls *The Fool's Way*. This is the mistake of the optimist. Lewis says that these people live their lives with a constant search for new, more passionate love affairs, more exciting vacations, a nicer house, a cooler car and new hobbies that one mistakenly believes will satiate our deepest longings. When they are not satisfied, the "fools" blame the object and think they simply need to move on to the next love, vacation, house, car or possession in the vain hope that it can provide the fulfillment that the old one was unable to provide. The fool's way leads inevitably to idolatry.

Although Dymer comes to the realization that sex with a succubus does not satisfy – the result was the birth of a monster – he believes foolishly that it was simply the wrong object.

'And she – she was no dream. It would be waste
To seek her there, the living in that den
Of lies.' The Master smiled. 'You are in haste!
For broken dreams the cure is, Dream again
And deeper. If the waking world, and men,
And nature marred your dream – so much the worse
For a crude world beneath its primal curse.'[46]

You just need to dream again – pursue a new object of your desires.

Another way of dealing with experiences of *Sehnsucht* is what Lewis calls *The Way of the Disillusioned "Sensible Man."* This is the mistake of the pessimist. These disillusioned, sensible people regard their longing as a chasing after wind – a pipe dream that naïve young people chase, but

[44] Ibid, book 2, ch. 5, p. 33.

[45] *MC*, third book, ch. 10, pp. 74–75.

[46] *Dymer* 6:24.

which these pessimists now have come to regard as an illusion, a chimera they have long since abandoned. They have learned not to have too high hopes in life, since they only end in disappointment. The longing itself is deceptive.

A third response to the experience of *Sehnsucht* lies somewhere between these two extremes. One should both enjoy creation and the life we live while at the same time restraining oneself and distancing oneself from it. Lewis did not advocate either the golden mean or the Hindu idea that one should act without thought to the consequences of one's actions. We need both sides: enjoyment *and* renunciation. With only one side, one will end up with a false view of reality and a life out of balance. Lewis calls this way *The Christian Way*. If "nature makes nothing in vain,"[47] then there must be an object that can satisfy our longing. When Lewis finally came to the recognition that nothing in this finite world can satiate this desire for the numinous, he concluded that the object for his desire must also be infinite.

Evaluation

The argument from desire is a different type of argument than the classic arguments for God's existence. It lacks both the deduction of the ontological argument and the induction of the cosmological. Like the teleological and moral arguments, the argument from desire is abductive – Lewis presents what he believes to be the best explanation of our human experience and observations. Our experiences and observations are naturally open to interpretation. Nonetheless, in spite of its natural limitations, I think the argument from desire has a certain ability to speak to a person's existential experiences and not just to her intellect. There is something here about the human condition that resonates within us.

Lewis reflected much later on his early experiences of *Sehnsucht*. He believed that even if his futile attempts at fulfilling his longing with something temporal had led him to sin, he still would not have wanted to reject the experience that gave rise to his misdirected endeavors.

> I have not (or not yet) reached a point at which I can honestly repent of my early experiences of romantic *Sehnsucht*. That they were occasions to much that I do repent, is clear; but I still cannot help thinking that this was my abuse of them, and that the

[47] *PRegress*, preface to third edition, p. xiii.

> experiences themselves contained, from the very first, a wholly good element. Without them my conversion would have been more difficult.[48]

Lewis used a number of metaphors to describe the function of *Sehnsucht* in a person's life. He once compared it with a spilled drink.

> I am quite ready to describe *Sehnsucht* as 'spilled religion', provided it is not forgotten that the spilled drops may be full of blessing to the unconverted man who licks them up, and therefore begins to search for the cup whence they were spilled. For the drops will be taken by some whose stomachs are not yet sound enough for the full draught.[49]

Sehnsucht acts like an *amuse-bouche* that leads some people to long and search for more. But as with all such signs, there is always a risk that a person's experience of *Sehnsucht* can be misunderstood.

> You will have notices that most dogs cannot understand *pointing*. You point to a bit of food on the floor; the dog, instead of looking at the floor, sniffs at your finger. A finger is a finger to him, and that is all.[50]

Instead of sniffing at the finger, one should see where the finger is pointing. Lewis interpreted his experiences of *Sehnsucht* as road signs pointing the way to God. Once he had followed the signs and met God, these signs began to play a less important role in his life, as he admits in *Surprised by Joy*.[51] That's because something – or Someone – else had become more important to him. Lewis wrote that it would indeed be odd if a person who had gotten lost in the woods and eventually stumbled upon a road with a sign pointing the way to the nearest town would sit down and venerate the sign. The purpose of the sign is not to draw attention to itself, except for the purpose of helping people find their way to their true destination. That's also what *Sehnsucht* does.

---

48 "Christianity and Culture" in *CR*, p. 23. Also in *EC*, p. 81.

49 Ibid in *CR*, p. 23. Also in *EC*, p. 81.

50 C.S. Lewis, "Transposition" in *WoG*, p. 114. Also in *EC*, p. 277.

51 *Surprised*, ch. 15, p. 238.

"All prayers always, taken at their word, blaspheme,
Invoking with frail imageries a folk-lore dream;
And all men are idolaters, crying unheard
To senseless idols, if thou take them at their word,
And all men in their praying, self-deceived, address
One that is not (so saith that old rebuke) unless
Thou, of mere grace, appropriate, and to thee divert
Men's arrows, all at hazard aimed, beyond desert.
Take not, oh Lord, our literal sense, but in thy great,
Unbroken speech our halting metaphor translate."[1]

[1] *PRegress*, book 8, ch. 4, p. 146.

Ray Baker

The Myth Became Flesh and Dwelt Among Us: On Scripture

Debates about the infallibility or inerrancy of the Bible were not current during Lewis's lifetime. These discussions did not really pick up speed until the 1970s and 80s, and even then, primarily in America.

Many skeptical researchers point to contradictions in the Bible and claim that the Bible cannot be fully trustworthy.[2] Lewis claimed just the opposite. He once wrote in a letter that people in the ancient world never had the same expectations of exactness that we demand of the Bible today, regardless of whether the texts are regarded as holy or not. "The very kind of truth we are often demanding was, in my opinion, never even envisaged by the Ancients."[3] He said that if the biblical authors were not completely honest, they would never have admitted not knowing the answer to something. The people who copied and spread the biblical manuscripts would not have retained the apparent mistakes (like when Jesus said that this generation would not pass away before he would come back) if they were not completely honest. People in the ancient world were not so stupid or uneducated as to be unaware of these problems and contradictions. Lewis considered the presence of these problems as evidence of the Bible's credibility.

In this chapter I will examine C.S. Lewis's views on Scripture, in particular his understanding of divine revelation, inspiration, myth, and the historicity of the biblical narratives.

Lewis always viewed himself as a researcher in literature, not as a theologian. As such he was not constrained by standard formulations and the "right answers" that have been provided by conservative theologians, even though he was a voracious reader and well aware of the issues in contemporary theological discourse. He looked at the Bible text from a completely different angle – partly with the eyes of someone who just loves good stories, but also as an expert in literature. Although he was skeptical of attempts to read the Bible as literature, this was true only in cases where reading the Bible as literature is all that is left once one has stripped the Bible of all its religious significance, truth claims and moral

---

[2] Ehrman 2009.

[3] Personal letter to Clyde Kilby dated May 7, 1959 in *Letters3*, p. 1046.

demands on the lives of its readers.[4] At the same time, he also questioned the value of many trendy theories within literary studies. "Especially poisonous is the kind of teaching which encourages [students] to approach every literary work with suspicion."[5]

Good readers

Before looking more specifically at how Lewis viewed the Bible, it would be helpful to see how he thought one should approach literature in general.

First, one must be a good reader. Good literature both deserves and demands good readers. A good reader is a person who receives a text as a goal in itself, enters into a new world and tries to see the world from the author's perspective and allows the poetic pictures to impact his/her fantasy in order to fulfill its purpose and produce a correct response in the reader. This is very different than the perspective today where literature professors proclaim the death of the author and focus on a reader-response hermeneutic where the reader's response to a text has interpretive precedence over the putative intentions of the author.

Lewis thought that a poor reader, on the other hand, takes in just enough to satisfy a temporary need. He or she reads a text only once "just to see what happens" and reads only for the sake of killing time.

Lewis stated that the task of an author is simply to try to embody with his or her art a reflection of eternal beauty and wisdom. Lewis criticized the cult of originality and novelty that characterizes much of the academic world today. In his inaugural lecture upon becoming professor in Cambridge he asked the question, "How has it come about that we use the highly emotive word 'stagnation', with all its malodorous and malarial overtones, for what other ages would have called 'permanence'?"[6]

> [A]n author should never conceive himself as bringing into existence beauty or wisdom which did not exist before, but simply and solely as trying to embody in terms of his own art some reflections of eternal Beauty and Wisdom.[7]

---

[4] C.S. Lewis, "The Literary Impact of the Authorized Version" in *SLE*, p. 144.

[5] *ExCrit*, ch. 9, p. 93.

[6] C.S. Lewis, *De Descriptione Temporum* (Cambridge: Cambridge University Press, 1954), p. 16.

[7] C.S. Lewis, "Christianity and Literature" in *CR*, p. 7. Also in *EC*, p. 416.

The cult of originality almost always becomes a straightjacket that restricts true creativity.

> No man who values originality will ever be original. But try to tell the truth as you see it, try to do any bit of work as well as it can be done for the work's sake, and what men call originality will come unsought.[8]

With his Platonist viewpoint, Lewis believed that truth and beauty are eternal values. The task of the artist and the author is not to create something new, but to find creative ways to reflect these eternal values. "The human mind has no more power of inventing a new value than of imagining a new primary colour, or, indeed, of creating a new sun and a new sky for it to move in."[9] Likewise, "Really great moral teachers never do introduce new moralities; it's quacks and cranks who do that."[10]

Lewis illustrates this idea with a priest in *The Great Divorce*. The priest is intent on presenting an unorthodox Christology in a lecture at the meeting of a theological association in hell:

> Jesus ... was a comparatively young man when he died. He would have outgrown some of his earlier views ... if he'd lived. As he might have done, with a little more tact and patience. I am going to ask my audience to consider what his mature views would have been. ... What a different Christianity we might have had if only the Founder had reached his full stature! I shall end up by pointing out how this deepens the significance of the Crucifixion. One feels for the first time what a disaster it was: what a tragic waste ... so much promise cut short.[11]

With a knowing wink Lewis showed where he believed such theological novelties have their origin!

The special function of literature is to lift a person above the mundane world of everyday language to a fantasy world of non-propositional communication. He calls literature a "little incarnation" that embodies realities that until this point have been invisible to us. It

---

[8] C.S. Lewis, "Membership" in *EC*, p. 340. Also in *WoG*, p. 175.

[9] *Abolition*, ch. 2, p. 44.

[10] C.S. Lewis, *Spenser's Images of Life*. Alastair Fowler, ed. (Cambridge: Cambridge University Press, 1967), p. 140.

[11] *Divorce*, ch. 5, p. 46.

expresses an experience which the reader instinctively recognizes as true. At its best, literature reflects ultimate reality.

What do you mean?

In an essay called "The Language of Religion" Lewis examined the ability of language to communicate anything meaningful about religious experience or ultimate reality. He shed light on three types of language:

First he discussed a *scientific or philosophical language.* This is an objective form of language that often includes technical terms.

> A 56-year old man died at 9:40 pm on March 23 at Mercy Hospital with a suspected myocardial infarction. An autopsy showed that the pericardium fibrin deposits but without an increased amount of liquid. The heart weighed 470 grams and was generally hypertrophied and dilated.

Scientific language focuses on the quantitative and communicates primarily through that which can be measured. But scientific language tells us nothing about either the pain the man suffered in the last minutes of life or the grief of his loved ones.

The second type of language is *normal language.* "A man died of a heart attack." It is a straight-forward, no nonsense type of communication.

Finally, we have *poetic language.* Poetic language is qualitative; it succeeds in conveying feelings in a way that neither scientific nor normal language is able. Poetic language may include simple humorous euphemisms like "He kicked the bucket" or "She keeled over." Or it may be poetic in a more strict sense:

> Remember him – before the silver cord is severed,
> or the golden bowl is broken;
> before the pitcher is shattered at the spring,
> or the wheel broken at the well,
> and the dust returns to the ground it came from,
> and the spirit returns to God who gave it.[12]

Or this example, "And you as well must die" by Edna St. Vincent Millay.[13]

---

[12] Ecclesiastes 12:6–7.

[13] <http://www.poemtree.com/poems/And-You-As-Well-Must-Die.htm>.

And you as well must die, belovèd dust,
And all your beauty stand you in no stead;
This flawless, vital hand, this perfect head,
This body of flame and steel, before the gust
Of Death, or under his autumnal frost,
Shall be as any leaf, be no less dead
Than the first leaf that fell, this wonder fled,
Altered, estranged, disintegrated, lost.
Nor shall my love avail you in your hour.
In spite of all my love, you will arise
Upon that day and wander down the air
Obscurely as the unattended flower,
It mattering not how beautiful you were,
Or how belovèd above all else that dies.

Poetic language has the potential of lifting us from our everyday experience and communicating experiences which we have not had, or using parts of our experience to direct our thoughts to something beyond our immediate experience. It helps us put into words thoughts and feelings that lie unexpressed in our subconscious. Lewis said that although science can tell us when and where we are likely to find an elm tree, "only poetry can tell you what meeting an elm is like."[14]

Lewis argued that religious language is not a special kind of language, but something in between ordinary and poetic language.

> The language of religion, which we may presently have to distinguish from that of theology, seems to me to be, on the whole, either the same sort we use in ordinary conversation or the same sort we use in poetry, or somewhere between the two.[15]

In normal language one might say, "I believe in God." If asked to clarify that statement, one could choose several routes of explanation. In scientific or theological language, one could explain: "I believe in an incorporeal entity personal in the sense that it can be the subject and object of love on which all other entities are unilaterally dependent."[16] But this does little to

---

[14] C.S. Lewis, *The Personal Heresy: A Controversy* (Oxford: Oxford University Press 1939), ch. 5, p. 110.

[15] C.S. Lewis, "The Language of Religion" in *CR*, p. 129. Also in *EC*, p. 255.

[16] Ibid in *CR*, p. 135. Also in *EC*, p. 261.

convey the sense of awe, wonder, fear or worship that people experience in their belief in God.

Thus we use poetic language about God: We can call God our heavenly father or King of kings and Lord of lords. We can say that the word became flesh and dwelt among us but that all we like sheep have gone astray. But these expressions are not merely expressions of emotions; they also have a communicative value and say something meaningful about God and our relationship to God.

> Theology certainly shares with poetry the use of metaphorical or symbolical language. The first Person of the Trinity is not the Father of the Second in a physical sense. The Second Person did not come 'down' to earth in the same sense as a parachutist: nor re-ascend into the sky like a balloon: nor did He literally sit at the right hand of the Father.[17]

Lewis criticized the tendency among some modern theologians to reject metaphors and poetic descriptions of God such as *heavenly father* based on the equivocal and deceptive nature of these images. He said that these theologians only succeed at substituting one metaphor with another.

> All language, except about objects of sense, is metaphorical through and through. To call God a 'Force' (that is, something like a wind or a dynamo) is as metaphorical as to call Him a Father or a King. On such matters we can make our language more polysyllabic and duller: we cannot make it more literal.[18]

It is only in speaking of physical phenomena that one can avoid using poetic language. "All language about things other than physical objects is necessarily metaphorical."[19]

> We are invited to restate our belief in a form free from metaphor and symbol. The reason why we don't is that we can't. We can, if you like, say 'God entered history' instead of saying 'God came down to earth.' But, of course, 'entered' is just as metaphorical as 'came down'. You have only substituted horizontal or undefined movement for vertical movement. We

---

[17] C.S. Lewis, "Is Theology Poetry?" in *EC*, p. 17.

[18] C.S. Lewis, "Horrid Red Things" in *Dock+*, p. 71. Also in *EC*, p. 129.

[19] "Is Theology Poetry?" in *EC*, p. 18.

> can make our language duller; we cannot make it less metaphorical.[20]

As such, it is impossible to speak of God in any meaningful way without the use of metaphors.

Revelation

Revelation is the idea within Christian theology whereby God chooses to show himself or communicate information about himself at different times and in different ways. Theologians commonly make the distinction between general revelation and special revelation.

General revelation is when God uses the normal workings of the created order to show himself: the majesty of the universe, the inherent feelings of love a person experiences, an innate longing for something more in life (the longing that Lewis called joy), the moral law written on human hearts, etc.

Special revelation is when God uses some supernatural means to communicate with people through miracles, visions, visits from angels, special words of prophecy, etc. Many theologians would include the Bible as a clear form of special revelation where God guided human authors to write what would be the word of God for humanity. The greatest form of special revelation according to Lewis was when God became man with the birth of Jesus Christ.

Lewis's concept of revelation was broader than that of most Christian theologians. He believed that God reveals himself in the masterpieces of world literature, in other religions, in ancient myths and legends and through human reason and intuition. God used the poets' minds and words to communicate small fragments of eternal truth even in the pagan myths. In Christianity, God himself is the poet whose language is made up of real people and historic events.

Scripture, for Lewis, bears witness to revelation without necessarily being revelation; scripture is divinely inspired but humanly generated.

> The total result is not 'the Word of God' in the sense that every passage, in itself, gives impeccable science or history. It carries the Word of God; and we (under grace, with attention to tradition and to interpreters wiser than ourselves, and with the

---

[20] Ibid in *EC*, p. 18.

use of such intelligence and learning as we may have) receive that Word from it not by using it as an encyclopaedia or an encyclical but by steeping ourselves in its tone or temper and so learning its overall message.[21]

To call the Bible the Word of God is in itself an example of religious language. The Bible is not the word of God in any ontological sense. "It is Christ Himself, not the Bible, who is the true word of God. The Bible, read in the right spirit and with the guidance of good teachers, will bring us to Him."[22] The Bible becomes the word of God for us when we allow ourselves to be formed and guided by what we read in the Bible.

Myth

As I mentioned, Lewis thought that religious language lay somewhere between normal language and poetic language. He believed, in spite of the natural limitations of human language, that poetic language is the best medium for communicating the eternal truths of God and about God. Poetic language includes analogies, metaphors, similes, parables, symbols and more. We have images like *God the father, the lamb of God, the good shepherd, the kingdom of heaven is like a mustard seed,* and *the kingdom of heaven is like a treasure hidden in a field.* All of these literary devices are included in what Lewis called myth. A myth is poetic or religious language about ultimate reality.

Lewis defined myth as "a real though unfocused gleam of divine truth falling on human imagination"[23] that makes it possible for the ineffable to be communicated. We can't see light; we can only see the things which light illuminates. A myth is like light – it illuminates God's truth.

A myth has several important characteristics. In the first place, one must make a distinction between myth and allegory. In an allegory one begins with a character quality and creates a personification whose identity is clear. Myth, on the other hand, starts with the physical as a symbol for the spiritual. One can always interpret an allegory, but a myth

---

[21] *Psalms*, p. 96.

[22] Personal letter to Mrs. Johnson dated November 8, 1952 in *LettersWHL*, p. 428. Also in *Letters3*, p. 246.

[23] *Miracles*, ch. 15, note 1, p. 176.

cannot always be explained or interpreted with a one-to-one correspondence.

Secondly, a myth is essentially non-literal. The magic lies not so much in the words themselves as in the reality which they reflect. A myth doesn't have to be historically accurate, but it may be historically true. A myth is an archetypical narrative that reflects, symbolizes and mediates eternal truths. Here one must be careful not to confuse the image with reality. There is no inherent contradiction between myth and fact. A myth can communicate truth without necessarily being factual.

> Now as myth transcends thought, Incarnation transcends myth. The heart of Christianity is a myth which is also a fact. The old myth of the Dying God, *without ceasing to be myth* comes down from the heaven of legend and imagination to the earth of history. It *happens* – at a particular date, in a particular place, followed by definable historical consequences. We pass from a Balder or an Osiris, dying nobody knows when or where, to a historical Person crucified (it is all in order) *under Pontius Pilate.* By becoming a fact it does not cease to be myth; that is the miracle.[24]

A third characteristic is that a myth is characterized by fantasy. There is little if any possibility that such a chain of events could take place in real life.

A myth also embodies fourthly a universal reality. The reality behind the images of the book of Revelation is much greater than that which is communicated with words.

In the fifth place, Lewis claimed that a myth produces the same response in its recipients. There is an emotional response – one "recognizes oneself" in a new way and comes to deeper insight into oneself, other people, the world in which one lives, and to God. The main point of the narrative about Adam and Eve in the Garden of Eden is not so much the fall into sin, even if that is also important. The most important thing we can learn is that even things that look good, and which can be logically defended, can still be wrong and have disastrous consequences for ourselves and others.

Finally, Lewis said that a myth acts as a bridge between two worlds. Beyond what Lewis considered to be the shallow question of whether a myth is historically factual, a myth forces us to come into closer contact

---

[24] C.S. Lewis, "Myth Became Fact" in *Dock+*, pp. 66–67. Also in *EC*, p. 141.

with truth than we could experience only through knowing the factual. Lewis was convinced that myth is the best way for God to communicate. It leads us into an understanding which surpasses that which we can know through facts or history.

Unlike Bultmann, who was a contemporary of Lewis, Lewis said, "We must not be ashamed of the mythical radiance resting on our theology."[25] The difference between Lewis and Bultmann was that Lewis held that a myth is a truth that God communicates. Bultmann said that myth is merely a human creation. Bultmann wanted to rid the Bible of myths – the process of demythologization. Lewis wondered, "Through what strange process has this learned German gone in order to make himself blind to what all men except him see?"[26] Lewis claimed that Bultmann was only substituting a rich mythology with a poorer one. "Hence what they now call 'demythologising' Christianity can easily be 're-mythologising' it – and substituting a poorer mythology for a richer."[27] Lewis called for more imagination in communicating God's eternal truths to humanity.

Historicity

So what does all this mean for Lewis's view of the historicity of Scripture? He wrote: "as a literary historian, I am perfectly convinced that whatever else the Gospels are they are not legends."[28] In his autobiography he reiterated: "I was by now too experienced in literary criticism to regard the Gospels as myths."[29] Elsewhere Lewis stated that finding a 'historical Jesus' totally different from what we find in the canonical gospels is a mode of 'research' he heartily distrusted.[30]

He laid out his understanding of the historicity of the biblical narrative thus:

> The earliest stratum of the Old Testament contains many truths in a form which I take to be legendary, or even mythical, ... but gradually the truth condenses, becomes more and more

[25] Ibid in *Dock+*, p. 67. Also in *EC*, p. 142.

[26] C.S. Lewis, "Modern Theology and Biblical Criticism" in *CR*, p. 156.

[27] *Malcolm*, ch. 10, p. 52.

[28] "What Are We to Make of Jesus Christ?" in *Dock+*, p. 158. Also in *EC*, p. 40.

[29] *Surprised*, ch. 15, p. 236.

[30] C.S. Lewis, *Paradise Lost*, ch. 1, p. 29.

> historical. From things like Noah's Ark or the sun standing still upon Ajalon, you come down to the court memoirs of King David. Finally you reach the New Testament and history reigns supreme, and the Truth is incarnate. And 'incarnate' here is more than a metaphor.[31]

> Jonah and the Whale, Noah and his Ark are fabulous; but the Court history of King David is probably as reliable as the Court history of Louis XIV.[32]

Referring to the belief that "every sentence of the Old Testament has historical or scientific truth," Lewis defined his own position:

> But this I do not hold, any more than St. Jerome did when he said that Moses described Creation 'after the manner of a popular poet' (as we should say, mythically) or than Calvin did when he doubted whether the story of Job were history or fiction.[33]

Lewis was careful to point out, however, that his opinion that certain Old Testament narratives are non-historical myths had nothing to do with a presuppositional skepticism against the occurrence of miracles in these narratives. In a letter to Corbin Scott Carnell, who had written to ask Lewis for clarification to a footnote in chapter 15 of *Miracles*, Lewis wrote:

> [T]he whole *Book of Jonah* has to me the air of being a moral romance, a quite different *kind* of thing from, say, the account of King David or the New Testament narratives, not *pegged*, like them, into any historical situation.
>
> In what sense does the Bible 'present' this story [Jonah] 'as historical'? Of course it doesn't *say*, 'This is fiction': but then neither does Our Lord *say* that His Unjust Judge, Good Samaritan, or Prodigal Son are fiction. (I would put *Esther* in the same category as Jonah for the same reason). How does a denial, a doubt, of their historicity lead logically to a similar denial of New Testament miracles? Supposing (as I think is the case), that sound critical reading revealed different *kinds* of narrative in the

---

[31] "Is Theology Poetry?" in *WoG*, p. 129. Also in *EC*, p. 16.

[32] "Answers to Questions on Christianity" in *Dock+*, question 10, pp. 57–58. Also in *EC*, p. 325.

[33] C.S. Lewis, "Scripture" in *The Joyful Christian* (NY: Macmillan Touchstone, 1996), p. 110.

> Bible, surely it would be illogical to conclude that these different kinds should all be read in the same way? This is not a 'rationalistic approach' to miracles. Where I doubt the historicity of an Old Testament narrative I never do so on the ground that the miraculous *as such* is incredible.[34]

Lewis writes that we should not interpret God's actions in a non-historical, mythical realm as literal truth.

> But there can be no defence for applying the same treatment to the miracles of the Incarnate God. They are recorded as events on this earth which affected human senses. They are the sort of thing we can describe literally. If Christ turned water into wine, and we had been present, we could have seen, smelled, and tasted. The story that He did so is not of the same order as His 'sitting at the right hand of the Father'. It is either fact, or legend, or lie. You must take it or leave it.[35]

Inspiration

Lewis allowed for the "inspiration" of later extra-biblical material. He once wrote in a personal letter to Clyde Kilby, "If every good and perfect gift comes from the Father of lights, then all true and edifying writings, whether in Scripture or not, must be *in some sense* inspired."[36]

At the same time, Lewis took the Bible's claims seriously. "The Scriptures come before me as a book claiming divine inspiration. I am not prepared to argue with the prophets."[37] He also wrote that "all Holy Scripture [including even the imprecatory psalms] is in some sense – though not all parts of it in the same sense – the word of God."[38]

In summary, we can say that Lewis had a high view of Scripture, although he did not formulate it in terms of infallibility or inerrancy as many evangelical scholars would have liked today. He defined inspiration in terms of God elevating a human text in order to communicate his word through it, rather than God sending down a divine word from heaven.

Yet God plays an active role in the writing of the biblical texts.

---

[34] Personal letter to Corbin Scott Carnell dated April 4, 1953 in *Letters3*, p. 319.

[35] "Horrid Red Things" in *Dock+*, p. 71. Also in *EC*, p. 130.

[36] Personal letter to Clyde S. Kilby dated May 7, 1959 in *Letters3*, p. 1045.

[37] "Historicism" in *CR*, p. 102. Also in *EC*, p. 622.

[38] *Psalms*, ch. 2, p. 19.

> Of course I believe the composition, presentation, and selection for inclusion in the Bible, of all the books to have been guided by the Holy Ghost. But I think He meant us to have sacred myth and sacred fiction as well as sacred history.[39]

The Bible is the word of God in the sense that God can use it to communicate his word to people, although not all parts of the Bible are equally conducive to communicating eternal truth. Although the Bible contains many stories that are most likely not historical events, God still uses them to convey eternal truths in much the same way as God uses non-historical stories like the parables of Jesus to convey eternal truth. Lewis did, however, insist on the historicity of the key events in the life of Christ: the incarnation, crucifixion and resurrection. The truth of Christian faith hangs on the historicity of these events.

Evaluation

Many of Lewis's less conventional ideas about the Bible were never written for publication; they were often presented as preliminary musings in personal letters.[40] He admitted as much in another letter to Edward Dell. "I cannot claim to have a clearly worked out position about the Bible or the nature of Inspiration. That is a subject on which I would gladly learn: I have nothing to teach."[41]

Kevin Vanhoozer comments, "It is difficult to extract a 'doctrine' of Scripture from Lewis's occasional writings, for Lewis was less interested in critical approaches to, or doctrines of, scripture than he was in the realities about which scripture speaks."[42]

According to Philip Ryken, Lewis had originally included a chapter on biblical infallibility in the first draft of *Letters to Malcolm*. In a section that was eventually removed before the book went to print, Lewis explained why he rejected the idea of biblical inerrancy. The first reason was his rejection of a strictly literal interpretation. A second reason was the Bible's own testimony of its origin as the result of normal human

---

[39] Personal letter to Janet Wise dated October 5, 1955 in *Letters3*, pp. 652–653.

[40] Philip Ryken, "Inerrancy and the Patron Saint of Evangelicalism" in John Piper and David Mathis, ed., *The Romantic Rationalist: God, Life, and Imagination in the Work of C.S. Lewis* (Wheaton: Crossway, 2014), p. 48.

[41] Personal letter to Edward T. Dell dated February 4, 1949 in *Letters2*, p. 914.

[42] Kevin J. Vanhoozer, "On Scripture" in MacSwain and Ward, p. 75.

processes, such as when Luke described the research that lay behind both the gospel that bears his name and the Acts of the Apostles.[43]

In addition to Luke's research process, Lewis for Clyde Kilby three other reasons for not believing in inerrancy. In the first place, Paul appears to make a distinction between that which Christ had revealed to him and his own ideas in 1 Corinthians 7:10, 12. Secondly, there are evident contradictions in the text, such as the divergent accounts of the death of Judas in Matthew and Acts or the genealogies of Jesus as relayed by Matthew and Luke. Thirdly, Lewis didn't think his belief that Job and Jonah were not historical was compatible with belief in biblical inerrancy as he understood it.[44]

It wasn't until after Lewis's death that discussions on the Bible's infallibility and inerrancy became current among evangelical theologians. The International Council of Biblical Inerrancy eventually hammered out what have today become standard definitions of important terms like the inspiration, infallibility and inerrancy of the Bible.

In the *Chicago Statement on Biblical Inerrancy* (1978), *infallibility* is defined as "the quality of neither misleading nor being misled and so safeguards in categorical terms the truth that Holy Scripture is a sure, safe, and reliable rule and guide in all matters."[45] The focus in this definition is redirected from the question of whether there are errors in the Bible to the question of whether the Bible is sufficient for the purposes for which God intended it.

Likewise, *inerrant* is defined as "the quality of being free from all falsehood or mistake and so safeguards the truth that Holy Scripture is entirely true and trustworthy in all its assertions."[46]

The authors of the Chicago statement address a number of the objections that people like Lewis had against this understanding of biblical inerrancy.

> The truthfulness of Scripture is not negated by the appearance in it of irregularities of grammar or spelling, phenomenal descriptions of nature, reports of false statements (*e.g.*, the lies of

---

[43] Ryken 2014, pp. 48–51.

[44] Personal letter to Clyde S. Kilby dated May 7, 1959 in *Letters3*, p. 1045.

[45] From the Chicago Statement on Biblical Inerrancy. Quoted in Norman Geisler, ed. *Inerrancy* (Grand Rapids: Zondervan Academic, 1980), p. 500. The full statement of the Chicago Statement on Biblical Inerrancy is available online: <http://library.dts.edu/Pages/TL/Special/ICBI_1.pdf>.

[46] Quoted in Geisler 1980, p. 500.

> Satan), or seeming discrepancies between one passage and another. ... When total precision of a particular kind was not expected nor aimed at, it is no error not to have achieved it. Scripture is inerrant, not in the sense of being absolutely precise by modern standards, but in the sense of making good its claims and achieving that measure of focused truth at which its authors aimed.[47]

One may legitimately wonder whether this definition of inerrancy dies the death of a thousand qualifications. Each exception could in itself possibly be a *prima facie* reason for rejecting claims of inerrancy.

Belief in the Bible's infallibility or inerrancy need not force a person to an unnatural literal interpretation. The Bible comprises many different literary genres. Besides narratives, there are also parables, poetry, legal texts, exaggeration, symbols, metaphors and apocalyptic texts. Did the events recounted in the parable of the prodigal son really happen?[48] Does it matter? Should we interpret John's description of Jesus in Revelation 1:14–16 literally? Does it matter if Jesus really rose from the dead? Ryken explains:

> [B]elief in inerrancy does not bind a person to a literal interpretation of scriptural passages that were not intended to be interpreted literally and that normal human processes of authorship are not incompatible with the inspiration and guiding of the Holy Spirit in guiding the human authors of the Bible.[49]

The problems come when some researchers claim that a certain story in the Bible is a myth or parable while others say that the same story is a historical narrative. Examples of this type would include Adam and Eve in the garden of Eden, Jonah and the great fish and the miracles of Jesus. It is easy to end up in one of two ditches, either by rejecting as legend something the author intended to report as a historical event (the mistake

---

[47] Quoted in Geisler 1980, pp. 500–501.

[48] Did the prodigal son and the good Samaritan really exist? Were people in that area gossiping about a guy who demanded his share of the inheritance which he then squandered? Was the assault and robbery on the road to Jericho a current event that every-one knew about? Could Jesus take neighborhood gossip and turn it on its head to give it new meaning? I wonder. Of course we'll never know, but Lewis's point remains – the value of these stories as bearers of truth is independent of their historicity.

[49] Ryken 2014, p. 50.

many liberal theologians may make) or by interpreting something literally when the author's intentions were more figurative (as some fundamentalists may do). This may even apply to imaginative interpretations of supposedly future events in the book of Revelation.

Lewis pointed to apparent contradictions in the Bible as one reason for rejecting biblical inerrancy. The Chicago statement encourages believers to strive to reconcile inconsistencies in the text, but even when this proves to be impossible (at least for the time being), we should still affirm the Bible as both infallible and inerrant.

> We affirm that canonical Scripture should always be interpreted on the basis that it is infallible and inerrant. ... Apparent inconsistencies should not be ignored. Solution of them, where this can be convincingly achieved, will encourage our faith, and where for the present no convincing solution is at hand we shall significantly honor God by trusting His assurance that His Word is true, despite these appearances, and by maintaining our confidence that one day they will be seen to have been illusions.[50]

Our knowledge of the world of the Bible has grown by leaps and bounds since Lewis's time. Today there are many reasonable explanations to questions that have baffled earlier generations of Bible readers. The discrepancies in the narrative surrounding the death of Judas may suffice as an example. According to Matthew 27:5 Judas went out and hanged himself. According to Acts 1:18 Judas fell and died in a field that he himself had purchased with the money for which he had betrayed Jesus. These two narratives may reflect two different cultural traditions. Matthew wrote for a Jewish audience who would be familiar with *midrash* as a genre. Familiar events, stories and quotes are cut and pasted in unexpected ways in order to give otherwise incomprehensible current events an interpretive key. Luke, who was writing within the Greco-Roman narrative tradition, describes in disgusting detail how ungodly people meet a painful, gruesome death.[51] The problem behind contradictions in the Bible is sometimes due more to our ignorance than to problems with the sources.

---

[50] Quoted in Geisler 1980, p. 500.

[51] Note also Luke's description of Herod's death in Acts 12:21–23. As a contrast to this, we see how he presents the death of the godly Stephen in Acts 7:55–56.

It is not my purpose to criticize Lewis for not believing in biblical inerrancy. His view of the Bible lies fairly close to the definitions of inerrancy that were later developed by the International Council on Biblical Inerrancy, even if one may have reservations about the definitions themselves. By these definitions, the Bible is said to be "free from all falsehood or mistake" while at the same time admitting the presence of contradictions and anachronisms in the text. The biggest problem I see with Lewis's bibliology is one that surfaces any time one attempts to draw some boundaries within theology. Lewis maintained that the historicity of certain biblical narratives is important, but not that of others. How does one determine where the line should be drawn between stories whose historicity is important and those where it is not? Lewis saw a clear boundary around the canonical narratives about the life and work of Jesus Christ as God incarnate. Beyond that, his conclusions seem somewhat more arbitrary. Lewis appears to claim that as a literary scholar, he just "knows" which stories are historical.

> The value of some biblical accounts (e.g., the Resurrection) depends very much on whether the events actually happened, but the value of others (e.g., the fate of Lot's wife) hardly at all. And the ones whose historicity matters are, as God's will, those where it is plain.[52]

Lewis's contention that one simply knows when a narrative's historicity is important is unsatisfying. On this ground, why should Jesus' death on the cross be regarded as an important historical event, but not the fall into sin, especially in light of Romans 5, where Paul makes a clear parallel between these two events and their implications for world history? Lewis criticized Bultmann's rejection of the Bible's miracle stories as unhistorical, but gave us no real tools for determining when their historicity is important.

[52] Personal letter to Clyde S. Kilby dated May 7, 1959 in *Letters3*, p. 1045.

"When I open Ovid, or Grimm, I find the sort of miracles
which really would be arbitrary. Trees talk, houses turn into trees,
magic rings raise tables richly spread with food in lonely places,
ships become goddesses, and men are changed into
snakes or birds or bears. It is fun to read about:
the least suspicion that it had really happened
would turn that fun into nightmare.
You find no miracles of that kind in the Gospels.
Such things, if they could be, would prove
that some alien power was invading Nature;
they would not in the least prove that it was the same power
which had made Nature and rules her every day.
But the true miracles express not simply a god, but God:
that which is outside Nature, not as a foreigner,
but as her sovereign."[1]

[1] C.S. Lewis, "Miracles" in *Dock+*, p. 32. Also in *EC*, p. 113.

God the Great Magician? Miracles and the Modern Mind

Christer Sturmark is a well-known secular humanist who has defended atheism in many public debates with Christian leaders in Sweden. In the past he often made the claim that he would be willing to believe in God if only he could see some empirical evidence that a miracle had taken place. One of my close friends and colleagues decided to take up the gauntlet that Sturmark had thrown down. My friend arranged for Sturmark to meet a tiny, joyful, old lady named Elise Lindqvist. Elise told how she had been diagnosed with tumors in her spine. When people from St. Clara's Church in central Stockholm anointed her with oil, laid hands on her and prayed, she was healed.[2] She has x-rays from both before the healing prayers and afterwards. She has medical records where doctors attest that they don't have any medical explanation, but that the tumors are gone. Elise showed this documentation to Christer Sturmark and told him what happened. When my colleague asked whether Sturmark would now be willing to acknowledge the existence of God, he poo-pooed the whole thing saying that he isn't a doctor and doesn't know how to interpret these medical reports, but that there must be a natural explanation. Now when Sturmark debates Christians he usually says that he would be willing to believe in God if he could see a real miracle, such as an amputated leg grow out again.

Miracles are something of a problem for many Christians. We believe that God can perform miracles, while at the same time being forced to admit that we have never experienced one ourselves. How could a reasonable, educated person in the twenty-first century still believe in miracles when they are so rare?

C.S. Lewis's book *Miracles* was first published in 1947 and revised for a second edition in 1960. In it Lewis argued that before one can answer the question of whether a certain miracle has taken place as a historical event, one must first answer a more foundational philosophical question about whether miracles are even logically possible.

---

[2] Now more than 80 years old, Elise leads an amazing ministry among prostitutes and other victims of trafficking at St. Clara's Church in Stockholm, a work for which she has been honored with a medal by the Queen of Sweden. She tells her life story, including her healing, in the book *Ängeln på Malmskillnadsgatan* (roughly "The Angel of the Red Light District").

In a chapter called "The Naturalist and the Supernaturalist" Lewis defined the terms *naturalist* and *supernaturalist*. Naturalists believe that the universe is a huge process where everything that happens occurs as a result of natural causes within a closed system. Supernaturalists, on the other hand, believe that some events whose causes cannot be completely accounted for by natural processes may be the result of temporary disruptions in the system or interventions by a power outside the system. An event may be considered supernatural if its causes cannot be fully explained by the laws of nature.

Lewis was a supernaturalist. He believed in God because he thought the idea of God gives a more satisfactory explanation than naturalism for two common phenomena in the world: rationality and morality. Lewis was nonetheless careful to point out that having good reason to affirm supernaturalism as a worldview is no guarantee that miracles actually take place.

> It by no means follows from Supernaturalism that Miracles of any sort do in fact occur. God (the primary thing) may never in fact interfere with the natural system He created. ... But if Naturalism is true, then we do know in advance that miracles are impossible.[3]

The argument from reason

> If the solar system was brought about by an accidental collision, then the appearance of organic life on this planet was also an accident, and the whole evolution of Man was an accident too. If so, then all our present thoughts are mere accidents – the accidental by-product of the movement of atoms. And this holds for the thoughts of the materialists and astronomers as well as for anyone else's. But if *their* thoughts – i.e., of Materialism and Astronomy – are merely accidental by-products, why should we believe them to be true? I see no reason for believing that one accident should be able to give me a correct account of all the other accidents. It's like expecting that the accidental shape taken by the splash when you upset a milk-jug should give you

[3] *Miracles*, ch. 2, p. 19.

> a correct account of how the jug was made and why it was upset.[4]

As Lewis defined it, metaphysical (or philosophical) naturalism is the view that nature is all that exists. Naturalists deny the existence of God, the soul, an afterlife or anything supernatural. Nothing exists outside or beyond the physical universe.

With his argument from reason Lewis sought to show that naturalism is self-refuting, or otherwise false and indefensible. Its role in the larger argument Lewis developed in *Miracles* is to show that only supernaturalism can adequately account for the phenomenon of reason. Rationality and morality are two reasons for thinking that supernaturalism is a better interpretive key to the universe than naturalism. If supernaturalism is true, then there is in principle no problem with saying that miracles may also occur.

According to Lewis:

> For this reason the question whether miracles occur can never be answered simply by experience. Every event which might claim to be a miracle is, in the last resort something presented to our senses, something seen, heard, touched, smelled, or tasted. And our senses are not infallible. If anything extraordinary seems to have happened, we can always say that we have been the victims of an illusion. If we hold a philosophy which excludes the supernatural, this is what we always shall say. What we learn from experience depends on the kind of philosophy we bring to experience. It is therefore useless to appeal to experience before we have settled, as well as we can, the philosophical question.[5]

More precisely, Lewis's argument from reason can be stated as follows:

The first premise is that no belief is rationally inferred if it can be fully explained in terms of non-rational (physical or naturalistic) causes.

> It is, of course, possible to suppose that when all the atoms of the universe got into a certain relation (which they were bound to get into sooner or later) they would give rise to a universal consciousness. And it might have thoughts. And it might cause

[4] "Answers to Questions on Christianity" in *Dock+*, question 6, pp. 52–53. Also in *EC*, pp. 320–321.

[5] *Miracles*, ch. 1, pp. 9–10.

> those thoughts to pass through our minds. But unfortunately its own thoughts, on this supposition, would be the product of non-rational causes and therefore, by the rule which we use daily, they would have no validity.[6]

The argument holds that if, as thoroughgoing naturalism entails, all of our thoughts are the effect of physical causes, then we have no reason for assuming that they are also the result of rational processes. According to naturalism, natural causes are both necessary and sufficient for rational thought. Knowledge, however, is apprehended by reasoning from ground to consequent. Therefore, if naturalism were true, there would be no way of knowing it or anything else not the direct result of a physical cause.

The second premise is that if naturalism is true, then all beliefs can be fully explained in terms of non-rational causes such as the movement of atoms or biological evolution.

> The theory that thought therefore is merely a movement in the brain is, in my opinion, nonsense, for if so, that theory itself would be merely a movement, an event among atoms, which may have speed and direction, but of which it would be meaningless to use the words 'true' or 'false.'[7]

Naturalists hold that the physical universe is all that exists; everything that happens in the universe can in principle be explained without recourse to supernatural or unnatural causes. For this reason, naturalists claim that all events must have physical causes, and that human thoughts can ultimately be explained in terms of material causes or physical events such as neurochemical events in the brain that are non-rational.

The third premise is that if naturalism is true, then no belief is rationally inferred.

A fourth premise is that we have good reason to accept naturalism only if it can be rationally inferred from good evidence.

There is thus no good reason to accept naturalism.

> If my own mind is a product of the irrational – if what seem my clearest reasonings are only the way in which a creature

[6] Ibid, ch. 4, p. 43.

[7] "Transposition" in *WoG*, p. 103. Also in *EC*, p. 273.

> conditioned as I am is bound to feel – how shall I trust my mind when it tells me about Evolution?[8]

Lewis asserted that by this logic, the statement *I have reason to believe naturalism is valid* is self-referentially incoherent in the same manner as the sentence *I never tell the truth.* To assume the veracity of the conclusion would eliminate the possibility of valid grounds from which to reach it. To summarize the argument in the book, Lewis quoted J.B.S. Haldane who appealed to a similar line of reasoning. Haldane stated:

> If my mental processes are determined wholly by the motions of atoms in my brain, I have no reason to suppose that my beliefs are true ... and hence I have no reason for supposing my brain to be composed of atoms.[9]

In short, naturalism undercuts itself. If naturalism is true, then we cannot sensibly believe it or virtually anything else.

In some versions of the argument from reason, Lewis extended the argument to defend a further conclusion: that human reason depends on an eternal, self-existent rational being (God). This extension of the argument from reason states:[10]

1) *Since everything in nature can be wholly explained in terms of non-rational (physical) causes, human reason (more precisely, the power of drawing conclusions based solely on the rational cause of logical insight) must have a source that is both non-rational and physical.*
2) *If human reason came from non-reason, it would lose all rational credentials and would cease to be reason.*
3) *So, human reason cannot come from non-reason (from 2).*
4) *So human reason must come from a source outside nature that is itself rational (from 1 and 3).*

---

[8] C.S. Lewis, "The Funeral of a Great Myth" in *CR*, p. 89. Also in *EC*, p. 28. Lewis's use of the word *irrational* was part of Anscombe's critique of a similar line of reasoning in chapter three of *Miracles*. She contended that according to naturalism, the development of thought should be regarded as non-rational rather than irrational. This was among the corrections Lewis later made to the second edition of *Miracles*.

[9] Quoted in *Miracles*, ch. 3, p. 24.

[10] These premises are a summary of the argument Lewis advances in chapter 4 of *Miracles*.

5) *This supernatural source of reason may itself be dependent on some further source of reason, but a chain of such dependent sources cannot go on forever. Eventually, we must reason back to the existence of an eternal, non-contingent source of human reason.*

6) *Therefore, there exists an eternal, self-existent, rational Being who is the ultimate source of human reason. This Being we call God (from 4–5).*

In another text Lewis writes that the incoherence of naturalism leads us to the conclusion that we "belong" to another world than the purely physical one of our empirical experience.

> There is only one way to avoid this deadlock [*viz.*, the incoherence of naturalism]. We must go back to a much earlier view. We must simply accept it that we are spirits, free and rational beings, at present inhabiting an irrational universe, and must draw the conclusion that we are *not derived from it*. We are strangers here. We come from somewhere else. Nature is not the only thing that exists.[11]

Philosophers such as William Hasker,[12] Alvin Plantinga[13] and Victor Reppert[14] have expanded on the argument from reason and credit Lewis with first bringing the argument to light in *Miracles*.

Anscombe's critique

Lewis was for many years an active participant in the Oxford Socratic Club, an association that organized interesting lectures, discussions and debates. Lewis had released the book *Miracles* in 1947. A few months later, on February 2, 1948 he debated the book's thesis with Elizabeth Anscombe, a Roman-Catholic philosopher and later professor at

[11] C.S. Lewis, "On Living in an Atomic Age" in *EC*, p. 365.

[12] William Hasker, *Metaphysics: Constructing a World View* (Downers Grove: InterVarsity Press, 1983), p. 49.

[13] Alvin Plantinga, *Warrant and Proper Function* (New York: Oxford University Press, 1993), pp. 216–238.

[14] Victor Reppert, *C.S. Lewis's Dangerous Idea: A Philosophical Defense of Lewis's Argument from Reason* (Downers Grove: InterVarsity Press, 2003); Victor Reppert, "Several Formulations of the Argument from Reason" *Philosophia Christi* 5/1 (2003): 9–33; Victor Reppert, "Defending the Dangerous Idea" in David Baggett, Gary R. Habermas and Jerry L. Walls, ed., *C.S. Lewis as Philosopher* (Downers Grove: InterVarsity Press, 2008), pp. 53–67.

Cambridge. Anscombe critiqued Lewis's argument from reason as he laid it out in chapter 3 of the book.

Anscombe's first objection was against Lewis's use of the word *irrational*.[15] Lewis had written that "We may in fact state it as a rule that *no thought is valid if it can be fully explained as the result of irrational causes*."[16] Anscombe's point was that there is an important distinction between irrational and non-rational causes to our thoughts and ideas. Irrational causes can be anything from wishful thinking, passions and vested interests to prejudices and narrow-mindedness. Non-rational causes may include brain tumors, electrical impulses to the brain, tuberculosis and fatigue. She agrees with Lewis that if one claims that irrational causes are an adequate foundation for an idea, then the idea lacks a rational foundation. Non-rational causes, on the other hand, do not necessarily lead to incorrect conclusions. Naturalists attempt to base rationality on non-rational causes, but this need not undermine the validity of reason.

Lewis conceded Anscombe's critique on this point and revised his argument for the book's second edition in 1960.

Secondly, Anscombe questioned Lewis's attempt at contrasting valid and invalid reasoning. She writes:

> What *can* you mean by 'valid' beyond what would be indicated by the explanation you would give for distinguishing between valid and invalid, and what in the naturalistic hypothesis prevents that explanation from being given and from meaning what it does?[17]

Her point is that it is meaningless to say that a certain line of reasoning is invalid if there is no such thing as valid reasoning. Lewis had argued that starting from natural, non-rational principles, that all reasoning would be invalid. Anscombe countered that it is legitimate for the naturalist to reason even if rationality only has non-rational causes, since the naturalist does not focus on what possible causes may lie behind the reasoning, only on whether the logic is valid or not.

---

[15] G.E.M. Anscombe, "A Reply to Mr. C.S. Lewis's Argument that 'Naturalism' is Self-Refuting" *Socratic Digest* (nr 4) in *The Collected Philosophical Papers of G.E.M. Anscombe, Vol 2: Metaphysics and the Philosophy of Mind* (Minneapolis: University of Minnesota Press, 1981), pp. 225–226.

[16] *Miracles*, ch. 3, p. 27. (Note: This quote is from the original 1947 edition. Subsequent editions have been corrected.)

[17] Anscombe 1981, p. 226.

Lewis acknowledged later that *valid* was a poor word choice for what he was trying to communicate. He only meant that if naturalism were true, then one would never be able to present an argument where the conclusion followed logically from the premises. He was trying to show that a person's thought processes can be veridical, that is, a reliable or trustworthy road to knowledge and truth, only if it is founded upon something other than non-rational causes.

Anscombe's third objection was that Lewis was equivocal in his use of words like *because, cause* and *reason.*[18] In normal language use one may give *because I want to drink some tea* as an adequate reason for why the water in the kettle is boiling. But an explanation based on purposes or final causes does not explain the physics behind why the water in the kettle is boiling. Lewis accepted this critique and revised the argument to make a clearer distinction between physical causes and final causes.

Many writers have commented on Lewis's state of mind after the debate. Some, like A.N. Wilson, state that Lewis was devastated.[19] Others have written that Lewis could concede Anscombe's points, but nothing more. According to Art Lindsley, Anscombe relayed that Lewis was his normal self when they met for dinner not long after the debate.[20]

Walter Hooper reflects:

> I think it may have been Miss Anscombe's rather bullying quality that left Lewis low and dispirited afterward. His former pupil, Derek Brewer, who dined with him two days later, says that he described the meetings 'with real horror' – 'His imagery was all of the god of war, the retreat of infantry thrown back under heavy attack'. Some who were at the meeting contend that Lewis lost to Miss Anscombe; others that the lady came out second best. Even the contestants said different things. Lewis told me he did not lose the argument. A few years later when I met Miss Anscombe in the common room of Somerville College and asked what she remembered of the meeting, she removed a cigar from her mouth only long enough to say, 'I won.'[21]

---

[18] Ibid, pp. 227–231.

[19] Wilson 1990, 2002, p. 213.

[20] Lindsley 2005, p. 107.

[21] Walter Hooper, "Oxford's Bonny Fighter" in James Como, ed., *C.S. Lewis at the Breakfast Table and Other Reminiscences* (New York: Macmillan, 1979), p. 163. It is said that

John Beversluis criticizes Wilson, "It is simply untrue that the post-Anscombe Lewis abandoned Christian apologetics. ... It is rhetorically effective to announce that the post-Anscombe Lewis wrote no further books on Christian apologetics, but it is pure fiction."[22]

Roughly half of Lewis's apologetic essays were written after the debate. There may be other explanations as to why Lewis did not write any full-length apologetic books after 1948. First, he had become a well-known author. The stream of letters from admirers from around the world increased steadily as his popularity rose. Lewis complained on many occasions about how his sense of duty "forced" him to devote several hours each day to responding to every letter that came in.[23] By the mid-1950s Lewis had also begun a relationship with Joy Davidman that would occupy much of his time.

Morality as an argument against naturalism

Lewis begins the book *Miracles* with two reasons for rejecting naturalism as a worldview. The first reason was the argument from reason. The second indicator that supernaturalism is a better worldview than naturalism is the human sense for morality.

"For when men say 'I ought' they certainly think they are saying something, and something true, about the nature of the proposed action, and not merely about their own feelings."[24]

On this point Lewis calls into question Hume's view of morality, namely that "morality is determined by sentiment. It defines virtue to be *whatever mental action or quality gives to a spectator the pleasing sentiment of approbation*; and vice the contrary."[25] Hume developed an idea that was later called Hume's law whereby one cannot prescribe how a person *ought* to act based on an empirical description of how she *actually* acts. No

---

Professor Anscombe denied Hooper's anecdote in Stephen Schofield, "Professor Anscombe Corrects Father Hooper" *Canadian C.S. Lewis Journal* (December 1979): 7.

[22] Quoted in Lindsley 2005, p. 107.

[23] Personal letter to Arthur Greeves dated December 23, 1941 in *Letters2*, p. 504. He often bewailed the burden of correspondence. He wrote: "But general correspondence – what is called 'having a pen-friend' – is quite impossible for me. The daily letter writing is the chief burden of my life." (Personal letter to Don Holmes dated February 17, 1959 in *Letters3*, p. 1023).

[24] *Miracles*, ch. 5, p. 51.

[25] David Hume, "Concerning Moral Sentiment" from *An Enquiry Concerning the Principles of Morals*, Appendix 1, ¶10. P. 70.

database, no matter how large, is adequate for telling a person what she should do. Hume did not believe that moral judgments reflect an external reality, but rather an internal state of mind. One decides how one should act by following one's feelings in any given situation.

Lewis summarizes Hume's thoughts on morality: "All moral judgements would be statements about the speaker's feelings, mistaken by him for statements about something else (the real moral quality of actions) which does not exist."[26] If Hume is correct on this point, then his ideas have serious implications for how people live their lives in the real world.

> [W]hen they tell us we 'ought to make a better world' the words 'ought' and 'better' must, on their own showing, refer to an irrationally conditioned impulse which cannot be true or false any more than a vomit or a yawn?[27]

The alternative to supernatural causes of our ideas about morality is the idea that our natural impulses also come from natural causes. With a mischievous grin Lewis asks, "Now that I know that my impulse to serve posterity is just the same kind of thing as my fondness for cheese ... do you think I shall pay much attention to it?"[28] Based on this, "[t]here can be no reason for trying to whip up and encourage the one impulse rather than the other."[29] His conclusion is: "If we are to continue to make moral judgements (and whatever we say we shall in fact continue) then we must believe that the conscience of man is not a product of Nature."[30]

Lewis is aware of several possible objections to his preliminary conclusions and asks: "If so stupendous a thing exists, ought it not to be obvious as the sun in the sky?"[31] He then responds to this objection with an example. A pane of glass makes it possible to see the landscape without drawing attention to itself. In the same way, the supernatural makes it possible for us to use our rational and moral abilities without drawing attention to itself. It happens almost unconsciously – just as we follow the rules of grammar when speaking or writing.

---

[26] *Miracles*, ch. 5, p. 51.

[27] Ibid, ch. 5, p. 52.

[28] Ibid, ch. 5, p. 53.

[29] Ibid, ch. 5, p. 53.

[30] Ibid, ch. 5, p. 53.

[31] Ibid, ch. 6, p. 57.

> All these instances show that the fact which is in one respect the most obvious and primary fact, and through which alone you have access to all the other facts, may be precisely the one that is most easily forgotten – forgotten not because it is so remote or abstruse but because it is so near and so obvious. And that is exactly how the Supernatural has been forgotten.[32]

Lewis continues and maintains that a person's inability to sense the supernatural is a relatively recent development in the history of humanity.

> All over the world, until quite modern times, the direct insight of the mystics and the reasonings of the philosophers percolated to the mass of the people by authority and tradition; they could be received by those who were no great reasoners themselves in the concrete form of myth and ritual and the whole pattern of life. In the conditions produced by a century or so of Naturalism, plain men are being forced to bear burdens which plain men were never expected to bear before.[33]

Lewis doesn't regard rationality and morality as proof of miracles. Simply as indicators that there may be a supernatural being who could momentarily suspend the laws of nature or interfere with natural processes. Whether or not this being actually does so is a different question. "From the admission that God exists and is the author of Nature, it by no means follows that miracles must, or even can, occur."[34]

Even if one assumes the existence of God, God could very well be the God of the deist – a God who created the world to function according to a consistent set of natural laws, but who then withdrew to allow it to continue without further disruption by its creator. Another possibility is that the laws of nature are inviolable. Empiricism gives us knowledge as to what has happened. This leads Lewis to question the ability of empiricism to tell us what *could* happen.

> But mere experience, even if prolonged for a million years, cannot tell us whether the thing is possible. … A miracle is by definition an exception. How can the discovery of the rule tell

[32] Ibid, ch. 6, p. 58.

[33] Ibid, ch. 6, p. 59.

[34] Ibid, ch. 7, p. 62.

you whether, granted a sufficient cause, the rule can be suspended?[35]

Miracles

The story of Christer Sturmark and Elise Lindqvist at the beginning of this chapter illustrates Lewis's point that one cannot determine whether a specific miracle has taken place until one has first resolved the more basic philosophical question of whether miracles are possible at all. Once Lewis has laid the a metaphysical foundation whereby supernaturalism would appear to be a better explanation of the human phenomena of rationality and morality, he turns his attention to the question of whether miracles actually occur. Supernaturalism is no guarantee in itself that miracle occur, only that it is not impossible. Through the rest of the book Lewis focuses on one of the most famous critiques of miracles in the history of Western thought. In 1748 David Hume included an argument against miracles in section ten of his book *An Essay Concerning Human Understanding*.[36]

During Hume's day, miracles were used as apologetic evidence. This differed somewhat from the way the resurrection of Christ is used in contemporary apologetics. The miracle claims of that time were more of the "crying-statues-of-the-Virgin-Mary" sort that had great popular appeal.

Hume doesn't claim that miracles were impossible, only that there could never be a case where there is such sufficient evidence for a miracle that the falseness of the witnesses' testimony could be more incredible than the miracle claim itself.

Hume's reasoning has two parts. He first presents a general statement about the laws of nature. He then puts forth several observations concerning the nature of witnesses and the conclusions one can draw from them. If Hume could succeed in undermining the credibility of people who claim to have seen miracles, he could then undermine the truth of other statements that otherwise could not be empirically confirmed.

Regarding the laws of nature, Hume begins with a definition of a miracle:

---

[35] Ibid, ch. 7, p. 63.

[36] Chapter 10.

> A miracle is a violation of the laws of nature; and as a firm and unalterable experience has established these laws, the proof against a miracle, from the very nature of the fact, is as entire as any argument from experience can possibly be imagined.[37]

Hume's definition differs significantly from Lewis, who defines miracle as "an interference with nature by supernatural power."[38]

According to Hume's definition, humanity's collective experience throughout the millennia has shown us that nature generally acts in certain predictable ways. We draw certain probable conclusions from our observations of nature and call these the laws of nature. Hume was keenly aware of the problem of induction – that the conclusions of inductive arguments are never necessary conclusions. We never know with certainty whether our conclusions are true, since the experiences and observations that lead to these conclusions are never exhaustive. There is always the possibility that we have only experienced what is in fact an anomaly or that there may be other events that would appear to contradict the conclusions we have formed based on our experience. In *diagram 1* the xs represent our collective human experience.

x x x x x
x x x x x
x x x x x
x x x x x
x x x x x

Diagram 1

We can say that humanity's collective experience forms a non-contradictory set. Based on our consistent experience, we draw certain conclusions about how the world works and call these the laws of nature, which are symbolized in *diagram 2* as a box around the xs.

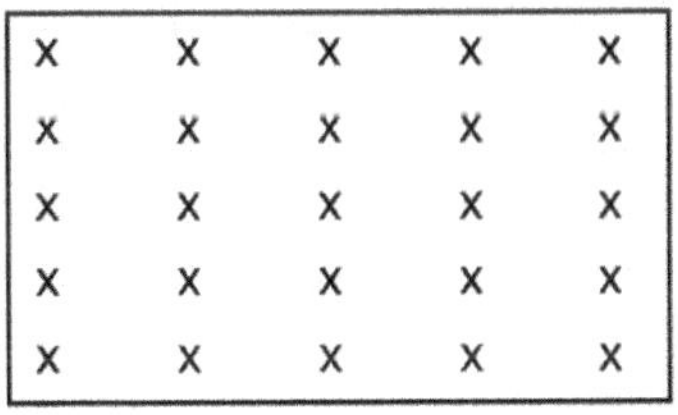

x	x	x	x	x
x	x	x	x	x
x	x	x	x	x
x	x	x	x	x
x	x	x	x	x

Diagram 2

[37] David Hume, Section X "Of Miracles" in *An Essay Concerning Human Understanding* (Oxford: Oxford University Press, 2007), p. 83.

[38] *Miracles*, ch. 2, p. 12.

x x x x x
x x x x x *
x x x x x
x x x x x
x x x x x

Diagram 3

But then something may happen that doesn't fit in with our experience up until that point – something we could not have predicted based on our observations of the regularity of nature. This anomaly is represented in *diagram 3* by an asterisk ∗.

At this point we have to figure out how to relate to this anomaly. We have four main options. First, we could accept this event as a miracle, caused by someone or something outside the system. This is not an option for David Hume and other naturalists who have decided *a priori* that miracles are not possible.

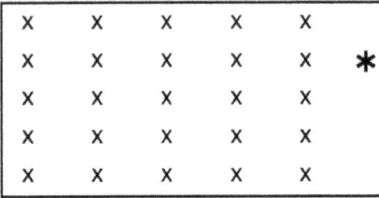

x x x x x
x x x x x *
x x x x x
x x x x x
x x x x x

Diagram 4

A second option is to redefine our previous understanding of the law of nature in light of the new event. We observe that many smokers (x) get lung cancer. Experience shows us that smokers face a much higher risk of coming down with lung cancer than non-smokers. Further observations show us that non-smokers who live with smokers also get lung cancer (∗) in larger numbers than non-smokers in a control group. We revise our earlier understanding of the relationship between smoking and lung cancer to include people who are exposed to second-hand smoke. Our understanding of the law of nature is expanded as shown in *diagram 4.*

A third option is to say that the anomaly (∗) actually belongs to a different set of events that can be described by a different law of nature. For example, our observations tell us that water freezes at zero degrees C. But then I notice that the sea does not freeze even though the water temperature is –1º C. The fact that salt water does not freeze at zero degrees is not a violation of a law of nature; it is consistent with a different set of uniform experiences that we describe as the law of nature that salt water has a lower freezing point than fresh water. The new law of nature is illustrated by the asterisks in *diagram 5.*

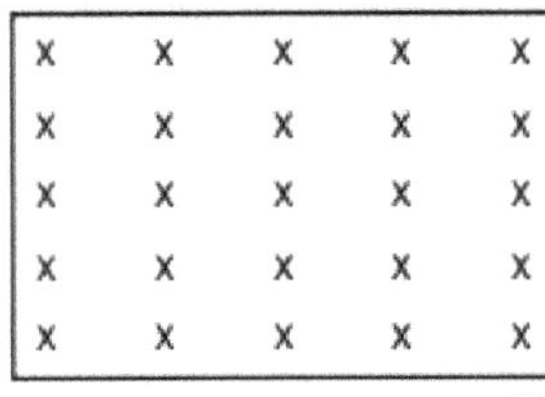
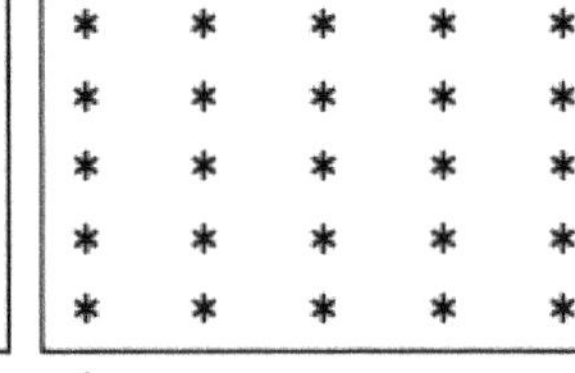

Diagram 5

A fourth option – the one that Hume pursues – is calling into question the credibility of the person making the miracle claims. In *diagram 6* this is represented by the rejection that anomaly (*) has taken place at all. Hume makes certain conclusions about the credibility of a witness based on his observations of many people who claim to have witnessed a miracle.

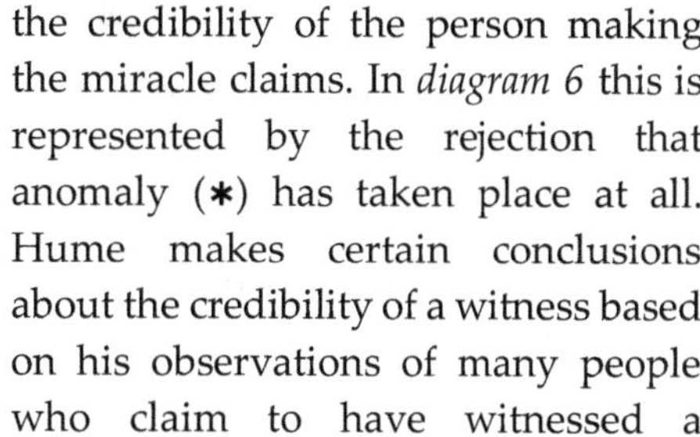

Diagram 6

What does a reliable witness look like? According to Hume, such a person must be so well educated such that one cannot doubt him. Such a person is a safeguard against all kinds of deception. He/she must be above reproach and must risk losing everything if his/her testimony proves to be false.

Not only that, the alleged miracle must have taken place in public, and in a part of the world where the deception could not avoid being revealed.

Hume also points out that people like gossip, exaggerations and rumors. "Do not the same passions, and others still stronger, incline the generality of mankind to believe and report with the greatest vehemence and assurance, all religious miracles?"[39]

Hume states that alleged miracles generally take place among ignorant and primitive peoples.

> [I]f a civilised people has ever given admission to any of them, that people will be found to have received them from ignorant and barbarous ancestors, who transmitted them with that inviolable sanction and authority, which always attends received opinions.[40]

Finally, Hume declares that miracle claims in different religions cancel each other out. Hume didn't just want to undermine the truth-claims of various religions, but also that of miracles themselves.

> Every miracle, therefore, pretended to have been wrought in any of these religions (and all of them abound in miracles), as its direct scope is to establish the particular system to which it is

[39] Hume, "Of Miracles," p. 86.

[40] Ibid, p. 86.

> attributed; so has it the same force, though more indirectly, to overthrow every other system.[41]

Hume's conclusion is that no miracle claims can be more probable than the possibility that the person making the miracle claim is either deceived or lying.

> No testimony is sufficient to establish a miracle, unless the testimony be of such a kind, that its falsehood be more miraculous, than the fact which it endeavours to establish … When anyone tells me that he saw a dead man restored to life, I immediately consider with myself, whether it be more probable that this person should either deceive or be deceived, or that the fact, which he relates, should really have happened. I weigh the one miracle against the other; and according to the superiority, which I discover, I pronounce my decision, and always reject the greater miracle. If the falsehood of his testimony would be more miraculous than the event which he relates; then, and not until then, can he pretend to command my belief or opinion.[42]

Lewis's critique of Hume

Lewis's first critique addresses Hume's metaphysical assumptions about the laws of nature and the possibility of miracles. Lewis contends that Hume's conclusion that miracles are not possible does not follow from his own philosophy. Hume states that the laws of nature are established by "a firm and unalterable experience", but because of the problem of induction – which Hume clearly recognized – and Hume's rejection of notions of causality, he should be cautious about making categorical statements about what is not possible.

> If we have no notion why a thing happens [follows from Hume's rejection of causality], then of course we know no reason why it should not be otherwise, and therefore have no certainty that it might not some day be otherwise.[43]

Because of the problem of induction, we can never know whether our experiences are a fair sample of all possible experiences in the universe.

---

[41] Ibid, p. 88.

[42] Ibid, p. 83.

[43] *Miracles*, ch. 8, p. 77.

Lewis writes: "[A]ll the observations that men have made or will make while the race lasts cover only a minute fraction of the events that actually go on."[44]

According to Hume, the laws of nature are human constructions about how nature probably operates. But Lewis sees a limitation in what one can know just by observing regularities in nature.

> [T]he Laws of Nature explain everything except the source of the events. ... The laws, in one sense, cover the whole of reality except – well, except that continuous cataract of real events which makes up the actual universe. They explain everything except what we should ordinarily call 'everything'. The only thing they omit is – the whole universe. ... Science, when it becomes perfect, will have explained the connection between each link in the chain and the link before it. But the actual existence of the chain will remain wholly unaccountable.[45]

The laws of nature reveal nothing about nature as a whole or what might possibly be outside of nature.

Lewis admits that the laws of nature will function in a consistent, predictable manner – as long as nothing or no one disrupts these natural processes.

> [I]f there was anything outside Nature, and if it interfered – then the events which the scientist expected wouldn't follow. That would be what we call a miracle. In one sense it wouldn't break the laws of Nature. The laws tell you what will happen if nothing interferes. They can't tell you whether something *is* going to interfere.[46]

Lewis gives the example of billiards. The laws of physics are such that when one shoots a billiard ball with a certain amount of force at a certain angle that one can predict with a high degree of accuracy how the balls will move on the table – as long as no trickster reaches in and grabs the ball or otherwise interrupts its normal path. This is exactly what Lewis maintains God does in performing a miracle.

---

44 Ibid, ch. 13, p. 135.

45 C.S. Lewis, "The Laws of Nature" in *Dock+*, p. 78. Also in *EC*, p. 330.

46 "Religion and Science" in *Dock+*, p. 74. Also in *EC*, pp. 144–145.

> [E]very prediction of what will happen in a given instance is made under the proviso 'other things being equal' or 'if there are no interferences'. Whether other things *are equal* in a given case and whether interferences may occur is another matter.[47]

This illustrates option number three above, where the anomaly may actually be an indicator that a wholly different set of rules is in play. Lewis says that these anomalies are what drive the scientific endeavor. "[S]cience actually proceeds by concentrating not on the regularities of Nature but on her apparent irregularities. It is the apparent irregularity that prompts each new hypothesis."[48]

That fact that anomalies take place is evidence that our experience of nature is not "firm and unalterable." Even if the cause of the anomaly is an outside agent and not a not-yet known law of nature, then once the interruption of the natural processes takes place, the laws of nature continue to function based on the new set of circumstances.

> Miraculous wine will intoxicate, miraculous conception will lead to pregnancy, inspired books will suffer all the ordinary processes of textual corruption, miraculous bread will be digested. The divine art of miracle is not an art of suspending the pattern to which events conform but of feeding new events into that pattern.[49]

Lewis thus concludes that Hume's argument is a case of circular reasoning.

> Unfortunately we know the experience against them to be uniform only if we know that all the reports of them are false. And we know all the reports to be false only if we know already that miracles have never occurred.[50]

Regarding Hume's claim that witnesses of miracles love rumors, gossip, exaggerations, and are unreliable, Lewis says that a more objective position would be to examine the witnesses' credibility without making an *a priori* judgment about their character. Although he doesn't address this point in *Miracles,* Lewis emphasizes this point in the story from *The*

---

[47] *Miracles*, ch. 8, p. 78.

[48] Ibid, ch. 13, p. 138.

[49] Ibid, ch. 8, p. 81.

[50] Ibid, ch. 13, pp. 134–135.

Lion, the Witch and the Wardrobe where the professor asks Peter and Susan to apply this principle to the fanciful stories Lucy has been telling about a fantasy land called Narnia.[51]

Lewis suggests moreover that Hume uses loaded terms like "ignorant" and "primitive" and *a priori* precludes the possibility that a rational, educated person could believe in miracles. Lewis believed that a good education and great knowledge are no guarantees that a person is honorable, virtuous or credible. Not only that, Lewis maintains that people in premodern times were not as ignorant of the laws of nature as Hume seems to suppose. When Joseph found out Mary was pregnant, he did not immediately believe it was a miracle. He understood that there will not normally be a pregnancy unless there has been sex.

> If there ever were men who did not know the laws of nature at all, they would have no idea of a miracle and feel no particular interest in one if it were performed before them. Nothing can seem extraordinary until you have discovered what is ordinary.[52]

That is, if a person doesn't understand that it does not normally snow in England in July then she would not be surprised if it in fact snowed in July.

Lewis responds to Hume's assertion that putative miracles in different religions cancel one another. In the first place, Lewis says that Hume's claim rests upon a false assumption. Hume appears to presuppose that all religions use miracles as apologetic evidence. Lewis points out that Hindus, for example, do not base the truth claims (if any) of their faith on the occurrence of miracles.

> All the essentials of Hinduism would, I think, remain unimpaired if you subtracted the miraculous, and the same is almost true of Mohammedanism. But you cannot do that with Christianity. ... A naturalistic Christianity leaves out all that is specifically Christian.[53]

In the second place, Lewis contends that for Hume's argument to be correct, two or more religions would have to present similar miracles as evidence for conflicting truth-claims, which they do not. Christianity's *sine*

---

[51] C.S. Lewis, "Back on this Side of the Door" in *Lion*, pp. 89–90.

[52] *Miracles*, ch. 7, p. 65.

[53] Ibid, ch. 10, pp. 91–92.

qua non is the resurrection of Christ. A similar event cannot be found in any other religion. The miracle claims of most religions have to do with supernatural healings. But even if Muslims or Buddhists are healed, it does not weaken Christianity's truth claim since Christians believe that the goodness and providence of God extend to all of humanity, regardless of religious confession. Lewis writes, "I do not think that it is the duty of a Christian apologist ... to disprove all the stories of the miraculous which fall outside the Christian records, nor of a Christian man to disbelieve them."[54]

The very idea that an adherent of an Eastern religion would use a miracle as apologetic evidence would appear to be highly counterproductive. In a worldview where the physical universe is regarded as an illusion, what would be the point of claiming that a god or holy person had powers over the physical universe?

> But what could be more absurd than that he who came to teach us that Nature is an illusion from which we must escape should occupy himself in producing effects on the Natural level – that he who comes to wake us from a nightmare should *add* to the nightmare? The more we respect his teaching the less we could accept his miracles.[55]

Regarding putative miracles within Buddhism, Lewis comments: "in fact, the religion would get on very much better without them because in that case the miracles largely contradict the teaching."[56]

Hume's criteria for a credible witness would exclude the primary sources to most of world history. By applying this standard consistently, we could not know anything about events which took place outside of large cities before the Renaissance.

Conclusion

The strength of Lewis's *Miracles* is his critique of Hume's metaphysical assumptions. He does not attempt to prove such key miracles as the incarnation and resurrection. His purpose is a bit more modest – to show

---

[54] Ibid, ch. 15, p. 175.

[55] Ibid, ch. 15, p. 176.

[56] C.S. Lewis, "The Grand Miracle" in *Dock+*, p. 80. Also in *EC*, p. 3.

that the incarnation and the resurrection are in keeping with the style of what we otherwise know about God.

> I contend that in all these miracles alike the incarnated God does suddenly and locally something that God has done or will do in general. Each miracle writes for us in small letters something that God has already written, or will write, in letters almost too large to be noticed, across the whole canvas of Nature. They focus at a particular point either God's actual, or His future, operations on the universe ... Not one of them is isolated or anomalous: each carries the signature of the God whom we know through conscience and from Nature. Their authenticity is attested by the *style*.[57]

We recognize this style since God's miracles are somehow "natural" (even though they are by their very nature *super*natural). God does not make bread out of stones, but he makes lots of bread from a little bread. He makes dead people alive again, but he doesn't make stones come to life and start walking around. He speeds up natural processes or rouses natural processes which lie dormant, such as when Jesus healed people or cursed the fig tree which withered.

> Bread is not made there of nothing. Bread is not made of stones, as the Devil once suggested to Our Lord in vain. A little bread is made into much bread. The Son will do nothing but what He sees the Father do. There is, so to speak, a family *style*.[58]

We recognize God's style when God either speeds up natural processes,[59] slows down or reverses natural processes,[60] magnifies natural processes[61] or shrinks natural processes.[62] "Every year, from Noah's time till ours, God turns water into wine. ... Every year God makes a little corn into much corn."[63]

---

[57] *Miracles*, ch. 15, p. 177.

[58] "Miracles" in *Dock+*, p. 30. Also in *EC*, p. 111.

[59] Like when Jesus turned water to wine or cursed the fig tree that then withered.

[60] Like when Jesus healed people or raised people from the dead.

[61] Like in the miracles of feeding thousands where Jesus turned a few fish and a little bread to lots of food.

[62] Like in the incarnation where God creates in one person a bit of what God created in the beginning; or when Jesus controls a specific storm in the same way that God has ultimate control over the weather as a whole.

[63] "Miracles" in *Dock+*, p. 29. Also in *EC*, pp. 110–111.

Lewis's positive case for miracles is weaker, but his ideas that there is a certain style to real miracles is one that some people may find helpful. I believe that Lewis's critique of Hume and defense of the possibility of miracles, together with more modern approaches of showing the historicity of Jesus' resurrection, make a very powerful case for the truth claims of Christian faith.

"What reason have we, except our own desperate wishes, to believe that God is, by any standard we can conceive, 'good'? Doesn't all the prima facie *evidence suggest exactly the opposite?"*[1]

[1] *Grief*, ch. 2, p. 29.

God's Megaphone: The Problem of Pain

C.S. Lewis was no stranger to personal pain. As a boy, he lost both of his parents: his mother, who died of cancer, and his father, who in his grief abandoned Jack and his brother emotionally and sent them away to boarding schools in England. As a young man he directly encountered the ugliness of war.

The Problem of Pain was Lewis's first real book of Christian apologetics, written in 1940. In *The Problem of Pain* Lewis considers the problem of suffering from a purely theoretical standpoint. Twenty years later Lewis would write another book about pain and suffering. This second book has a very different character, as he writes as a way of processing the personal pain he was suffering over the loss of his wife Joy Davidman after an extended battle with cancer. This book is *A Grief Observed.*

The Problem of Pain begins with observations of pain and suffering in our world. In the natural world creatures prey upon one another. In the natural world life is sustained through the death of other things. Humans not only experience pain; they also have the capacity to anticipate and fear pain.

Lewis explains that this was one of the main reasons he abandoned his childhood faith to become an atheist. When one sees all the apparently senseless suffering and random acts of evil in the world, one can easily come to the conclusion that "either there is no spirit behind the universe, or else a spirit indifferent to good and evil, or else an evil spirit."[2]

Yet, if there is so much pain in the world, why did people ever attribute creation to a benevolent creator?

> If the universe is so bad, or even half so bad, how on earth did human beings ever come to attribute it to the activity of a wise and good Creator? ... The spectacle of the universe as revealed by experience can never have been ground for religion: it must always have been something in spite of which religion, acquired from a different source, was held.[3]

---

[2] *ProbPain*, ch. 1, p. 15.

[3] Ibid, ch. 1, p. 15.

He argues that it is unreasonable to think that the idea of God as all-loving and all-powerful simply emerged out of the minds of men. One may speculate that religion may come from the minds of simpler humans whose ignorance of suffering produced a naïve view of the world and thus the idea of a benevolent creator. But Lewis argues that this simply doesn't fit with the historical record. It is obvious that people have always been aware of pain and suffering. He humorously encourages readers who believe that to lay down their books and reflect on the fact that all the major world religions developed in a world without anesthesia.

Instead, Lewis states that Christian faith developed as a response to the Numinous – a sense of awe mixed with fear of the unknown. Nothing about the natural world would lead humanity to experience this type of awe or fear. So where does this awe come from? Either awe is a random artifact of the human mind, or it is a real experience – a revelation. The problem with the first explanation is that awe has shown no tendency of disappearing from the human experience, even from the most advanced and sophisticated humans.

Without a transcendent creator God who ultimately defines good and evil, there are no grounds upon which to substantiate the difference between the two. Lewis states that "pain would be no problem unless, side by side with our daily experience of this painful world, we had received what we think a good assurance that ultimate reality is righteous and loving."[4]

Without God we would not know that a certain set of events is undesirable. On an animal level we may dislike pain and shy away from things that cause us pain, but there's nothing that says we should not inflict pain on others or that certain moral principles that do not directly lead to the infliction or experience of pain should be established. Although people in different times and cultures may have different opinions about which specific actions are morally right or wrong, there is a common sense that there is such a thing as a right or wrong action. People are aware of this – both when other people break the moral standards we expect them to obey, and when we ourselves go against the standards we set up for ourselves and for others. Lewis claims that morality, like awe, is not something that merely comes from nature, and that it thus must come to us as revelation. Without God as the revealer or guarantor of some

[4] Ibid, ch. 1, p. 24.

standard of morality one could only conclude that that's how the world is. Period.

> Either he was a raving lunatic of an unusually abominable type, or else He was, and is, precisely what he said. There is no middle way. If the records make the first hypothesis unacceptable, you must submit to the second.[5]

The problem of pain

The problem of pain is a fundamental theological dilemma and perhaps the most serious objection to Christian faith. It is closely related to the problem of evil. One may make a distinction and say that the focus of the problem of evil is on the abstract, philosophical question while the problem of pain focuses more on the existential experience of suffering. Although Lewis calls his book *The Problem of Pain,* his approach to the issue is quite theoretical – he presents a number of reflections on the problem of evil. This illustrates the tendency among many authors to use the two terms synonymously.

Even within the broader category of theistic religion, the issue of evil and suffering is a serious problem. Christianity aggravates the problem by insisting that God is both all-powerful and completely loving. Lewis repeats a classic formulation of the argument:

> If God were good, He would make His creatures perfectly happy, and if He were almighty He would be able to do what he wished. But the creatures are not happy. Therefore God lacks either goodness, or power, or both.[6]

This is the problem of pain in its simplest form.

1) *If God were all-powerful he would be able to do what he wants.*
2) *If God were good, he would make his creatures perfectly happy. Perhaps it would be better to formulate this premise: "If God were completely good, he would want his creatures to be perfectly happy."*
3) *The creatures are not happy.*

---

[5] Ibid, ch. 1, pp. 23–24.

[6] Ibid, beginning of ch. 2, p. 26.

4) God is lacking in either goodness, power or both.

There are several approaches to this problem of evil. One can call into question any one of the premises 1–3 or one can show how God may have good reasons for allowing the creatures' unhappiness. Lewis uses both approaches.

First, Lewis attempts to call into question premises 1–3 by saying that the use of the terms *good, almighty* and *happy* are equivocal.

> The possibility of solving [the problem] depends on showing that the terms 'good' and 'almighty,' and perhaps also the term 'happy,' are equivocal: for it must be admitted from the outset that if the popular meanings attached to these words are the best, or the only possible, meaning, then the argument is unanswerable.[7]

In the remaining nine chapters, Lewis will develop this basic statement through an in-depth reflection on the meaning of divine omnipotence, divine goodness and human happiness (and pain).

1) If God were all-powerful he would be able to do what he wants.

What do we mean when we say that God is all-powerful or omnipotent? Can God do anything at all? Lewis answers in the affirmative – with certain reservations. God cannot do the logically impossible.

> You may attribute miracles to Him, but not nonsense. This is no limit to His power. If you choose to say 'God can give a creature free will and at the same time withhold free will from it,' you have not succeeded in saying *anything* about God: meaningless combinations of words do not suddenly acquire meaning simply because we prefix to them the two other words 'God can.' It remains true that all *things* are possible with God: the intrinsic impossibilities are not things but nonentities. It is no more possible for God than for the weakest of His creatures to carry out both of two mutually exclusive alternatives; not because His power meets an obstacle, but because nonsense remains nonsense even when we talk it about God.[8]

---

[7] Ibid, beginning of ch. 2, p. 26.

[8] Ibid, ch. 2, p. 28.

The law of non-contradiction still applies. Probing further into divine omnipotence, Lewis applies this principle to possible worlds God could have created. He says that it is impossible for God to create a world "of free souls without at the same time creating a relatively independent and 'inexorable' Nature."[9] The laws of nature imply the possibility, though not a necessity, of evil and suffering, for "not all states of matter will be equally agreeable to the wishes of a given soul."[10] People, if they are free, may take advantage of the fixed laws of nature to hurt one another. Even though we may wish for an omnipotent God to interrupt the laws of nature for the sake of not allowing people to use their free will to harm anyone else, such an action would eventually lead to a wholly meaningless universe, in which nothing important depends on human choices.

> We can, perhaps, conceive of a world in which God corrected the results of this abuse of free-will by His creatures at every moment: so that a wooden beam became soft as grass when it was used as a weapon, and the air refused to obey me if I attempted to set up in it the sound waves that carry lies or insults. But such a world would be one in which wrong actions were impossible, and in which, therefore, freedom of the will would be void; nay, if the principle were carried out to its logical conclusion, evil thoughts would be impossible, for the cerebral matter which we use in thinking would refuse its task when we attempted to frame them. All matter in the neighbourhood of a wicked man would be liable to undergo unpredictable alterations.[11]

We cannot desire freedom to choose and yet hold God responsible for not preventing our choosing of evil. Either we have freedom or we do not. Either we choose or we do not. We cannot have it both ways. We cannot blame God for our evil actions when we freely chose them. We cannot excuse ourselves and accuse God when freedom was truly granted to us. Our understanding of what it means for God to be omnipotent must be viewed from this informed perspective. In other words, we cannot have our cake and eat it too.

---

[9] Ibid, ch. 2, p. 29.

[10] Ibid, ch. 2, p. 32.

[11] Ibid, ch. 2, p. 33.

All this presupposes a second strategy for answering the problem of evil. Not only can one show that terms like *omnipotent, almighty* or *all-powerful* must be carefully defined, one can show (or assume, as Lewis does here) that human freedom is of such inherent value that God would allow even the most horrendous evils that humans can inflict upon others.

Perhaps this is not the best of all logically possible worlds, but it may well be the only feasible one. When we ask what God could have done, we're ascribing the idea of human choice to God. But a perfectly good God cannot question which end is best to pursue; there is no debate about which world is best – God already knows.

> *2) If God were good, he would want to make his creatures perfectly happy.*

In chapter three of *The Problem of Pain* Lewis goes on to look at how the words *goodness* and *loving* are used.

> The problem of reconciling human suffering with the existence of a God who loves, is only insoluble so long as we attach a trivial meaning to the word 'love', and look on things as if man were the centre of them.[12]

Since God is said to be loving, good and powerful in spite of the reality of pain and suffering, it is "abundantly clear" that we need to be more precise in how we use these words. Lewis writes: "[S]ince I have reason to believe, nevertheless; that God is Love, I conclude that my conception of love needs correction."[13]

Here again we see that Lewis points to the equivocal use of the words *goodness* and *loving*. Was it good for God to make a world that was destined to lead to human suffering? According to Lewis, God's idea of goodness is almost certainly unlike ours. "Divine 'goodness' differs from ours, but it is not sheerly different: it differs from ours not as white from black but as a perfect circle from a child's first attempt to draw a wheel."[14]

That is, our use of words like *good* and *loving* are analogical; they are similar to the way we use those words when speaking of God, but not identical. The terms cannot be used univocally (in the exact same sense) when speaking both of humans and God since humans and God are two

---

[12] Ibid, ch. 3, p. 47.

[13] Ibid, ch. 3, p. 40.

[14] Ibid, ch. 3, p. 39.

very different types of beings. Yet if the use of the words is too different, then we cannot not say anything meaningful about God at all.

> If God is wiser than we His judgment must differ from ours on many things, and not least on good and evil. What seems to us good may therefore not be good in His eyes, and what seems to us evil may not be evil. On the other hand, if God's moral judgment differs from ours so that our black may be His white, we can mean nothing by calling Him good; for to say, 'God is Good,' while asserting that His goodness is wholly other than ours, is really only to say, 'God is we know not what.'[15]

Lewis claims that when people speak of the love or goodness of God, they simply mean that God is kind. That is, that God wants people to be "happy" in some vague sense – "not happy in this way or in that, but just happy."[16]

> We want, in fact, not so much a Father in Heaven as a grandfather in heaven – a senile benevolence who, as they say, 'liked to see young people enjoying themselves' and whose plan for the universe was simply that it might be truly said at the end of each day, 'a good time was had by all.'[17]

But God's love is not mere kindness. "Kindness ... cares not whether its object becomes good or bad, provided only that it escapes suffering,"[18] while love wants what is best for someone, even if a certain amount of suffering may be an inadvertent by-product. A "kind" God would want us to be happy, but a loving God may want something for us that transcends our fleeting feelings of happiness.

To demand that God be kind is to express disappointment with the God who is there. "To ask that God's love should be content with us as we are is to ask that God should cease to be God."[19] It is an attempt to create God in our image. "I do not think I should value much the love of a friend who cared only for my happiness and did not object to my becoming dishonest."[20]

---

[15] Ibid, ch. 3, p. 37.

[16] Ibid, ch. 3, p. 40.

[17] Ibid, ch. 3, p. 40.

[18] Ibid, ch. 3, pp. 40–41.

[19] Ibid, ch. 3, p. 48.

[20] Ibid, ch. 3, p. 48.

Therefore Lewis insists that love in its truest, deepest sense is "more stern and splendid than mere kindness."[21] The awareness of a distinction between love and kindness and the recognition of what it means to be the object of God's love make it easier to comprehend why love is not incompatible with suffering. Because God loves us, God will not rest until we become wholly lovable. From that perspective, the suffering of a creature in need of alteration is a mere corollary to God's goodness.

3) The creatures are not happy.

This brings us to the third premise in the problem of evil: *3) The creatures are not happy.* Here Lewis believes some clarification needs to be made. Creatures are not happy, but this is not an inherent problem in the creation. People are unhappy because they have freely chosen not to live according to the intent of their creator. The problem with this premise is that the perception of humankind's sinful condition, and hence of a real need for alteration – a thing obvious even to ancient pagans – has largely disappeared from the modern horizon, rendering the Christian call to repentance and conversion unintelligible. To talk to modern people, Lewis insists, "Christianity now has to preach the diagnosis – in itself a very bad news – before it can win the hearing for the cure."[22]

We must get to the source of the problem. The source is not God, but humanity. "The doctrine of the Fall asserts that the evil which thus makes the fuel or raw material of the second and more complex kind of good is not God's contribution but man's."[23] Through the abuse of their freedom, people have alienated themselves from God and become the unhappy creatures that now fill our world.

Lewis's first observation about human pain and suffering is that it sometimes comes about as a natural consequence of sinful human choices. But not all suffering can be explained in this way. The proper understanding of this situation is that God is not only not the cause of human unhappiness, but God has done everything possible to relieve humans of their unhappiness by providing a means of reconciliation between humans and between humans and God. "We are not merely imperfect creatures who must be improved: we are ... rebels who must lay down our arms."[24]

---

[21] Ibid, ch. 3, p. 40.

[22] Ibid, ch. 4, p. 55.

[23] Ibid, ch. 5, p. 84.

[24] Ibid, ch. 6, p. 91.

Besides suffering that is a direct result of human sin, some of the suffering and pain that a person may experience in this life serves the purpose of calling our attention to the fact that we are on the wrong path in life – one that leads to destruction. "God whispers to us in our pleasures, speaks in our conscience, but shouts in our pains: it is His megaphone to rouse a deaf world."[25]

Although we may think our suffering and pain to be evil, some of it is actually a good that God sends or allows for the sake of leading us back to the correct path through life. The process of renunciation and surrender that characterizes salvation and sanctification can sometimes be very painful.

In *Voyage of the Dawn Treader,* one of the books in *The Chronicles of Narnia,* we meet "a boy called Eustace Clarence Scrubb, and he almost deserved it."[26] Eustace is a spoiled, mean-spirited brat. He loves to manipulate other people. In the book Eustace and the others come to an island where he discovers that he has been transformed into a dragon. Becoming a dragon was not so unusual; it was the natural consequence of what he was in the process of becoming. On the inside he was already a monster; now his outside matched the inside. Later Eustace recounts what happened when he met the Christ-figure Aslan the lion.[27]

> "Well, anyway, I looked up and saw the very last thing I expected: a huge lion coming slowly towards me. And one queer thing was that there was no moon last night, but there was moonlight where the lion was. So it came nearer and nearer. I was terribly afraid of it. You may think that, being a dragon, I could have knocked any lion out easily enough. But it wasn't that kind of fear. I wasn't afraid of it eating me, I was just afraid of it – if you can understand. Well, it came close up to me and looked straight into my eyes. And I shut my eyes tight. But that wasn't any good because it told me to follow it."
>
> "You mean it spoke?"
>
> "I don't know. Now that you mention it, I don't think it did. But it told me all the same. And I knew I'd have to do what it told me, so I got up and followed it. And it led me a long way

---

[25] Ibid, ch. 6, p. 93.

[26] *Dawntreader,* ch. 1 "The Picture in the Bedroom" in *The Complete Chronicles of Narnia* (NY: HarperCollins, 1998), p. 293.

[27] Ibid, ch. 7 "How the Adventure Ended" in *The Complete Chronicles of Narnia* (NY: HarperCollins, 1998), pp. 326–327.

into the mountains. And there was always this moonlight over and round the lion wherever we went. So at last we came to the top of a mountain I'd never seen before and on top of this mountain there was a garden – trees and fruit and everything. In the middle of it there was a well.

"I knew it was a well because you could see the water bubbling up from the bottom of it: but it was a lot bigger than most wells – like a very big, round bath with marble steps going down into it. The water was clear as anything and I thought if I could get in there and bathe it would ease the pain in my leg. But the lion told me I must undress first. Mind you, I don't know if he said any words out loud or not.

"I was just going to say that I couldn't undress because I hadn't any clothes on when I suddenly thought that dragons are snaky sort of things and snakes can cast their skins. Oh, of course, thought I, that's what the lion means. So I started scratching myself and my scales began coming off all over the place. And then I scratched a little deeper and, instead of just scales coming off here and there, my whole skin started peeling off beautifully, like it does after an illness, or as if I was a banana. In a minute or two I just stepped out of it. I could see it lying there beside me, looking rather nasty. It was a most lovely feeling. So I started to go down into the well for my bath.

"But just as I was going to put my feet into the water I looked down and saw that they were all hard and rough and wrinkled and scaly just as they had been before. Oh, that's all right, said I, it only means I had another smaller suit on underneath the first one, and I'll have to get out of it too. So I scratched and tore again and this underskin peeled off beautifully and out I stepped and left it lying beside the other one and went down to the well for my bathe.

"Well, exactly the same thing happened again. And I thought to myself, oh dear, how ever many skins have I got to take off? For I was longing to bathe my leg. So I scratched away for the third time and got off a third skin, just like the two others, and stepped out of it. But as soon as I looked at myself in the water I knew it had been no good.

"Then the lion said – but I don't know if it spoke – 'You will have to let me undress you.' I was afraid of his claws, I can tell

> you, but I was pretty nearly desperate now. So I just lay flat down on my back and let him do it.
>
> "The very first tear he made was so deep that I thought it had gone right into my heart. And when he began pulling the skin off, it hurt worse than anything I've ever felt. The only thing that made me able to bear it was just the pleasure of feeling the stuff peel off. You know – if you've ever picked the scab off a sore place. It hurts like billy-oh but it is such fun to see it coming away."
>
> "I know exactly what you mean," said Edmund.
>
> "Well, he peeled the beastly stuff right off – just as I thought I'd done it myself the other three times, only they hadn't hurt – and there it was lying on the grass: only ever so much thicker, and darker, and more knobbly-looking that the others had been. And there was I as smooth and soft as a peeled switch and smaller than I had been. Then he caught hold of me – I didn't like that much for I was very tender underneath now that I'd no skin on – and threw me into the water. It smarted like anything but only for a moment. After that it became perfectly delicious and as soon as I started swimming and splashing I found that all the pain had gone from my arm. And then I saw why. I'd turned into a boy again."

In *The Great Divorce,* Lewis gives a colorful example of a ghost or damned soul who comes to the outskirts of heaven on a day-trip from hell. This ghost or former man has a red lizard on his shoulder. The man decides that he would rather return to hell than to make the necessary changes to be allowed to enter heaven.[28]

> "Yes. I'm off," said the Ghost. "Thanks for all your hospitality. But it's no good, you see. I told this little chap," (here he indicated the lizard), "that he'd have to be quiet if he came – which he insisted on doing. Of course his stuff won't do here: I realise that. But he won't stop. I shall just have to go home."
>
> "Would you like me to make him quiet?" said the flaming Spirit – an angel, as I now understood.
>
> "Of course I would," said the Ghost.
>
> "Then I will kill him," said the Angel, taking a step forward.

---

[28] *Divorce*, ch. 11, p. 90.

"Oh – ah – look out! You're burning me. Keep away," said the Ghost, retreating.

"Don't you want him killed?"

"You didn't say anything about killing him at first. I hardly meant to bother you with anything so drastic as that."

"It's the only way," said the Angel, whose burning hands were now very close to the lizard.

"Shall I kill it?"

"Well, that's a further question. I'm quite open to consider it, but it's a new point, isn't it? I mean, for the moment I was only thinking about silencing it because up here – well, it's so damned embarrassing."

"May I kill it?"

"Well, there's time to discuss that later."

"There is no time. May I kill it?"

"Please, I never meant to be such a nuisance. Please – really – don't bother. Look! It's gone to sleep of its own accord. I'm sure it'll be all right now. Thanks ever so much."

"May I kill it?"

"Honestly, I don't think there's the slightest necessity for that. I'm sure I shall be able to keep it in order now. I think the gradual process would be far better than killing it."

"The gradual process is of no use at all."

"Don't you think so? Well, I'll think over what you've said very carefully. I honestly will. In fact I'd let you kill it now, but as a matter of fact I'm not feeling frightfully well today. It would be silly to do it now. I'd need to be in good health for the operation. Some other day, perhaps."

"There is no other day. All days are present now."

"Get back! You're burning me. How can I tell you to kill it? You'd kill me if you did."

"It is not so."

"Why you're hurting me now."

"I never said it wouldn't hurt you. I said it wouldn't kill you."

We may summarize Lewis's thinking about this third premise (that the creatures are not happy) with this quote:

> In the fallen and partially redeemed universe we may distinguish (1) the simple good descending from God, (2) the

> simple evil produced by rebellious creatures, and (3) the exploitation of that evil by God for His redemptive purpose, which produces (4) the complex good to which accepted suffering and repented sin contribute.[29]

As long as people resist the sometimes painful work of salvation and sanctification God wants to do in their lives, they will be unhappy.

> Let me implore the reader to try to believe, if only for a moment, that God, who made these deserving people, may really be right when he thinks that their modest prosperity and the happiness of their children are not enough to make them blessed: that all this must fall from them in the end, and that if they have not learned to know Him they will be wretched.[30]

Lewis confesses that no one likes to suffer. "Pain hurts. That is what the word means. I am only trying to show that the old Christian doctrine of being made 'perfect through suffering' is not incredible. To prove it palatable is beyond my design."[31]

The proper good of a creature is to surrender to its creator. Surrender is the most common image Lewis uses of salvation. However, the human spirit, hardened as it is through years of usurpation, will not "even begin to try to surrender self will as long as all seems to be well with it."[32] Thus, the function of pain, on the lowest level, is to shatter the illusion that all is well, to plant "the flag of truth within the fortress of a rebel soul."[33]

The pain that God allows for the sake of salvation and sanctification must run its complete course or else there is a significant risk that once the pain ceases, we will once again be distracted from the path God has set before us. Lewis explains that when he suffers,

> At first I am overwhelmed, and all my little happinesses look like broken toys. Then, slowly and reluctantly, bit by bit, I try to bring myself into the frame of mind that I should be in at all times. … And perhaps, by God's grace, I succeed, and for a day or two become a creature consciously dependent on God and drawing its strength from the right sources. But the moment the

---

[29] *ProbPain*, ch. 7, pp. 110–111.

[30] Ibid, ch. 6, p. 97.

[31] Ibid, ch. 6, p. 105.

[32] Ibid, ch. 6, p. 92.

[33] Ibid, ch. 6, p. 95.

> threat is withdrawn, my whole nature leaps back to the toys … And that is why tribulations cannot cease until God either sees us remade or sees that our remaking is now hopeless.[34]

At the same time, pain may lead us away from God. The worst case scenario is that it may lead a person to a final, defiant rebellion against God. I shall return to Lewis's thoughts on this possibility in the next chapter of this book, "My Will be Done: Hell According to C.S. Lewis."

Summary

In the book *The Problem of Pain*, Lewis lays out the following argument:

1) *If God were all-powerful he would be able to do what he wants.*

This is true *per se*, but one must be careful not to assume that God can do the logically impossible, such as create a world of free creatures who never do evil.

2) *If God were completely good, he would want his creatures to be perfectly happy.*

Here one must be careful not to conflate happiness with goodness or kindness.

3) *The creatures are not happy.*

This is true, but it was not part of God's original plan for the creation to be unhappy. Now that people have placed themselves in a situation where they are unhappy, God may sometimes take advantage of that unhappiness to bring people back to the right relationship with God. That's where they may experience the happiness God desired for them in creation and which God desires in a restored creation.

4) *God is lacking in either goodness, power or both.*

Lewis maintains that this conclusion commits the fallacy of the exhaustive hypotheses. That God may be lacking in goodness or power are not the only logical alternatives. God may be perfectly good and all-powerful but have reasons for allowing human suffering such as allowing it as a by-product of the greater good of human freedom, or as an alarm clock to wake people to the fact that they are living lives that are harmful to

---

[34] Ibid, ch. 6, p. 107.

themselves and to others so that they may mend their ways and enjoy a greater good, heaven.

When suffering becomes personal

In *The Problem of Pain,* Lewis offered the reader this overly humble confession: "You would like to know how I behave when I am experiencing pain, not writing books about it. You need not guess for I will tell you; I am a great coward."[35] Twenty years later Lewis wrote about pain again, this time about his own suffering. In *A Grief Observed* he satisfied, albeit inadvertently, the alleged curiosity of his readers. But he did not come across as a coward; nor did his firm grasp of "a theory of suffering" prove altogether irrelevant. True, his faith in God was challenged; he uttered blasphemies; he doubted God's existence; worst of all, he went through the very objections to God's goodness that he had already refuted in *The Problem of Pain.* They all seemed valid to a disabled mind under the sway of seemingly unbearable pain. But then he came to his senses: "Why do I make room in my mind for such filth and nonsense? Do I hope that if feeling disguises itself as thought I shall feel less?"[36]

When feeling disguises itself as thought, one might be tempted to believe in any kind of nonsense. Nowhere is it truer than in the problem of pain.

In *A Grief Observed* Lewis does not develop a logical argument of the sort he presented in The Problem of Pain. The book appears to be relatively unstructured; it is, as the title indicates, Lewis's personal reflections about suffering, grief, doubt and faith in connection with his wife's cancer and subsequent death. Just like the roller-coaster emotions expressed in the book of Psalms, Lewis weaves a tapestry of questions, complaints and thoughtful reflections.

Among other things, he criticizes Freud's critique of religion. Lewis's experience of love to H.[37] is for him a good sign that faith in God is not a substitute for sex and love, as Freud claimed. If that were true, we would no longer need this simulacrum once we experience true love and sex.

---

[35] Ibid, ch. 6, p. 105.

[36] *Grief,* ch. 2, p. 45.

[37] In *Grief,* Lewis calls his departed loved one H., which was the first initial of his wife Helen Joy Davidman Gresham.

Lewis expresses his pain and says that words that were intended to bring comfort only have the desired effect if the one to be comforted has a sufficient level of spiritual maturity.

> What St. Paul says can comfort only those who love God better than the dead, and the dead better than themselves. If a mother is mourning not for what she has lost but for what her dead child has lost, it is a comfort to believe that the child has not lost the end for which it was created. And it is a comfort to believe that she herself, in losing her chief or only natural happiness, has not lost a greater thing, that she may still hope to 'glorify God and enjoy Him forever.'[38]

Well-meaning friends tried to comfort Lewis by saying that Joy was "in God's hands." Lewis dismisses such empty phrases. "But if so, she was in God's hands all the time, and I have seen what they did to her here."[39] He continues and asks how such suffering could be compatible with our ideas about the goodness of God.

> If God's goodness is inconsistent with hurting us, then either God is not good or there is no God: for in the only life we know He hurts us beyond our worst fears and beyond all we can imagine. If it is consistent with hurting us, then He may hurt us after death as unendurably as before it.[40]

If the dead are still conscious in the afterlife, as many Christians believe, the question arises: "Why should the separation (if nothing else) which so agonizes the lover who is left behind be painless to the lover who departs?"[41] If God did not care enough to protect them from suffering before death, why should death make any difference?

In addition to castigating the inability of "comforting" words to ease our pain, Lewis airs some awful thoughts that bubble up to the surface in the face of suffering. Lewis is not afraid that God does not exist, but that God may not be what we have imagined. What if God is actually cruel, or if God is playing a nasty prank on us?

It is difficult for us to imagine an evil god who lures us into his trap by using pleasure as a bait – simply for the sake of seeing how we respond

[38] Ibid, ch. 2, p. 26.

[39] Ibid, ch. 2, p. 27.

[40] Ibid, ch. 2, pp. 27–28.

[41] Ibid, ch. 2, p. 27.

to suffering. Or could it be as many Calvinists think, that God only appears to be evil because *we* are evil?

> Now God has in fact – our worst fears are true – all the characteristics we regard as bad: unreasonableness, vanity, vindictiveness, injustice, cruelty. But all these blacks (as they seem to us) are really whites. It's only our depravity that makes them look black to us.[42]

Unless we define a word like *good* in somewhat analogical terms whether we apply it to God or to humans, it will be impossible to say anything meaningful about God.

> If cruelty is from His point of view 'good,' telling lies may be 'good' too. Even if they are true, what then? If His ideas of good are so very different from ours, what He calls Heaven might well be what we should call Hell, and vice-versa.[43]

> Why do I make room in my mind for such filth and nonsense? Do I hope that if feeling disguises itself as thought I shall feel less? Aren't all these notes the senseless writhings of a man who won't accept the fact that there is nothing we can do with suffering except to suffer it?[44]

God could certainly allow temporary pain in order to serve a higher purpose or greater good, but how would we know that? How do we know whether God is a benevolent surgeon or an evil vivisector? Lewis writes that not even our convictions that God is good – whatever that means – can protect us from the apparent truths that pain hurts and all normal people shun it. "What do people mean when they say, 'I am not afraid of God because I know He is good'? Have they never even been to a dentist?"[45]

If one has reason – in spite of personal suffering – to believe in a good God, then one must somehow learn to make peace with suffering. One must continue to think rationally, even when it feels as though the rug is being yanked from beneath our feet and our entire life and faith begin to fall uncontrollably to the ground. Lewis states nonetheless that it is not a

---

[42] Ibid, ch. 2, p. 32.

[43] Ibid, ch. 2, p. 32.

[44] Ibid, ch. 2, p. 33.

[45] Ibid, ch. 3, p. 43.

good idea to abandon Christian faith in the midst of suffering. "You can't see anything properly while your eyes are blurred with tears."[46] When the ground of our very being is shaken, we must strive to calm ourselves before we can make a fair assessment of the situation. Lewis compares this to attempting to rescue a drowning person. It's only when he or she stops panicking and flailing about that he or she can be rescued without jeopardizing the safety of the rescuer.

Lewis calms himself and asks: "what new factor has H.'s death introduced into the problem of the universe? What grounds has it given me for doubting all that I believe? I knew already that these things, and worse, happened daily."[47] Why should we allow our feelings to trump what we otherwise have good reason for believing to be true? Yet in spite of the rational decision to not make any long-range decisions when our feelings and our judgment are clouded by suffering, we may still be tempted to wonder whether everything "we otherwise have good reason for believing to be true" might not actually be as ephemeral as a house of cards that can easily be blown down by the slightest puff of wind.

In a text reminiscent of Pascal's wager, Lewis writes that we have to place a bet.

> Your bid – for God or no God, for a good God or the Cosmic Sadist, for eternal life or nonentity – will not be serious if nothing much is staked on it. And you will never discover how serious it was until the stakes are raised horribly high, until you find that you are playing not for counters or for sixpences but for every penny you have in the world. Nothing less will shake a man – or at any rate a man like me – out of his merely verbal thinking and his merely notional beliefs. He has to be knocked silly before he comes to his senses. Only torture will bring out the truth. Only under torture does he discover it himself.[48]

However, he is not calling for a fideistic leap of faith – faith in spite of reason. Lewis believes there are good reasons to continue believing in God in spite of personal suffering. He does not rescind the answers he presented earlier in *The Problem of Pain*.

---

[46] Ibid, ch. 3, p. 45.

[47] Ibid, ch. 3, p. 36.

[48] Ibid, ch. 3, pp. 37–38.

One possible explanation of why God may allow personal suffering is that God has good reasons, even if God doesn't always reveal those reasons to humanity.

> Now if pain is an evil then the infliction of pain, considered in itself, must clearly be an evil act. ... Most of us think that it can rightly be inflicted for a good purpose – as in dentistry or just and reformatory punishment.[49]

Good purposes may lead us to deeper insights about our faith. It is not, as many people believe, a question of God wanting to put us to the test to see how strong our faith is. "God has not been trying an experiment on my faith or love in order to find out their quality. He knew it already. It was I who didn't."[50] It's about razing idolatrous images of God and giving us a more realistic picture of what a relationship with God could look like.

Lewis eventually lands with confidence in the conviction that what we truly need is Christ, "not something that resembles Him."[51] We must recognize that our image of God may not necessarily be an image that comes *from* God. "It has to be shattered time after time. He shatters it Himself. He is the great iconoclast. Could we not almost say that this shattering is one of the marks of His presence?"[52]

The problem that Lewis sees is that every attempt to explain God's possible reasons for allowing suffering inevitably fails when we apply it to the question of animal suffering.

> But the absence of 'soul' in that sense makes the infliction of pain upon them not easier but harder to justify. For it means that animals cannot deserve pain, nor profit morally by the discipline of pain, nor be recompensed by happiness in another life for suffering in this.[53]

Do our "rational" reasons hold water? Do they provide us with a strong faith that can weather the fiercest storms, or will it be like a house of cards? Even if the house of cards should fall, what do we do then? Start again. But one will never know whether the new construction is any stronger than the one that fell. At least not until it is also put to the test.

---

49 C.S. Lewis, "Vivisection" in *Dock+*, pp. 224–225. Also in *EC*, pp. 693–694.

50 *Grief,* ch. 3, p. 52.

51 Ibid, ch. 4, p. 65.

52 Ibid, ch. 4, p. 66.

53 "Vivisection" in *Dock+*, p. 225. Also in *EC*, p. 694.

When Lewis saw how Joy sank deeper and deeper into the abyss of pain, he probably prayed that he would be willing to take her pain if only she could be released from it. I think that is what many loved ones would pray on behalf of a suffering child, spouse or parent. But isn't that exactly what happens in death? Our loved one is relieved from her pain while those of us who remain are left to bear it in their place.

"God in His mercy made
The fixed pains of Hell.
That misery might be stayed,
God in His mercy made
Eternal bounds and bade
Its waves no further swell.
God in his mercy made
The fixed pains of Hell."[1]

"I know that many wiser and better Christians than I in these days do not like to mention heaven and hell even in a pulpit."[2]

"The Landlord does not condemn them to lack of hope:
they have done that themselves. …
Left to itself, the desire without the hope would soon
fall back to spurious satisfactions, and these souls
would follow it of their own free will
into far darker regions at the very bottom of the black hole."[3]

"Men say that his love and his wrath are one thing."[4]

---

[1] *PRegress*, book 10, ch. 3, pp. 207–208.

[2] "Learning in War Time" in *WoG*, p. 48. Also in *EC*, p. 579.

[3] *PRegress*, book 10, ch. 3, p. 207.

[4] Ibid, book 10, ch. 3, p. 207.

Ray Baker

My Will Be Done: Hell According to C.S. Lewis

Hell was a theme to which Lewis returned with surprising regularity. Besides two extended texts – *The Great Divorce* and chapter 8 in *The Problem of Pain* – he touched on this burning question in a number of different contexts. Ironically, there is very little about hell and the fate of the ungodly in *The Screwtape Letters,* a book whose focus lies more on the Christian life than on what comes after death.

C.S. Lewis was a scholar who has thought much over human's fate after death. His reflections on hell – both in his fiction and his non-fiction – are almost without comparison in insight and creativity. In this chapter I will synthesize his ideas on the duration, quality, purpose and finality of hell and highlight some areas where I believe Lewis could have been more logically consistent.

C.S. Lewis shared the sentiments of many people today. "There is no doctrine which I would more willingly remove from Christianity than this, if it lay in my power. ... If a game is played, it must be possible to lose it."[5] But since Jesus so clearly warned against hell, Lewis believed that one must take his words seriously. Yet how does one reconcile the possibility that some people may end up in hell with a classic Christian concept of a loving God? He writes,

> I am not going to try to prove the doctrine tolerable. Let us make no mistake; it is not tolerable. But I think the doctrine can be shown to be moral by a critique of the objections made, or felt, against it.[6]

To understand Lewis's concept of hell, one must first look at his understanding of humanity and of God. Lewis believed that if one doesn't like the idea of eternal reward and eternal punishment, it is often because one has a faulty concept of God. One cannot understand God's greatness and character while at the same time trivializing both God's goodness and the sin that makes it impossible for sinful people to dwell in God's presence.

---

[5] *ProbPain*, ch. 8, p. 118.

[6] Ibid, ch. 8, p. 120.

The nature of God, the nature of humanity

According to Lewis, divine sovereignty and human freedom go hand-in-hand in an almost inexplicable way. Today many people would call his position *compatibilism*. Starting from our temporal perspective, we humans cannot understand how God, who is eternal, can allow people to choose freely while at the same time remaining sovereign. Yet both ideas seem to stand together in such a way that we cannot understand one without the other. Lewis writes:

> 'Work out your own salvation in fear and trembling' – pure Pelagianism. But why? 'For it is God who worketh in you' – pure Augustinianism. It is presumably only our presuppositions that make this appear nonsensical. We profanely assume that divine and human action exclude one another like the actions of two fellow-creatures so that 'God did this' and 'I did this' cannot both be true of the same act except in the sense that each contributed a share.[7]

The tension between free will and divine sovereignty is only one of many apparent paradoxes in the Christian faith, along with pleasure and renunciation, reason and imagination, and "thick" and "clear" religions. Typical of Lewis, he did not think that the solution to these paradoxes lay in an Aristotelian golden mean. Rather one should hold to both extremes, but in balance.

Lewis believed firmly that people are free and that they therefore are morally responsible for their actions.

> We know that we can act and that our actions produce results. Everyone who believes in God must therefore admit ... that God has not chosen to write the whole of history with His own hand. Most of the events that go on in the universe are indeed out of our control, but not all. It is like a play in which the scene and the general outline of the story is fixed by the author, but certain details are left for the actors to improvise.[8]

---

[7] *Malcolm*, ch. 9, pp. 49–50.

[8] C.S. Lewis, "Work and Prayer" in *Dock+*, p. 105. Also in *EC*, p. 161.

In *Perelandra,* Ransom comes to the conclusion that "Predestination and freedom were apparently identical."[9] In another context, Lewis wrote, "Free will is the *modus operandi* of destiny."[10] It is necessary to affirm both ideas, even if they seem from a human, temporal perspective to be contradictory.

> For every attempt to see the shape of eternity except through the lens of Time destroys your knowledge of Freedom. Witness the doctrine of predestination which shows (truly enough) that eternal reality is not waiting for a future in which to be real; but at the price of removing Freedom which is the deeper truth of the two.[11]

He illustrates the relation between predestination and human freedom with our understanding of the nature of light. Sometimes light appears to observers as particles, while at other times it manifests itself as a wave. It is likewise easier for humans to see God's sovereignty at some points while human freedom comes more into focus at others.

> [B]ut till (if ever) we can see the consistency it is better to hold two inconsistent views than to ignore one side of the evidence. The real inter-relations between God's omnipotence and Man's freedom is something we can't find out. ... It is plain from Scripture that, in whatever sense the Pauline doctrine [of election] is true, it is not true in any sense which excludes its (apparent) opposite.[12]

From God's atemporal perspective, there is no contradiction. "For the Enemy [God] does not foresee the humans making their free contributions in a future, but sees them doing so in His unbounded Now. And obviously to watch a man doing something is not to make him do it."[13] For God then, there is no such thing as *fore*knowledge or *pre*destination.

He presents a similar line of thought in *The Discarded Image.*

> Eternity is quite distinct from perpetuity, from mere endless continuance in time. Perpetuity is only the attainment of an

[9] *Perelandra,* ch. 11, p. 149.

[10] C.S. Lewis, "On Stories" in *OOW,* p. 15. Also in *EC,* p. 500.

[11] *Divorce,* ch. 13, p. 141.

[12] Personal letter to Emily McLay dated August 3, 1953 in *LettersWHL,* p. 252; Also in *Letters3,* p. 355.

[13] *Screwtape,* letter 27, p. 150.

> endless series of moments, each lost as soon as it is attained. … God is eternal, not perpetual. Strictly speaking, He never foresees; He simply sees. Your 'future' is only an area, and only for us a special area, of His infinite Now. He sees (not remembers) your yesterday's acts because yesterday is still 'there' for Him; he sees (not foresees) your tomorrow's acts because He is already in tomorrow. As a human spectator, by watching my present act, does not at all infringe its freedom, so I am none the less free to act as I choose in the future because God, in that future (His present) watches me acting.[14]

God can be sovereign without determining everything that happens in the world. Without true human freedom, people cannot be held morally accountable for their actions. "[S]ince the two conceptions, in the long run, mean the same thing – to think of this bad man's perdition not as a sentence imposed on him but as the mere fact of being what he is."[15] Likewise, without human freedom, there can be no justice in judgment.

The nature of God

Lewis believed that both divine justice and divine mercy demand the idea of hell. Without a hell one would have just cause to question God's justice. If God knows all the evil that people cause yet ignores it, God is no longer just, but an enabler. It is unfair both to the guilty and to the innocent to turn a blind eye to human evil.

God's standards for right and wrong are not arbitrary – they are grounded in God's nature. That's why evil people will not be permitted to continue in their sin forever and believe mistakenly that they've "won." God's justice demands that people come to the realization that evil is evil and that goodness and morality have their source in the nature of God.

Hell is also an expression of divine mercy and grace. Hell was created as a "… tourniquet on the wound through which the lost soul else would bleed to a death she never reached."[16]

The pain that the sinner experiences in hell, whether physical or psychological, is also an expression of God's mercy in that it prevents human evil from harming even more people.

---

[14] *Discarded*, ch. 4, p. 89.

[15] *ProbPain*, ch. 8, p. 123.

[16] *PRegress*, book 10, ch. 4, p. 180.

Human nature

When God created humanity, it was with the intention that human beings would live in a relationship with God. To illustrate this, let's call it humanity's "factory settings." People have unfortunately changed these factory settings through their sinful choices. Now the new default setting is that humanity is separated from God and headed for destruction.

I once had a computer that gradually became slower and slower. A friend of mine who is much more knowledgeable than I about these things took a look at my computer and concluded that I'd downloaded a lot of programs and files that conflicted with each other as well as several viruses. The best solution would be to save my documents and restore all the factory settings. The computer worked much better after that.

Just like my computer, once we realize that our "settings" in life no longer work, we can go back to the factory settings. In theological terms this is called repentance and salvation.

Lewis believed that for people to be held morally responsible for their actions, they must also be free. One can choose to promote the good of creation and general revelation, which is found in every person, or one can choose to follow the sinful tendencies that are also there as a result of original sin. The free moral choices one makes can lead to a lasting character – a virtuous life or a character that makes it impossible for a person to heed the voices that call one to a virtuous life. In *The Magician's Nephew*, Aslan says of Uncle Andrew: "[he] has made himself unable to hear my voice. If I spoke to him, he would hear only growlings and roarings. Oh Adam's sons, how cleverly you defend yourselves against all that might do you good!"[17] When this happens as a result of the consistent choices one makes through life, one can no longer distinguish between good and evil.

Since we are created to live in a relationship with God, we are dependent upon God for our continued existence. When one becomes separated from God, or when God defers to people's wishes to be left alone in hell, they will die both physically and spiritually.

Lewis's understanding of hell

In this section, I would like to highlight Lewis's answers to a number of common questions about hell: *What does hell look like? How does one end up*

[17] *Magician*, ch. 14 "The Planting of the Tree", p. 67.

there? and *What kind of fate can one expect there?* Lewis's answers to these three questions will even cast some light on his thoughts regarding the duration, quality, purpose and finality of hell.

What does hell look like?

Lewis's theology shows clear signs of influence from Augustine, who in turn was strongly influenced by both Plato[18] and the Neoplatonist Plotinus. Plotinus believed that God was pure Being, the greatest good. Everything else can be placed on a scale where the beings closest to God are also those who share divine character qualities like existence. The farther away from God one comes, the more one is lacking in these divine attributes.

One can see similar ideas in Lewis's theology of hell. In *The Great Divorce,* heaven and celestial beings are portrayed as really real. The ungodly, who come to the outskirts of heaven on a day trip from hell, are presented as shadows or ghosts. Their voluntary distance from God makes them both less corporeal and less real. On the outskirts of heaven, even the grass and the water are so hard that it hurts for the ghosts to come into contact with them.[19] When a mother (who has been reduced to a ghost in hell) wants to meet her son who died in childhood, she receives the answer that she needs "to be thickened up a bit" first before her son would be able to see her at all.[20]

Lewis describes the ontologically "real" nature of heaven:

---

[18] Andrew Walker, "Scripture, revelation and Platonism in C.S. Lewis" *Scottish Journal of Theology* 55/1 (2002): 19–35. "Lewis's Platonism is unmistakable ... Lewis found in Platonism a comprehensive way to reconcile reason's dialectic with the reasons of the heart. To settle for anything less than such a reconciliation, he felt, would be to betray his experience of art, mind, and the everyday world." "[M]any aspects of Lewis's thought are Platonic to the core." (Corbin Scott Carnell, *Bright Shadow of Reality: Spiritual Longing in C.S. Lewis* (Grand Rapids: Eerdmans, 1974), pp. 67, 71). It is also comic to note that according to *The Great Divorce* (chapter 1), the chthonic bookshops in the gray city sell the collected works of Aristotle. Perhaps Plato's books are available in celestial bookshops?

[19] This hierarchy of being is nicely illustrated by Lewis's application of the term *Shadowlands* to normal, earthly, human life. The name Shadowlands also betrays a striking connection to Plato's cave allegory, where humans can only sense the shadows and simulacra of an unseen reality. Life on earth is characterized by a certain degree of goodness and existence – more than that which characterizes hell and its denizens, but less real than heaven and its inhabitants. In *The Last Battle* Digory explains the hierarchy of existence and how the old Narnia the children knew was "only a shadow or copy of the real Narnia, which has always been here and always will be here" (*LBattle,* ch. 15 "Further Up and Further In", pp. 519–520. In this context Digory also exclaims, "It's all in Plato, all in Plato!"

[20] *Divorce,* ch. 11.

> [T]he heavenly real, certainly no less than the natural universe and perhaps very much more, is a realm of objective facts – hard, determinate facts, not to be constructed *a priori,* and not to be dissolved into maxims, ideals, values, and the like. One cannot conceive a more completely 'given,' or, if you like, a more 'magical,' fact than the existence of God as *causa sui.*[21]

In *Reflections on the Psalms,* Lewis describes God as "an utterly concrete Being (far more concrete than we)."[22] In this sense Lewis shows clear traces of Plato without it being simply labeled Platonism. In contrast to Platonism, Lewis's idea of the really real – God – is also physical.

Based on this hierarchy of being, Lewis believed that even the eternal fate of the godly will be corporeal.

> Christianity is almost the only one of the great religions which thoroughly approves of the body – which believes that matter is good, that God Himself once took on a human body, that some kind of body is going to be given to us even in Heaven and is going to be an essential part of our happiness, our beauty, and our energy.[23]

This hierarchy of being illustrates an important aspect of Lewis's theology of hell. The closer a being is to God, the higher ontological status it has. In the same token, the farther one comes from God, the less real one also becomes. There are no "people" in hell; only the remains of human beings. These remains are what is left over when all the good that is part of human nature gradually disappears through one's persistent choices to live apart from God. When one rejects God, one also rejects all the good things that God wishes to give to people: joy, beauty, friendship, generosity, love, goodness, benevolence, maybe even existence itself. The only things that remain are one's selfishness, bitterness, spite, revenge, and a total lack of grace and forgiveness. Lewis illustrates this idea in *The Great Divorce* where hell is presented as a gray, rapidly expanding city where people move farther and farther away from each other since they cannot tolerate the others' presence.[24]

---

[21] *Malcolm,* ch. 19, p. 104.

[22] *Psalms,* ch. 8 "Nature", p. 87.

[23] *MC,* book 3, ch. 5, pp. 55–56.

[24] *Divorce,* ch. 2.

In one of the conversations in *The Great Divorce*, a ghost tries to understand the true nature of things in hell. He receives an explanation from writer George MacDonald, who in this book is a spokesman for Lewis' own ideas.[25]

> 'Then those people are right who say that Heaven and Hell are only states of mind?' 'Hush,' said he sternly. 'Do not blaspheme. Hell is a state of mind – ye never said a truer word. And every state of mind, left to itself, every shutting up of the creature within the dungeon of its own mind – is, in the end, Hell. But Heaven is not a state of mind. Heaven is reality itself. All that is fully real is Heavenly. For all that can be shaken will be shaken and only the unshakable remains.'[26]

Lewis drew a clear contrast between what humans were intended to be by the creator, and what they will become in hell as a consequence of their choices.

> To be a complete man means to have the passions obedient to the will and the will offered to God: to have been a man – to be an ex-man or 'damned ghost' – would presumably mean to consist of a will utterly centered in its self and passions utterly controlled by the will.[27]

Lewis's idea about hell as a rubbish dump for the remains of what once were humans has clear parallels with *gehenna*, the Greek word for hell in the New Testament. *Gehenna* in turn comes from the valley of ge-Hinnom, an area just outside the city wall of Jerusalem where ancient Judeans had sacrificed children to false gods in times of moral and spiritual decay. The area is said in popular imagination to have been so contaminated that it became the site of the city's rubbish tip where perpetual smoke rose from the burning rubbish.

Another image for hell comes from *The Screwtape Letters*, where hell is pictured as an all-encompassing bureaucracy. Lewis did not believe there is fire and brimstone in hell, nor in a devil who runs around

---

[25] There are certain similarities here between MacDonald and Virgil in Dante's *Inferno*. Both act as insightful guides into unknown worlds beyond the grave.

[26] *Divorce*, ch. 9, pp. 68–69.

[27] *ProbPain*, ch. 8, pp. 125–126.

tormenting people with a pitchfork.[28] As a professor of literature, it was important for Lewis to emphasize that one must not "confuse the doctrine with the *imagery* by which it may be conveyed"[29] when the Bible describes the fate of the godless in hell.

How does one end up in hell?

Lewis's answer to this question is closely related to his understanding of salvation. According to Lewis, people are saved only when they stop fighting against God and surrender to God's will and plan for their lives. It is only then that they become truly human. A good illustration is the story of the dreadful boy Eustace in *The Voyage of the Dawn Treader*.[30] Eustace's consistently selfish actions led his body to be transformed into a dragon that matched his evil soul. Only when he surrendered completely to Aslan did he become fully human on both the inside and the outside.

The most important aspect of Lewis's answer to this question is that he didn't believe that God sends anyone to hell. "It's not a question of God 'sending' us to Hell. In each of us there is something growing up which will of itself be Hell unless it is nipped in the bud."[31] "A man can't be taken to hell, or sent to hell: you can only get there on your own steam."[32] Nor is hell a judgment or punishment meted out by God. "We are therefore at liberty ... to think of this bad man's perdition not as a sentence imposed on him but as the mere fact of being what he is."[33]

The people who end up in hell do so as a natural consequence of the choices made in life. They choose to live their lives without God, and God in love and justice defers to their moral maturity even when it entails self-destructive choices.

> There are only two kinds of people in the end: those who say to God, 'Thy will be done,' and those to whom God says, in the end, '*Thy* will be done.' All that are in Hell, choose it. Without

---

[28] Incidentally, there is good reason for a healthy dose of skepticism when it comes to contemporary tales of putative "journeys" to hell. In these tales, Satan is invariably portrayed as some kind of king or lord over hell, punishing the souls who are there. The biblical image is that hell was created as a place of punishment *for* Satan (Matt 25:41). The idea of Satan tormenting people in hell has greater similarities to the Book of Enoch, Dante's *Inferno* and *Paradise Lost* than it does with the Bible.

[29] *ProbPain*, ch. 8, p. 124.

[30] *Dawntreader*, ch. 6.

[31] C.S. Lewis, "The Trouble with X" in *Dock+*, pp. 154–155. Also in *EC*, p. 360.

[32] *DT*, p. 49.

[33] *ProbPain*, ch. 8, p. 124.

> that self-choice there could be no Hell. No soul that seriously and constantly desires joy will ever miss it. Those who seek find. To those who knock it is opened.'[34]

Those who refuse to surrender to God continue in their rebellion against God. "I willingly believe that the damned are, in one sense, successful, rebels to the end; that the doors of hell are locked on the *inside*."[35] It is thus not God who locks them up in hell, but the rebels themselves who distance themselves from God until God finally removes all blessing from them. God had never intended for any person to end up in hell. "The saved go to a place prepared for them, while the damned go to a place never made for men at all."[36]

What kind of fate can one expect in hell?

Many people have the idea that heaven will be boring. Sometimes we hear people say that they'd rather go to hell where they can play poker and drink beer with their buddies. At least there, they'll have some fun. Lewis claimed it was the exact opposite. God created people as sensuous beings with the capacity to enjoy friendship, sex, good food and drink (including beer). It is only in fellowship with God in heaven that the natural human capacity to experience pleasure will continue. Hell will be boring: friendship, beauty and all the good things one enjoys in life will be blatantly absent. The only thing left will be the unbridled human vices that make a person unbearable.

Lewis was aware of the common objection to the doctrine of hell due to the disproportionality between finite sin and everlasting punishment. He speculated freely at this point and presented several possible solutions. First, he called into question the temporality of hell. That is, he wondered whether hell really entails an endless expanse of time. "That the lost soul is eternally fixed in its diabolical attitude we cannot doubt: but whether this eternal fixity implies endless duration – or duration at all – we cannot say."[37] Likewise, "Our Lord ... usually emphasises the idea, not of duration but of *finality*."[38]

Second, Lewis speculated on the nature of time. In the alternative worlds of *The Chronicles of Narnia* and in his space trilogy, time often flows

---

[34] *Divorce*, ch. 9, pp. 72–73.

[35] *ProbPain*, ch. 8, p. 127.

[36] Ibid, ch. 8, pp. 124–125.

[37] Ibid, ch. 8, p. 127.

[38] Ibid, ch. 8, pp. 126–127.

differently than it does in our world. He writes in *The Problem of Pain* that it is possible that time also has breadth in addition to length, and that time should be viewed as a plane and not as a line. An omniscient God would also know whether granting a person more time would make it easier for him to repent. If more opportunities (even more chances after death) would make a difference, God would give them.

One could illustrate this with a hardened criminal who upon release from prison would perhaps like to stay out of prison, but who lacks the willpower to make the necessary changes in lifestyle.[39] In the same way, there is at least a theoretical possibility for someone in hell to repent and be saved, and thus be released from suffering, but considering the total absence of divine goodness and grace in hell, the chances that anyone in point of fact does that are negligible.

Discussions of one's fate in hell naturally raise the question of how the godly could enjoy being in heaven with the knowledge that some of their loved ones are suffering in hell.

Lewis answered this question with yet another question: "Are we more merciful than God?"[40] We cannot allow our subjective feelings to determine how we are to interpret the goodness of God. In *The Great Divorce*, Lewis tells the story of Sarah and Frank Smith. Sarah is in heaven. Her husband Frank comes on an excursion from hell to the outskirts of heaven where he meets Sarah. Just as he always did in life, Frank tries to manipulate Sarah into feeling sorry for him in hell, but to no avail. Sarah finally goes her way filled with joy and a song in her heart.

> What some people say on earth is that the final loss of one soul gives the lie to all the joy of those who are saved. … That sounds very merciful: but see what lurks behind it. … The demand of the loveless and the self-imprisoned that they should be allowed to blackmail the universe: that till they consent to be happy (on their own terms) no one else shall taste joy: that theirs should be the final power; that Hell should be able to *veto* Heaven.[41]

According to Lewis, hell can never blackmail heaven. The damned will never be able to hold the final joy of the saved as hostage.

---

[39] This point is insightfully raised by Jonathan Kvanvig in *The Problem of Hell* (New York: Oxford University Press, 1993), p. 120.

[40] *ProbPain*, ch. 8, p. 126.

[41] *Divorce*, ch. 13, p. 120.

Evaluation

It would appear that Lewis is somewhat inconsistent in his thoughts on hell. Some aspects of his theory seem to fit more naturally with annihilationism or conditionalism, the idea that the ungodly will eventually cease to exist as an eternal, irrevocable punishment. If one's situation in hell means that one is separated from all blessings (the capacity to experience pleasure, joy, friendship, beauty) as Lewis maintains, it would be consistent to claim that one is also separated from the capacity for existence. According to Lewis, people become something less than fully human as a result of sin. It is only through surrender to God and salvation that they can be restored to full humanity. In hell, the corruption continues, which makes people not only less and less human, but less and less real.[42] Lewis wrote that "a damned soul is nearly nothing."[43] Among other things, he described hell as "... 'the darkness outside,' the outer rim where being fades away into nonentity."[44] Yet several pages earlier, he explained why he did not believe in ultimate annihilation. There he gave the analogy of a log on a fire. It ceases to be a log, but it does not cease to exist. It continues to exist in new forms: ashes, gases, heat, light, etc. Lewis argued that total annihilation is not a possibility due to certain physical laws.

There are several problems here. First, it could be argued that Lewis's ideas are at odds with the Christian doctrine of *creatio ex nihilo*. If God can create something from nothing, then it is not too difficult to believe that God can cause something that exists to cease existing.

Of course this applies to the material universe. The laws of nature that govern the material world do not necessarily apply to the immaterial world. Lewis clearly rejected the physicalism and naturalism of his day, which insisted that the material universe is all that exists. He held to a mind-body dualism wherein human beings have both physical and spiritual dimensions. In spite of this, it would appear that Lewis commits something of a category error when he assumes that the immaterial dimension is also governed by the laws of nature. The laws of nature that govern the material world do not necessarily apply to other dimensions

---

[42] Lewis never placed much emphasis on the ontological argument for God's existence, but he shared its presupposition that being is better than non-being.

[43] *Divorce*, ch. 13, p. 139.

[44] *ProbPain*, ch. 8, p. 127.

beyond the physical. In other words, that which is physically impossible due to certain laws of nature may nonetheless be logically and metaphysically possible. It is not physically possible for a person to lift a fully-grown horse into the air. Yet there is nothing illogical about the idea that a person with extraordinary strength like Pippi Longstocking or Superman could do it. Matter and energy cannot be destroyed; they take on new forms. This does not mean that the immaterial human soul could not be annihilated or otherwise cease to exist. Based on his understanding of both God and human nature, I maintain that Lewis would have been more logically consistent if he had concluded that God would defer to a person's will to live life without God even when that choice leads to a final cessation of existence.

A second problem for Lewis relates to the nature of human freedom. He seems inconsistent when he presupposes a compatibilist definition of human freedom ("Predestination and freedom were apparently identical") on one hand while at the same time claiming that God's omnipotence is voluntarily limited for the sake of deferring to human free choices[45] – something that presupposes libertarian incompatibilism.

Lewis appears to define human freedom in compatibilist terms when it relates to salvation and libertarian incompatibilism when it comes to damnation.

> Well, I would say that the most deeply compelled action is also the freest action. By that I mean, no part of you is outside the action. It is a paradox. I expressed it in *Surprised by Joy* by saying that I chose, yet it really did not seem possible to do the opposite.[46]

This apparent inconsistency is perhaps nowhere more clear than in Lewis's account of own salvation in *Surprised by Joy*. He writes that he had a free choice "in a sense," but that it was not necessarily a libertarian free choice.

> I say, 'I chose,' yet it did not really seem possible to do the opposite. ... You could argue that I was not a free agent, but I am more inclined to think that this came nearer to being a

45 "Finally, it is objected that the ultimate loss of a single soul means the defeat of omnipotence. And so it does." Lewis, *ProbPain*, ch. 8, p. 129. Yet Lewis regarded this as a miracle in itself – that the Almighty would both freely limit himself and make adjustments for even self-destructive human choices.

46 "Cross-Examination" in *Dock+*, p. 261. Also in *EC*, p. 553. Compare *Surprised*, ch. 14.

> perfectly free act than most that I have ever done. Necessity may not be the opposite of freedom.[47]

In addition, Lewis describes himself as "the most reluctant convert in all England" and God as one who loves the prodigals whom he brings in "kicking, struggling, resentful, and darting his eyes in every direction for a chance of escape."[48] Hardly a description of libertarian free choice.

In the name of consistency, Lewis has two options. He could presuppose libertarian human freedom for both salvation and damnation or he could recognize that people are not free in a libertarian sense. Libertarian freedom preserves the goodness of God *vis-à-vis* people in hell. However, it takes its toll on God's sovereignty. Is God really in control of the universe at all? Prayer would be limited to confession of sin and praising God for divine attributes. There would be no point in making any petition of God that involves human choices or actions. "Lord, please save my father" and "Lord, please help me get that job" become meaningless. Nor would thanking God for blessings that involve human choice be meaningful. "Lord, thank you that this wonderful person and I choose to love each other and get married – because we know that you didn't have anything to do with us becoming the wonderful people we are, or orchestrating the course of human events so that we would meet each other and fall in love."

A more realistic option given Lewis's overall theology would be to recognize that people are not free at all; they are slaves under sin. When one is saved by Christ one is still not free in a libertarian sense. There is an enemy of our souls who has a vested interest in leading people away from God and keeping them in sin. At the same time, there is also a good God who does everything possible to influence people to want to be saved.

A presumption of compatibilism for both salvation and damnation would mean that God somehow "causes" some people to freely lock themselves into hell – in a similar manner to God's way of compelling others to freely accept the gift of grace. In this case, the problem of God's goodness would remain. That is, if God has even a little part in people ending up in hell, then God bears part of the blame, so to speak. This is the very problem Lewis tries to circumvent by positing that God does not send anyone to hell and that the gates of hell are locked from the inside.

---

[47] *Surprised*, ch. 14, p. 224.

[48] Ibid, ch. 14, p. 229.

A third area of difficulty for Lewis relates to the classic Christian understanding of the resurrection of the body – the idea that both the godly and the ungodly will be raised from the dead to receive their eternal rewards and punishments (John 5:28–29). Lewis portrays the human "remains" in hell as incorporeal "damned ghosts." Lewis does not deny the resurrection of the body – on the contrary, God and the highest levels of the hierarchy of being are the ultimately real and "concrete." The problem is that he seems to do injustice to the idea of the bodily resurrection – at least in relation to the ungodly. Based on his hierarchy of being, he claims that our present physical bodies are only "half real and phantasmal"[49] in comparison with the body the godly will receive in the resurrection of the dead, while the ungodly have a nearly incorporeal existence.

A fourth problem is not as big as some others. Lewis writes in *The Problem of Pain*[50] that Jesus' talk of hell as a legal judgment is a figure of speech similar to Jesus' other metaphors for hell, destruction and deprivation. In spite of this, and although Lewis rejects the idea that suffering in hell is a punishment or judgment, he commonly refers to the people in hell as "the damned." Consider these passages already quoted in this chapter:

> To be a complete man means to have the passions obedient to the will and the will offered to God: to have been a man – to be an ex-man or '*damned* ghost' – would presumably mean to consist of a will utterly centered in its self and passions utterly controlled by the will.[51]

> I willingly believe that *the damned* are, in one sense, successful, rebels to the end; that the doors of hell are locked on the inside.[52]

> The saved go to a place prepared for them, while *the damned* go to a place never made for men at all.[53]

Of course, one could say that this is only a figure of speech, or that by their free choices, the ungodly damn themselves, but this still presumes some

[49] Personal letter to Arthur Greeves dated August 19, 1947 in Walter Hooper, ed., *The Letters of C.S. Lewis to Arthur Greeves (1914–1963)* (New York: Collier/Macmillan, 1986), p. 511.

[50] *ProbPain*, ch. 8, p. 126.

[51] Ibid, ch. 8, pp. 125–126. My emphasis.

[52] Ibid, ch. 8, p. 127. My emphasis.

[53] Ibid, ch. 8, pp. 124–125. My emphasis.

kind of judgment and punishment, not merely the natural consequences of one's choices.

This leads to a fifth problem for Lewis related to his understanding of punishment and retribution. Lewis is quite clear in his texts that deal specifically with the doctrine of hell that he rejects the idea that hell is retributive in purpose in favor of a theory of self-determination. Yet this seems to be at odds with his writings on a closely related topic. In 1953 Lewis published the article "The Humanitarian Theory of Punishment" in the legal journal *Res Judicatae*.[54] In this article he rejects what he calls the "humanitarian" theory of punishment, which would reform the penal system by treating criminals as sufferers from an illness. According to this humanitarian theory, the purpose of punishment should not be retributive, but either deterrence by example or remedial in the healing or treatment of the criminal. Lewis urges a "return to the traditional or Retributive theory not solely, not even primarily, in the interests of society, but in the interests of the criminal."[55] He believes that this view "carries on its front a semblance of mercy which is wholly false."[56] If one views deterrence as the primary purpose of the penal system, then it is not necessary that the one being punished is truly the one who committed the crime. If one rejects this idea as unjust, Lewis claims it is only because one has a residual concept of justice based on a retributive understanding of desert. Regarding the remedial view of punishment, Lewis writes,

> To be 'cured' against one's will and cured of states which we may not regard as disease is to be put on a level with those who have not yet reached the age of reason or those who never will; to be classed with infants, imbeciles, and domestic animals.[57]

That is to say, the legal right to govern one's own affairs and the moral responsibility for one's actions are taken away.

Lewis illustrates this conviction in a creative way in *That Hideous Strength*. The book is on one level, as Lewis himself admitted, a creative critique of the modernist anthropology he criticized in *The Abolition of Man*. In *That Hideous Strength*, the evil institution N.I.C.E. applies the

---

[54] C.S. Lewis, "The Humanitarian Theory of Punishment" *Res Judicatae* 6 (1953): 224–230. Also in *Dock+*, pp. 287–294 and *EC*, pp. 698–709.

[55] Ibid, p. 224; Also in *Dock+*, p. 287 and *EC*, p. 698.

[56] Ibid, p. 230; Also in *Dock+*, p. 293 and *EC*, p. 704.

[57] Ibid, p. 229; Also in *Dock+*, p. 292 and *EC*, p. 703.

humanitarian theory on the general populace for the purpose for manipulating and controlling people.

> As regards crime in general, they had already popularised in the press the idea that the Institute should be allowed to experiment pretty largely in the hope of discovering how far humane, remedial treatment could be substituted for the old notion of 'retributive' or 'vindictive' punishment.[58]

Justice demands that punishment be in proportion to the crime committed. The humanitarian theory – and other similar utilitarian perspectives on punishment – do not depend on concepts of desert and thus do not preserve the idea of proportionality as a foundation of justice.

> For desert was always finite: you could do so much to the criminal and no more. Remedial treatment, on the other hand, need have no fixed limit; it could go on till it had effected a cure, and those who were carrying it out would decide when *that* was.[59]

Instead of administering an impartial justice, N.I.C.E. wanted to "treat" everyone who refused to conform to their plans to take over the world.

> The executive of the N.I.C.E. has no connection with politics: and if it ever comes into relation with criminal justice, it does so in the gracious role of a rescuer – a rescuer who can remove the criminal from the harsh sphere of punishment into that of remedial treatment.[60]

When it comes to crimes against the civil law, Lewis advocates a return to the concept of desert and retribution as the only view that respects the individual's freedom and responsibility. Yet in the very similar case of crimes against God's laws, Lewis removes the concept of desert and retribution in favor of self-determination. Could not Lewis's critique of the humanitarian theory of punishment also be turned against his view of hell? He writes:

> But do not let us be deceived by a name. To be taken without consent from my home and friends; to lose my liberty; to

---

[58] *Hideous*, part 3, ch. 4, p. 47.

[59] Ibid, part 3, ch. 4, p. 47.

[60] Ibid, part 6, ch. 4, p. 84.

> undergo all those assaults on my personality which modern psychotherapy knows how to deliver; to be re-made after some pattern of 'normality' hatched in a Viennese laboratory to which I never professed allegiance; to know that this process will never end until either my captors have succeeded or I grown wise enough to cheat them with apparent success—who cares whether this is called Punishment or not?[61]

Lewis is unwilling to call consignment to hell a punishment, but isn't this the very type of playing with words of which he accuses the humanitarian theory of punishment? One could easily say that taking a sinner from his home and friends, causing him to lose his liberty, to force him to undergo all the assaults on his personality that consignment in hell knows how to deliver; to be re-made after some pattern of 'normality' hatched in a heavenly laboratory to which he never professed allegiance; to know that this process will never end – who cares whether this is called punishment or not?

A final problem for Lewis is the difficulty of harmonizing his theory with the Bible. Lewis claims that hell is not an issue of judgment or punishment, but rather the natural consequences of a person's free choices. The ungodly will certainly suffer in hell, but it is not because God judges them or consigns them to hell. It is difficult to integrate this idea with biblical passages that speak of hell as a punishment (Matthew 25:46; 2 Thessalonians 1:9), God's wrath (John 3:36; Romans 9:22; Revelation 14:10 and 19:15), and that God casts the ungodly into a lake of fire (Revelation 20:15). Even if one interprets the lake of fire metaphorically, as Lewis does, taking God's active role in casting the ungodly into the lake of fire and reinterpreting it as a person's free choice to lock himself into hell from the inside remains problematic. Henri Blocher makes the keen observation that "the Biblical picture of the wrathful Lord and Judge of all hardly suggests a mere passive role. There is something suspicious in the zeal to exonerate God of responsibility in judgement – theodicy built on insignificance?"[62] Jürgen Moltmann rightly criticizes interpretations like this as "atheistic" perspectives.[63]

---

[61] "The Humanitarian Theory of Punishment", p. 227; Also in *Dock+*, p. 290 and *EC*, p. 701.

[62] Henri Blocher, "Everlasting Punishment and the Problem of Evil" in Nigel M. de S. Cameron, ed., *Universalism and the Doctrine of Hell* (Carlisle: Paternoster, 1992), p. 300.

[63] "The logic of hell seems to me not merely inhumane but also extremely atheistic: here the human being in his freedom of choice is his own lord and god. His own will is his

Conclusion

If one defines salvation in terms of surrender, as Lewis does, then universalism presents a logical dilemma. God must either violate people's free will and save them even though they don't want to surrender, or else it must be possible for them to finally reject God. Surrender is a must. God is a "gentleman" who will not force himself on anyone.

> In the long run the answer to all those who object to the doctrine of hell is itself a question: 'What are you asking God to do?' To wipe out their past sins and, at all costs, to given them a fresh start, smoothing every difficulty and offering every miraculous help? But He has done so, on Calvary. To forgive them? They will not be forgiven. To leave them alone? Alas, I am afraid that is what He does.[64]

C.S. Lewis is always a creative and innovative Christian thinker. Even if his speculations on the fate of the ungodly are fraught with problems, his ideas have inspired generations of Christian thinkers who continue to reflect on these important questions.

---

heaven – or his hell. God is merely the accessory who puts that will into effect. If I decide for heaven, God must put me there; if I decide for hell, he has to leave me there. … Free human beings forge their own happiness and are their own executioners. They do not just dispose over their lives here; they decide on their eternal destinies as well. So they have no need of any God at all." (Jürgen Moltmann, "The Logic of Hell" in Richard Bauckham, ed., *God Will Be All in All: The Eschatology of Jürgen Moltmann* (Minneapolis: Fortress, 2001), p. 45).

[64] *ProbPain*, ch. 8, p. 128.

"Perfect love, we know, casteth out fear. But so do several other things – ignorance, alcohol, passion, presumption, and stupidity."[1]

"The glory of God, and, as our only means to glorifying Him, the salvation of human souls, is the real business of life."[2]

"By the way, did you ever meet, or hear of,
anyone who was converted from scepticism
to a 'liberal' or 'demythologized' Christianity?"[3]

[1] C.S. Lewis, "The World's Last Night" in *EC*, p. 51.

[2] "Christianity and Culture" in *CR*, p. 14. Also in *EC*, p. 73.

[3] *Malcolm*, ch. 22, p. 119.

The Battle Between Reason and Emotions: The Christian Life

The Christian life is often compared with a journey. John Bunyan's classic *Pilgrim's Progress* (1678) is one of the most widely distributed books of all times. The image of the Christian life as a journey continues to speak to many people today. A journey is exciting. It is dynamic and organic, in contrast to a static faith that seems engraved in stone. Jesus himself used the journey metaphor when he called people to follow the narrow path that leads to life and avoid the broad road that leads to destruction.[4]

Lewis made use of this metaphor in the first book he published after his conversion, *The Pilgrim's Regress*. The point is that without a clear guide, there's always a risk of getting lost. Sometimes the quickest way forward is to retrace one's path to get back onto the right road again.[5]

Evangelists, social commentators and talking heads on television sometimes claim that we are headed in the wrong direction. Even if Lewis shared the opinion that many things in our culture have gone wrong, he did not think that the secularized West was headed back to a pagan past.

> It is hard to have patience with those Jeremiahs, in Press or pulpit, who warn us that we are 'relapsing into Paganism'. It might be rather fun if we were. It would be pleasant to see some future Prime Minister ... trying to kill a large and lively milk-white bull in Westminster Hall. But we shan't. What lurks behind such idle prophecies, if they are anything but careless language, is the false idea that historical process allows mere reversal; that Europe can come out of Christianity 'by the same door as in she went' and find herself back where she was. It is not what happens. A post-Christian man is not a Pagan; you might as well think that a married woman recovers her virginity by divorce. The post-Christian is cut off from the Christian past and therefore doubly from the Pagan past.[6]

---

[4] Matthew 7:13–14.

[5] *MC*, first book, ch. 5, p. 28.

[6] *Temporum*, p. 15. In another text he adds the image of government ministers who offer sandwiches to the dryads in Hyde Park ("Is Theism Important?" in *Dock+*, p. 172 and *EC*, p. 54).

The road forward both for individuals and culture is to turn back to the one who is the way, the truth and the life.[7] In this chapter I shall examine some of Lewis's ideas about the Christian life. In particular, I will look at his ideas on doubt and faith, sanctification and calling.

Faith

Lewis defined faith as "the power of continuing to believe what we once honestly thought to be true until cogent reasons for honestly changing our minds are brought before us."[8] Faith is not a matter of blindly accepting something even when it defies reason. Faith is founded upon facts and true statements. We believe something because it is reasonable, not because it is absurd. And we continue to believe it until we are given good reasons to change our minds. Lewis did not regard shifting emotions as good reason for changing one's mind.

In the essay "Is Theism Important?" Lewis wrote about two ways of using the word *faith*. These correspond to the Latin words *fides* and *fiducia*. Lewis did not use these Latin words in this text, but rather called them *Faith-A* and *Faith-B*. Faith-A (*fides*) relates to things we hold to be true. It is a conviction that a certain statement is an accurate reflection of an external reality. Faith-B (*fiducia*) is the personal response to the truths one affirms with Faith-A. Faith-A lays the epistemological foundation to which Faith-B is an existential commitment. Lewis explained: "Philosophical arguments for the existence of God are presumably intended to produce Faith-A. No doubt those who construct them are anxious to produce Faith-A because it is a necessary precondition of Faith-B."[9] Arguments for the existence of God may provide grounds for a personal commitment to the God who is there.

Ever since the Enlightenment, many people have taken it for granted that one cannot *know* anything about religion and religious claims; one may simply *believe*. During the twentieth century many Christians accepted this epistemological watershed. American fundamentalist Christians isolated themselves in a little bubble after the humiliating defeat in the so-called "Scopes Monkey Trial" (1925). In many countries bishops and theologians failed to develop a thorough apologetic when

[7] John 14:6.

[8] C.S. Lewis, "Religion: Reality or Substitute?" in *CR*, p. 42. Also in *EC*, p. 135.

[9] C.S. Lewis, "Is Theism Important?" in *Dock+*, p. 173. Also in *EC*, p. 55.

facing the challenges of logical positivism, choosing rather to forfeit the match with attitudes like "Christian faith isn't about *proof*" and "It doesn't matter whether Jesus really rose from the dead a long time ago; the main thing is that he lives in the preaching of the church."

In many places in Europe and North America, Christian leaders stopped emphasizing the truth claims of Christianity in favor of the pragmatic and therapeutic effects of faith. Although Lewis believed that Christian faith also has a pragmatic value, he was unwilling to give up its truth claims.

> In lecturing to popular audiences I have repeatedly found it almost impossible to make them understand that I recommended Christianity because I thought its affirmation to be objectively *true*. They are simply not interested in the question of truth or falsehood. They only want to know if it will be comforting, or 'inspiring', or socially useful. (In English we have a peculiar difficulty here because in popular speech 'believe in' has two meanings (a) to accept as true, (b) To approve of – e.g. 'I believe in free trade'. Hence when an Englishman says he 'believes in' or 'does not believe in' Christianity, he may not be thinking about *truth* at all. Very often he is only telling us whether he approves or disapproves of the Church as a social institution.)[10]

Lewis maintained that one can never discuss the value of Christianity in any meaningful sense without first taking a clear stand on how one views Christianity's truth claims.

Doubt

Even Christians who base their Faith-B upon Faith-A sometimes face doubts. Paradoxically, many people who have a clear intellectual idea that God is love sometimes wonder why they never feel "kissed" by God. Lewis said that the Christian life is a struggle – but not between faith and reason on opposite ends of a tug-of-war. Rather, "The battle is between faith and reason on one side and emotion and imagination on the other."[11]

---

[10] C.S. Lewis, "Modern Man and his Categories of Thought" in *EC*, p. 619.

[11] *MC*, third book, ch. 11, p. 139. Similar ideas are expressed in "Religion: Reality or Substitute?" in *CR*, p. 43 and *EC*, p. 136.

It is precisely one's emotions that tempt a believer to abandon her convictions, to withdraw her commitment to God.

Perhaps one could diagnose two forms of doubt: intellectual doubt and emotional doubt.

First, there is intellectual doubt. This type of doubt comes when one begins to question the foundational ideas of the Christian faith: the existence of God, the resurrection of Jesus, the reliability of the Bible, etc. Many people may also get hung up on other questions or problems that are not as decisive for Christianity's truth claims, such as how we should interpret the creation narratives of Genesis, the stance of Christians on various political and ethical issues and historical atrocities that have been committed in the name of God, such as the crusades, the inquisition, witch-hunts and the suppression of scientific inquiry.

The best way to deal with intellectual doubt is to study. This is where apologetics can have both an internal and an external function. Internally, the study of apologetics can strengthen the faith of those who already believe so that they understand *why* they believe as they do. Externally, the study of apologetics can give non-believers good reasons for why they should believe. The study of apologetics and embracing the logical reasons for Christian commitment is the best way of dealing with intellectual doubt.

Intellectual questions may nonetheless sometimes mask what is in reality emotional doubt. The true issue is a person's rebellion against the call to bow the knee before God, even though he may use intellectual questions as a smokescreen to hide the real problem.

This emotional doubt is probably more common than intellectual doubt. It can be expressed in many different ways: doubt about the goodness of God, doubt that one is truly saved, existential feelings of anxiety or depression, feelings that one's sins are not forgiven, worries about the future, fear of hell and more. There can be many causes, including medical causes, traumatic experiences (abuse, illness, accidents, divorce, death), peer pressure, hypocritical Christians and a misguided concept of God.

Lewis experienced this kind of emotional doubt after the death of his wife Joy in 1960.

> Not that I am (I think) in much danger of ceasing to believe in God. The real danger is of coming to believe such dreadful things about Him. The conclusion I dread is not 'So there's no

> God after all,' but 'So this is what God's really like. Deceive yourself no longer.'[12]

But this was not the first time Lewis had felt this kind of emotional doubt. Much earlier, in the midst of the intellectual tug-of-war that led him to faith in Christ, he wrote to his childhood friend Arthur Greeves:

> I think the trouble with me is lack of faith. I have no rational ground for going back on the arguments that convinced me of God's existence; but the irrational deadweight of my old sceptical habits, and the spirit of this age, and the cares of the day, steal away all my lively feeling of the truth, and often when I pray I wonder if I am not posting letters to a non-existent address. Mind you I don't think so – the whole of my reasonable mind is convinced: but I often *feel* so. However, there is nothing to do but to peg away. One falls so often that it hardly seems worth while picking oneself up and going through the farce of starting over again as if you could ever hope to walk. Still, this seeming absurdity is the only sensible thing I do, so I must continue it.[13]

Much later he concluded that the best way to deal with emotional doubt is to refuse to allow one's feelings to trump sound reason.

> Now Faith … is the art of holding on to things your reason has once accepted, in spite of your changing moods. For moods will change, whatever view your reason takes. I know that by experience. Now that I am a Christian I do have moods in which the whole thing looks very improbable: but when I was an atheist I had moods in which Christianity looked terribly probable. This rebellion of your moods against your real self is going to come anyway. That is why Faith is such a necessary virtue: unless you teach your moods 'where they get off,' you can never be either a sound Christian or even a sound atheist, but just a creature dithering to and fro, with its beliefs really dependent on the weather and the state of its digestion.[14]

---

[12] *Grief*, ch. 1, pp. 6–7.

[13] Personal letter to Arthur Greeves dated December 24, 1930 in *Letters1*, pp. 944–945.

[14] *MC*, book 3, ch. 11, p. 77.

Beyond learning to master one's feelings, Lewis recommended reminding oneself of the facts of the Christian faith and expressing these truths to God in worship and prayer. The Christian faith has to be nourished.

Although Lewis did not mention apologetics in this context, it can also play a vital role in dealing with emotional doubt. It's not enough to simply sing hymns, pray the Lord's prayer and recite the apostles' creed if we have forgotten *why* we believe.

Prayer

Lewis assigned prayer an important role in dealing with doubt. But praying is not easy. With the fall of the Soviet Union at the beginning of the 1990s, a Western journalist visited a monastery in Ukraine where he met a number of Orthodox monks. The reporter asked one of the brothers what they do all day. The monk answered that they pray. This response confused the secularized journalist, who tried to clarify his question, "I mean, don't you *work*?" The monk looked patiently at him and said, "Yes – I told you that we *pray*." Anyone who has ever struggled with God in prayer knows just what he means.

I suppose that everyone has at some point wondered whether prayer makes any sense. Lewis articulated what many people think.

> I don't think it at all likely that God requires the ill-informed (and contradictory) advice of us humans as to how to run the world. If He is all-wise, as you say He is, doesn't He know already what is best? And if He is all-good won't He do it whether we pray or not?[15]

Lewis's answer to this objection was also an explanation as to why he didn't believe in determinism. People who says they don't need to pray since God already knows everything and can and will give us everything we need might just as well stop doing anything at all. In a humorous but incomplete draft Lewis wrote:

> 'Praying for things', said I, 'always seems to me like advising God how to run the world. Wouldn't it be wiser to assume that He knows best?' 'On the same principle', said he, 'I suppose you never ask a man next to you to pass the salt, because God knows best whether you ought to have salt or not. And I suppose you

[15] C.S. Lewis, "Work and Prayer" in *Dock+*, p. 104. Also in *EC*, p. 160.

> never take an umbrella, because God knows best whether you ought to be wet or dry.' 'That's quite different,' he protested. 'I don't see why,' said he. 'The odd thing is that He should let us influence the course of events at all. But since He lets us do it in one way I don't see why He shouldn't let us do it in the other.'[16]

If God has not predetermined whether we should be wet or dry or have salt on our food, then God has not determined the eventual outcome of our prayers. Lewis said that life is like a stage play where the dramatist and director sketch a broad outline of the play's plot and dénouement, but where they give the actors and actresses great freedom to improvise. Lewis explained that God gives people two ways of improvisation: through our actions and through our prayers.[17]

In several texts Lewis approvingly quoted Blaise Pascal: "God instituted prayer in order to allow His creatures the dignity of causality."[18] Through our actions and our prayer "we try to produce a state of affairs which God has not (or at any rate not yet) seen fit to provide 'on his own'."[19]

In his autobiography *Surprised by Joy* Lewis recounted how as a boy he had prayed that his mother, who was dying of cancer, would be healed. He believed (mistakenly, as it turned out) that God would be forced to heal his mother if only he managed to whip up within himself the right state of mind.

> No clause of my prayer was to be allowed to pass muster unless it was accompanied by what I called a 'realization,' by which I meant a certain vividness of the imagination and the affections. My nightly task was to produce by sheer will power a phenomenon which will power could never produce, which was so ill-defined that I could never say with absolute confidence whether it had occurred, and which, even when it did occur, was of very mediocre spiritual value.[20]

---

[16] C.S. Lewis, "Scraps" in *Dock+*, p. 217. Also in *EC*, p. 347.

[17] "Work and Prayer" in *Dock+*, p. 106. Also in *EC*, p. 161.

[18] Ibid in *Dock+*, p. 106. Also in *EC*, p. 161.

[19] Ibid in *Dock+*, p. 106. Also in *EC*, p. 162.

[20] *Surprised*, ch. 4, p. 61.

Even after her death he tried to pray. And failed every time to conjure up the right emotions. This gradually contributed to him leaving his childhood faith and becoming an atheist.

An important theme in *The Screwtape Letters* is how demons can distract people from praying. One way of doing this is to trick people into believing they must reject the bedtime prayers they mechanically recited as a child. Demons desire to get people to believe they must conjure up a certain feeling to show that they *really* believe.[21] But this is a faith based on feelings and not on facts and sound reason. Feelings have nothing in common with true faith, as we have seen earlier. A faith that is built upon a state of mind will eventually fall once the feelings fail.

The demon Screwtape concludes that "the prayers offered in the state of dryness are those which please Him best."[22]

When we pray, we enter into a collaboration with the triune God. We pray to the Father through the Son and with the help and guidance of the Holy Spirit. "[T]he whole threefold life of the three-personal Being is actually going on in that ordinary little bedroom where an ordinary man is saying his prayers."[23]

> Its very first words are *Our Father*. Do you now see what those words mean? They mean quite frankly, that you are putting yourself in the place of a son of God. To put it bluntly, you are *dressing up as Christ*. If you like, you are pretending. Because, of course, the moment you realise what the words mean, you realise that you are not a son of God. You are not being like The Son of God, whose will and interests are at one with those of the Father: you are a bundle of self-centred fears, hopes, greeds, jealousies, and self-conceit, all doomed to death. So that, in a way, this dressing up as Christ is a piece of outrageous cheek. But the odd thing is that He has ordered us to do it. ... Now, the moment you realise 'Here I am, dressing up as Christ,' it is extremely likely that you will see at once some way in which at that very moment the pretence could be made less of a pretence and more of a reality.[24]

---

[21] *Screwtape*, letter 4.

[22] Ibid, letter 8, p. 40.

[23] *MC*, fourth book, ch. 2 "The Three-Personal God", p. 163.

[24] Ibid, fourth book, ch. 7, "Let's Pretend", p. 101.

When children play "cops and robbers," or "house," or pretend to be schoolteachers or soldiers or shopkeepers, they are "testing" the types of roles they may assume in real life as adults.[25] Lewis said that when we call God our father, we are pretending to be like Christ. We have yet to become like Christ, but the theological truth is that believers are *in* Christ and that through adoption we become children of God and co-heirs with Jesus.[26] We are practicing for a time in the future when we will be like Christ when we see him face-to-face.[27]

Sanctification

The road to holiness is long and difficult. Human life seems to be characterized more by sin and failure than by victory over temptation. I suppose that every believer has wondered at some point where the line goes between resisting temptation (a victory) and sinning in one's heart (a defeat). Lewis stated that only the person who stands against temptation really understands how strong temptation is. "A silly idea is current that good people do not know what temptation means. This is an obvious lie. Only those who try to resist temptation know how strong it is."[28] The person who yields to temptation never experiences its full strength.

Sanctification means being able to both enjoy creation while renouncing it. The answer does not lie in some kind of Aristotelian golden mean (Lewis was, after all, a Platonist). Nor does it lie in Eastern concepts of action without desires for our actions or their possible consequences. The Christian answer is that we must hold both pleasure and renunciation simultaneously, but in balance. If we only have the one side, we will get a warped view of creation and imbalance in life. The person who only seeks pleasure makes the mistake of the fool and the hedonist. When something fails to satisfy, the fool believes mistakenly that there was something wrong with this particular object and goes on to seek satisfaction in some other thing. The person who follows the fool's path turns away from taking pleasure in creation and ends up with a compelling desire for finding comfort in oneself.

---

[25] Why don't children pretend to be psychologists, statisticians or database managers?

[26] Romans 8:1, 15–17.

[27] 1 Corinthians 13:12.

[28] *MC*, third book, ch. 11, p. 77.

The opposite extreme are the people who live only in renunciation. They know that nothing material can ultimately satisfy. Therefore they suppress the apparently insatiable desire they have and miss out on the simple joys that creation truly can bring to a person.

People do not like to talk about renunciation; there are far more hedonists than ascetics in our world. Many people associate ideas of renunciation with suppression and self-denial. Self-mortification may seem like a heavy burden to those who do not understand the benefit one gains in a living relationship with God. Lewis was especially fond of Jesus' paradoxical words that "whoever would save his life will lose it, but whoever loses his life for my sake will find it."[29]

Lewis concurred with Pascal, whom he quoted: "One shows one's greatness ... not by being at an extremity but by being simultaneously at two extremes."[30] To embrace two seemingly conflicting ideas is a recurring theme in Christian theology. Humans are both body and soul. Jesus was both God and man. Believers are both righteous and sinners (*simul justus et peccator*).

We cannot imagine what a redeemed and restored creation would look like. It is sometimes said that people in heaven will be asexual. This may seem like a punishment, or at the very least, like a form of deprivation. But this is merely a question of our perspective compared to God's.

In *Miracles* Lewis wrote about a boy who loves chocolate. Eating chocolate is just about the best thing he can imagine. Once, when hearing that sexual intercourse is the highest physical pleasure, he asks whether the lovers eat chocolate during intercourse. When he hears that they generally do not, he may associate sexuality with the negative idea of not getting any chocolate. He doesn't understand that the lovers refrain from eating chocolate because they are enjoying an even greater pleasure.[31] Our ideas about eternal life often suffer from this same type of limited experience.

Lewis maintained that a proper attitude is to take pleasure in creation while at the same time holding one's desire in control. He described in *Perelandra* how Ransom discovers a curious new kind of fruit on another planet. He tastes it and finds that it is delicious. His immediate reaction is to want another, but then realizes that he's no longer hungry or thirsty.

---

[29] Matthew 16:25.

[30] C.S. Lewis, "A Panegyric for Dorothy L. Sayers" in *EC*, p. 568.

[31] *Miracles*, ch. 16, pp. 260–261.

He is attracted to the pleasure of having another one, but decides against it.[32] Lewis wrote of Ransom, "He had always disliked the people who encored a favourite air in an opera – 'That just spoils it' had been his comment. But this now appeared to him as a principle of far wider application and deeper moment."[33]

In another book he wrote, "It would be rash to say that there is any prayer which God *never* grants. But the strongest candidate is the prayer we might express in the single word *encore.*"[34]

Living with pleasure and renunciation in balance means living in the present, with an appreciation for the quotidian details of life. It reminds us of the biblical book of Ecclesiastes, where we are called to enjoy life with our spouse and delight in the simple pleasures of life: food, work, friendship, etc.

Calling

Lewis reminded his readers many times that he was not a professional theologian, even though he was probably more widely read in theology than many "real" theologians. He was a professor of literature and seemed to believe that we can learn more about God by *being* a Christian than by studying God as an academic discipline. "I've always been glad myself that Theology is not the thing I earn my living by. … The performance of a *duty* will probably teach you quite as much about God as academic Theology would do."[35]

Many Christians mistakenly believe that pastors, missionaries and those who receive holy orders are the truly spiritual, while everyone else can at best enjoy a "secondary" kind of piety. This is a remnant from the Roman Catholic middle ages. The Protestant perspective, by contrast, is the priesthood of all believers. Through Jesus every person has the right to approach the throne of God and receive mercy and find grace at times when we need this help.[36] The farmer, the statistician, the database manager and psychologist can all honor God with their work just as much as the minister, missionary or monk.

---

[32] *Perelandra,* ch. 3, p. 38.

[33] Ibid, ch. 4, p. 43.

[34] *Malcolm,* ch. 5, p. 27.

[35] Personal letter to Sheldon Vanauken dated January 5, 1951 in *Letters3,* p. 83.

[36] Hebrews 4:16.

Lewis reacted against the idea that Christians should retreat from the world and live in a Christian bubble. Leaving the bubble only for forays in evangelism was an idea that Lewis thought "implies that our life can, and ought, to become exclusively and explicitly religious." He rejected such ideas and concluded that it won't happen – regardless of what one actually thinks of the matter.[37] Christians must continue their engagement with society, not merely rejecting culture but showing the way to transform culture for the better.

> If you attempted, in either case, to suspend your whole intellectual and aesthetic activity, you would only succeed in substituting a worse cultural life for a better. You are not, in fact, going to read nothing, either in the Church or in the line: if you don't read good books, you will read bad ones. If you don't go on thinking rationally, you will think irrationally. If you reject aesthetic satisfactions, you will fall into sensual satisfactions.[38]

Christ is lord over every area of life. That's why Lewis wrote, "All our merely natural activities will be accepted, if they are offered to God, even the humblest, and all of them, even the noblest, will be sinful if they are not."[39]

Satan tries to subvert the lordship of Christ over everything by foisting upon people the false dichotomy of the sacred and the profane. In resisting this, Lewis pleaded, "We must attack the enemy's line of communication. What we want is not more little books about Christianity, but more little books by Christians on other subjects – with their Christianity *latent*."[40]

The fiercest challenges to Christian faith are rarely the ones that are most obvious. The most dangerous ideas are the ones that creep in by undermining assumptions that people merely take for granted.

> It is not the books written in direct defence of Materialism that make the modern man a materialist; it is the materialistic assumption in all the other books. In the same way, it is not books on Christianity that will really trouble him [a non-Christian]. But he would be troubled if, whenever he wanted a

---

[37] "Learning in War Time" in *WoG*, p. 51. Also in *EC*, p. 581.

[38] Ibid in *WoG*, p. 52. Also in *EC*, p. 581.

[39] Ibid in *WoG*, p. 54. Also in *EC*, p. 582.

[40] "Christian Apologetics" in *Dock+*, p. 93. Also in *EC*, p. 150.

> cheap popular introduction to some science, the best work on the market was always by a Christian.[41]

For this reason Lewis recommended that more Christians become experts in all manner of intellectual inquiry and thus become salt and light by writing about their academic disciplines from a Christian perspective. "I believe that any Christian who is qualified to write a good popular book on any science may do much more by that than by any directly apologetic work."[42] It is an apologetic that according to Lewis would likely lead more people to faith than any book on the shelf labeled *Apologetics*.

No job for cowards

A recurring metaphor Lewis used for God is that of a dentist. Some people just made Lewis scratch his head. "What do people mean when they say, 'I am not afraid of God because I know He is good'? Have they never even been to a dentist?"[43] For some reason many people are afraid of the dentist and avoid going to the dentist as much as possible in spite of knowing that the dentist only wants to help us have better dental health. Well, a visit to the dentist is often fraught with feelings of shame. Maybe you've eaten too many sweets, smoked too much, not brushed properly and never used floss. Maybe it's been "a while" since your last visit to the dentist. You have not taken care of your teeth like you should, and there's no hiding that from the dentist.

Nor is it possible to hide our bad habits and shortcomings from an omnipotent God. The road to sanctification – just like dental health – can be painful.

> Christ says 'Give me All. I don't want so much of your time and so much of your money and so much of your work: I want You. I have not come to torment your natural self, but to kill it. No half-measures are any good. I don't want to cut off a branch here and a branch there, I want to have the whole tree down. I don't want to drill the tooth, or crown it, or stop it, but to have it out. Hand over the whole natural self, all the desires which you think innocent as well as the ones you think wicked – the whole outfit.

[41] Ibid in *Dock+*, p. 93. Also in *EC*, p. 150.

[42] Ibid in *Dock+*, p. 93. Also in *EC*, p. 150.

[43] *Grief*, ch 3, p. 43.

> I will give you a new self instead. In fact, I will give you Myself: my own will shall become yours.'[44]

The Christian life is no job for cowards. It is a struggle between reason and emotions. Our faith stands on a more sure foundation than shifting emotions. In *The Screwtape Letters,* Screwtape describes how "dangerous" it is for the demons' agenda when Christians build their faith on something other than feelings.

> Our cause is never more in danger, than when a human, no longer desiring, but intending, to do our Enemy's will, looks round upon a universe from which every trace of Him seems to have vanished, and asks why he has been forsaken, and still obeys.[45]

---

[44] *MC,* fourth book, ch. 8, p. 105.

[45] *Screwtape,* letter 8, p. 47.

Books by C.S. Lewis

Monographs

This annotated bibliography presents Lewis's books in chronological order. Canadian laws stipulate that literary works enter the public domain fifty years after the death of the author, as opposed to 75 years in the United States and United Kingdom. As such, many full-text editions of Lewis's work can be found for free on Canadian websites.

Spirits in Bondage: A Cycle of Lyrics (published under the pseudonym Clive Hamilton). London: William Heinemann, 1919. A collection of poems written before Lewis came to faith.

Dymer (published under the pseudonym Clive Hamilton). London: J.M. Dent, 1926. An epic poem Lewis wrote before becoming a Christian. Protagonist Dymer's longing for something "more" leads him to leave the dystopian "perfect city" on a journey to satisfy his longing. The full text of Dymer is also included in *Narrative Poems,* 1969.

The Pilgrim's Regress: An Allegorical Apology for Christianity, Reason, and Romanticism. London: J.M. Dent, 1933. Revised edition published in London by Geoffrey Bles, 1943. Lewis's first book as a Christian, which he allegedly wrote in just fourteen days.[1] This book is an allegory that leads one's thoughts to *Pilgrim's Progress. The Pilgrim's Regress* has certain thematic similarities with *Dymer*. In both books the protagonist leaves a life which he considers oppressive in order to follow his longing. Both characters try to satisfy their longing with objects that are incapable of satisfying. Sex with female figures leads to unwanted offspring that the fathers perceive as a threat. Yet the two books end differently, as *The Pilgrim's Regress* reflects a Christian faith that Lewis did not have when he wrote *Dymer*.

The Allegory of Love – A Study in Medieval Tradition. London: Oxford University Press, 1936. A respected work of literary criticism. Lewis

[1] John Piper, "C.S. Lewis, Romantic Rationalist" in John Piper and David Mathis, ed., *The Romantic Rationalist: God, Life and Imagination in the Work of C.S. Lewis* (Wheaton: Crossway, 2014), p. 24.

examines the idea of love – especially chivalrous love – in medieval literature, while also analyzing allegory as a genre.

Out of the Silent Planet. London: John Lane, 1938. The first part of the so-called space trilogy. Protagonist Ransom is kidnapped and transported to another planet. Once he arrives on Mars, not a whole lot happens; the book is mostly geographical and metaphysical descriptions of the new world. It is nonetheless interesting to note that Lewis's space trilogy was fairly unique among early science fiction books in that it is the humans who are the evil creatures while other extraterrestrial beings are the "good guys." Walter Hooper comments: "He was probably the first writer to introduce the idea of having *fallen* terrestrial invaders discover on other planets ... *unfallen* rational beings who were in no need of redemption and with nothing to learn from us."[2] Together with *Perelandra* and *That Hideous Strength,* the trilogy is a critique of H.G. Wells. They successfully avoid the dual pitfalls of a dystopian vision of life on the one hand and a naively optimistic utopia on the other.

The Personal Heresy – A Controversy (together with E.M.W. Tillyard). Oxford: Oxford University Press, 1939. A published debate between Lewis and Tillyard over literary criticism and the interpretation of poetry. Lewis defines "the personal heresy" as the idea that one must understand an author as a person before one can understand the author's work.

The Problem of Pain. London: Geoffrey Bles, 1940. Includes among other things Lewis's earliest text on hell and an important chapter on animal suffering – written long before the advent of the animal rights movement.

The Screwtape Letters. London: Geoffrey Bles, 1942. A collection of sometimes quite humorous letters from an older, more experienced demon to his apprentice on the art of tempting humans. The letters were originally published in serial form in a British newspaper before they were released in book form. Surprisingly the book has almost nothing to say about hell; the focus lies rather on the Christian life. A new edition with the addition of the text

---

[2] Footnote to "The Seeing Eye" in *CR*, p. 174.

"Screwtape Proposes a Toast" was released in 1961 in London by Geoffrey Bles.

A Preface to Paradise Lost. Oxford: Oxford University Press, 1942. Against the backdrop of other epic poems like *Beowulf, The Aeneid, The Odyssey* and *The Iliad,* Lewis presents a definitive work on Milton's *Paradise Lost*. His reflections on the epic genre give some insight into how he conceived his own epic poem *Dymer*.

Perelandra. London: John Lane, 1943. Part two in the space trilogy. In this episode, the scientist Ransom travels to Venus (which the inhabitants call Perelandra) and witnesses a new fall into sin. The serpent in this paradise is the evil scientist Dr. Weston.

The Abolition of Man. Oxford: Oxford University Press, 1943. Peter Kreeft calls this book one of the two most prophetic books of the twentieth century (alongside Huxley's *Brave New World*). This is a book with lots of philosophy. Lewis criticizes positivistic theories of education that deny the natural law. He also predicts what would later become postmodern relativism and constructivist pedagogy.

Broadcast Talks. London: Geoffrey Bles, 1942. Published in the United States with the title *The Case for Christianity*. New York: Macmillan, 1943. This book is Lewis's manuscript to a number of radio broadcasts he made for the BBC, where he explained and defended the basics of Christian faith. *Broadcast Talks* later became the "first and second books" of *Mere Christianity*.

Christian Behaviour – A Further Series of Broadcast Talks. London: Geoffrey Bles, 1943. This booklet was the manuscript to Lewis's second series of radio broadcasts about Christian faith. Here he outlines his thoughts on morality. It later became the "third book" in *Mere Christianity*.

Beyond Personality – The Christian Idea of God. London: Geoffrey Bles, 1944. This is the third book that comprises part (the so-called "fourth book") of *Mere Christianity*. Lewis develops the ideas first laid out in the earlier broadcasts in order to explain the implications of belief in the triune God of Christianity.

Mere Christianity. London: Geoffrey Bles, 1952. This classic work is not to be missed! The text was originally presented as a series of radio broadcasts on the BBC during World War II. *Mere Christianity* is comprised of revised editions of three previously published books: *The Case for Christianity / Broadcast Talks, Christian Behaviour* and *Beyond Personality*.

That Hideous Strength. London: John Lane, 1945. Although this book is part three of Lewis's space trilogy, the plot takes place on earth. Colleagues of the scientist Weston found N.I.C.E., a research institute that bears more than a passing likeness to the tower of Babel. The purpose of N.I.C.E. is to direct and manipulate both nature and society. *That Hideous Strength* is an imaginative presentation of the theories Lewis lays out in *The Abolition of Man*. People who make a pact with the forces of evil discover all too late that they have been enslaved – a theme that directs one's thoughts to Dr. Faust. Lewis explains some of the thoughts that lie *That Hideous Strength* in the essay "A Reply to Professor Haldane."

The Great Divorce. London: Geoffrey Bles, 1945. An occasionally humorous tale of a daytrip by bus from hell to the outskirts of heaven. The main character is guided by the Scottish writer George MacDonald who acts as a mouthpiece for Lewis's own ideas. There are clear parallels between MacDonald and Virgil in Dante's *Divine Comedy*.

Miracles: A Preliminary Study. London: Geoffrey Bles, 1947. Revised second edition published in London by Collins Fontana in 1960. A classic critique of Hume's famous objections to the possibility of miracles. The book begins with two important arguments against naturalism based on the human phenomena of rationality and morality.

Arthurian Torso – Containing the posthumous fragment of The Figure of Arthur by Charles Williams and a Commentary on the Arthurian Poems of Charles Williams by C.S. Lewis. Oxford: Oxford University Press, 1948. Lewis's friend and fellow "Inkling" Charles Williams wrote many poems and several books set against the backdrop of King Arthur's court. *Arthurian Torso* is a book of technical literary criticism where Lewis comments on Williams's poems as well as an unfinished manuscript that Williams left at his untimely death at the age of 58. The book is a difficult read for those who are not thoroughly familiar with Williams's work. Nonetheless, it does contain a rare insight into a typical meeting of The Inklings.

The Lion, the Witch and the Wardrobe. London: Geoffrey Bles, 1950. The first published book of *The Chronicles of Narnia*, even though the book's plot comes chronologically after *The Magician's Nephew.* The adventure begins when four siblings are sent to the countryside to live with a kind professor during the London blitz of World War II. They discover the fantasy land Narnia where they meet the majestic lion Aslan and a white witch. The book contains a famous allegory of Christ's substitutionary death.

Prince Caspian – The Return to Narnia. London: Geoffrey Bles, 1951. Part of *The Chronicles of Narnia.* This is the second book in order of publication, but the fourth book in chronological order. The siblings return to Narnia to help Prince Caspian regain his kingdom.

The Voyage of the "Dawn Treader". London: Geoffrey Bles, 1952. Part of *The Chronicles of Narnia,* where it is the third book in order of publication, but the fifth book in chronological order. In this tale the English children travel along with King Caspian on a mission to find seven lost knights of Narnia. Their adventures take them to Aslan's country at the end of the world.

The Silver Chair. London: Geoffrey Bles, 1953. The fourth book of *The Chronicles of Narnia* in order of publication, but the sixth book in chronological order. The children flee from some bullies through a secret door that leads to Narnia. In Narnia they are given the task of finding the abducted Prince Rilian. In an occasionally heavy narrative the protagonists struggle with mental confusion in the midst of uncertain conceptions of what is real and what is illusion.

The Horse and His Boy. London: Geoffrey Bles, 1954. This is the fifth book of *The Chronicles of Narnia,* but third in chronological order after *The Lion, the Witch and the Wardrobe.* In this fast-paced book, a brave boy and his talking horse have many adventures in fleeing from the evil Calormenes.

English Literature in the Sixteenth Century, Excluding Drama. Oxford: Clarendon Press, 1954. Lewis's *magnum opus* as a literary scholar. The book is the result of a research project that took almost twenty years. As a part of the series *Oxford History of English Literature* (OHEL) Lewis sometimes called it his "Oh Hell" book. The book is a detailed survey of sixteenth-century English literature. He calls into question the conventional idea that the Renaissance and the development of the scientific method represent a foundational paradigm shift in Western thought. He argues that there is a greater continuity between the middle ages and the modern world than what is commonly acknowledged. The book has also been published with the title *Poetry and Prose in the Sixteenth Century.*

De Descriptione Temporum. Cambridge: Cambridge University Press, 1955. Lewis's inaugural lecture as professor in Cambridge. Lewis contends that dissecting history into various periods with labels is an exercise in futility.

The Magician's Nephew. London: The Bodley Head, 1955. Although it was the sixth book of *The Chronicles of Narnia* in order of publication, it is the first book in chronological order. The children Digory and Polly discover an alternative reality when Uncle Andrew casts a spell on them. The children meet an evil queen and witness the creation of Narnia.

Surprised by Joy: The Shape of My Early Life. London: Geoffrey Bles, 1955. Lewis's autobiography from early childhood until his conversion to faith in Christ. He describes how experiences of joy as an unsatisfied longing compelled him to search for the "myth" that became reality.

The Last Battle. London: The Bodley Head, 1956. The last book in *The Chronicles of Narnia.* The book has a dark tone as all hell breaks loose before Aslan come and wins the final victory over the forces of evil.

Till We Have Faces: A Myth Retold. London: Geoffrey Bles, 1956. In this remix of the ancient Greek myth of Eros and Psyche, two princesses – one beautiful and one common – have both gotten themselves into situations beyond their control. Lewis called this book one of his favorites – in spite of poor reviews. He wrote in a personal letter to a school girl, "I am so glad you like *Till We Have Faces,* because so few people do. It is my biggest 'flop' for years, and so of course *I* think it my best book."[3]

Reflections on the Psalms. London: Geoffrey Bles, 1958. In spite of the title, this book is no commentary or devotional guide to the Psalter. Rather, it is a collection of essays with sometimes very tenuous connection to the Psalms. Some texts, such as chapter 11 – "Scripture" shed light on Lewis's views of the Bible as the word of

[3] Personal letter to the young girl Joan Lancaster dated April 20, 1959 in *Letters3*, p. 1040.

God and what he considered the mythological elements of the Old Testament. Chapter 12 – "Second Meanings in the Psalms" is also valuable for its help in seeing Jesus Christ through the psalms.

The Four Loves. London: Geoffrey Bles, 1960. A word study over four words for love found in ancient Greek: *storge* (affection), *phileo* (friendship), *eros* and *agape*.

Studies in Words. Cambridge: Cambridge University Press, 1960. Perhaps not the most relevant book for readers who are more interested in Lewis's theology and apologetics. Here he examines the etymology of words such as *nature, sad, wit, free, sense, conscious and conscience, world* and *life*.

A Grief Observed. London: Faber and Faber, 1961. This book was originally published under the pseudonym N.W. Clerk. Here Lewis airs his reflections on life, death and grieving in the wake of his wife's death. Lewis struggles with his faith in a good God when both he and his wife have suffered so much. The book, which began as a series of journal entries, was an important tool in his own process of working through his grief.

An Experiment in Criticism. Cambridge: Cambridge University Press, 1961. An important albeit underappreciated little book. Lewis lays the foundation of his literary criticism, which in turn is the foundation of his bibliology and its relationship to myth, historicity and how readers should approach a text.

The Discarded Image – An Introduction to Medieval and Renaissance Literature. Cambridge University Press, 1964. Lewis argues that modern readers must lay aside their worldview and attempt to enter into the medieval mindset of the author in order to appreciate the literature of that time. More specifically, he guides the reader into the world of medieval philosophy, cosmology, biology and education. This book presents a formidable challenge for readers who are not already well-versed in the world of medieval and Renaissance literature. In just one typical chapter Lewis refers to more than 60 different authors and works.

Letters to Malcolm: Chiefly on Prayer. London: Geoffrey Bles, 1964. Imaginary "letters" that all deal more or less with prayer. Lewis wrote somewhat ironically in this book on prayer: "But however badly needed a good book on prayer is, I shall never try to write it."[4]

Spenser's Images of Life. Cambridge: Cambridge University Press, 1967 (edited by Alastair Fowler). Edmund Spenser's *The Faerie Queen* (1590–1596) was in Lewis's opinion the most challenging poem in the English language. This book was compiled by Alastair Fowler from Lewis's lecture notes. As such, it lacks the polish that one normally associates with Lewis's books. Here again, this book of literary criticism is also a rather challenging read for those who are not so versed in literary criticism.

Essay collections

The most extensive collection of essays and other short texts by Lewis is found in *Essay Collection & Other Short Pieces,* Leslie Walmsley, ed. Yet most of Lewis's short texts of literary criticism are missing from this anthology. Walmsley's anthology has subsequently been divided and republished in two volumes under the titles: *Essay Collection (Vol. 1): Literature, Philosophy and Short Stories* and *Essay Collection (Vol. 2): Faith, Christianity and the Church.* For readers interested primarily in Lewis's theological and apologetic texts, I would recommend Walmsley's *Essay Collection* or the unabridged version of *God in the Dock.*

In this section I present in alphabetical order an overview of the published anthologies of Lewis's essays and short prose texts. A collocation of the individual titles appears below under the heading "Essays and Articles by Lewis".

A surprising number of the books in this section have been edited by Walter Hooper. Although one may have opinions as to whether Hooper was merely "cashing in" on his few months as Lewis's secretary or whether he is guilty of something more sinister, I think he, probably more than any other individual, is responsible for Lewis's continuing popularity today through his tireless publishing and republishing of Lewis's works.

A Mind Awake – An anthology of C.S. Lewis. Clyde S. Kilby, ed. New York: Harcourt Brace Jovanovich, 1968.

[4] *Malcolm*, ch. 12, p. 63.

Christian Reflections. Walter Hooper, ed. Grand Rapids: Eerdmans, 1967. An anthology of essays that deal primarily with literary criticism. Includes some important texts where Lewis outlines his views on religious language, myth and historicity as well as other issues that have some pertinence to his bibliology. This collection was also published with the title *The Seeing Eye and Other Selected Essays from Christian Reflections* (New York: Ballantine, 1967).

Christian Reunion and Other Essays. Walter Hooper, ed. London: Collins Fount, 1990. Another anthology of previously published texts edited by Walter Hooper.

Compelling Reason: Essays on Ethics and Theology. Walter Hooper, ed. London: HarperCollins, 1996. Old texts by Lewis in a new package by Walter Hooper (who else?).

Essay Collection and Other Short Pieces. Leslie Walmsley, ed. New York: HarperCollins, 2000. Includes six short stories and excerpts from a number of personal letters where Lewis discusses theological and ethical questions.

Essay Collection, Vol. 1: Literature, Philosophy and Short Stories. Leslie Walmsley, ed. New York: HarperCollins, 2002.

Essay Collection, Vol. 2: Faith, Christianity and the Church. Leslie Walmsley, ed. New York: HarperCollins, 2002.

Fern-seeds and Elephants and Other Essays on Christianity. Walter Hooper, ed. London: Collins, 1975. Yet another anthology of previously published Lewis texts edited by Walter Hooper.

First and Second Things: Essays on Theology and Ethics. Walter Hooper, ed. London: CollinsFount, 1985. One more anthology of previously published Lewis texts edited by Walter Hooper.

God in the Dock: Essays on Theology and Ethics. Walter Hooper, ed. Grand Rapids: Eerdmans, 1970. Published in the United Kingdom with the title *Undeceptions* (London: Geoffrey Bles, 1970). The title *God in the Dock* is not obvious for most American readers. The word *dock* does not refer to where one moors a boat, but to the "stand" in a British courtroom where the defendant stands during a trial. Note that an abridged version of his book has also been published with the title *God in the Dock: Essays on Theology*. Walter Hooper, ed. (London:

Collins Fount Paperbacks, 1979). The abridged version includes 13 texts; the longer one has 48 texts.

Image and Imagination: Essays and Reviews. Walter Hooper, ed. Cambridge: Cambridge University Press, 2013. Yet another anthology previously published Lewis texts edited by Walter Hooper. Includes around 50 essays, prefaces to and reviews of other books. One advantage with this collection is that most of the texts are not found in other Lewis anthologies. A disadvantage is that most of these texts are Lewis's reviews of other people's books.

Of Other Worlds: Essays and Stories. Walter Hooper, ed. New York: Harcourt Brace & World, 1966. One more anthology of previously published Lewis texts edited by Walter Hooper.

Of This and Other Worlds. Walter Hooper, ed. London: HarperCollins, 1982. Another anthology of previously published Lewis texts edited by Walter Hooper.

On Stories and Other Essays on Literature. Walter Hooper, ed. New York: Harcourt Brace Jovanovich, 1966, 1982. I think you can see a certain pattern here: yet another anthology of previously published Lewis texts edited by Walter Hooper.

Present Concerns. Walter Hooper, ed. London: Fount, 1986. Need I say more?

Rehabilitations and Other Essays. Oxford: Oxford University Press, 1939. An early anthology (without the involvement of Walter Hooper) that includes among other things the important essay "Christianity and Literature" in which Lewis outlines his views of the Bible as myth.

Screwtape Proposes a Toast and Other Pieces. London: 1965.

Selected Literary Essays. Walter Hooper, ed. Cambridge: Cambridge University Press, 1969. No prize for guessing correctly: another anthology of previously published Lewis texts edited by Walter Hooper.

Studies in Medieval and Renaissance Literature. Walter Hooper, ed. Cambridge: Cambridge University Press, 1966. Yep – an anthology of previously published Lewis texts edited by Walter Hooper. The interesting and unique thing about this anthology is its focus on specialized texts of literary criticism.

The Grand Miracle and Other Selected Essays on Theology and Ethics. Walter Hooper, ed. New York: Ballantine, 1982. Twenty-six texts already published in *God in the Dock.*

The Weight of Glory and Other Addresses. New York: Macmillan, 1949. Published in the United Kingdom with the title *Transpositions and Other Addresses* (London: Geoffrey Bles, 1949). An expanded edition was released in 1979. An anthology of short prose texts – articles, sermons and essays. Along with *Essay Collection* and the longer version of *God in the Dock,* this is one of the better anthologies.

The World's Last Night and Other Essays. New York: Harcourt Brace Jovanovich, 1960. A collection of essays.

They Asked for a Paper, London: Geoffrey Bles, 1962.

Timeless at Heart: Essays on Theology. Walter Hooper, ed. London: Collins Fount, 1987. Bingo! Still another anthology of previously published Lewis texts edited by Walter Hooper.

Letter collections

Lewis editor Walter Hooper comments: "Lewis was one of the last great letter-writers"[5] even though he himself considered correspondence to be one of the great burdens of life – "hours of loathsome letter-writing every day."[6] Today there are approximately 3300 extant letters from Lewis to a large number of friends and correspondents. Hooper estimates that if every letter Lewis wrote had been preserved for posterity the number would easily be doubled. Lewis's letters have been published in a number of different collections, but the definitive collection is *Collected Letters* in three volumes. Although some of the letters give us unique insights into Lewis's thoughts regarding a number of questions where he perhaps was not yet ready to publish his ideas, way too many of the letters are of the banal *I'm-so-glad-you-liked-my-book* variety. One wonders how many more carefully reasoned books Lewis would have been able to write if he hadn't felt so obligated to answer every single letter that was sent to him.

The Letters of C.S. Lewis. W.H. Lewis, ed. London: Geoffrey Bles, 1966; New York: Harcourt Brace & World, 1966. An early letter collection. All

[5] Walter Hooper, preface to *Letters3,* p. vii.

[6] Personal letter to Mary Willis Shelburne dated October 17, 1963 in *Letters3,* p. 1464.

the letters in this collection were later included in the definitive *Collected Letters* in three volumes. A valuable addition to lewisiana is Warnie's introduction "Memoir".

Letters to an American Lady. Clyde S. Kilby, ed. Grand Rapids: Eerdmans, 1967. A collection of letters to Mrs. Mary Willis Shelburne, an American widow who, interspersed with discussions of literature, worried about her children and often complained about her financial situation. Lewis arranged a monthly stipend to be sent to her through his American publisher. At its height, Lewis wrote up to three letters a week to Mrs. Shelburne. The letters are also included in *Collected Letters.*

They Stand Together: The Letters of C.S. Lewis to Arthur Greeves (1914–1963). Walter Hooper, ed. New York: Macmillan, 1979. A collection of letters that stretch over almost 50 years. Greeves was Lewis's childhood friend from Belfast and probably his closest friend after his brother Warnie. These letters are also included in *Collected Letters.*

Letters to Children. Lyle W. Dorsett and Marjorie Lamp Mead, ed. New York: Macmillan, 1985. A collection of letters Lewis wrote to children. At times humorous and insightful, although generally with rather mundane contents.

Letters – C.S. Lewis & Don Giovanni Calabria – A Study in Friendship. Martin Moynihan, ed. and trans. Ann Arbor MI: Servant Books, 1988. Don Giovanni Calabria was an Italian priest (who was later canonized as a saint by the Roman Catholic Church) who had read *The Screwtape Letters* and wanted to write to Lewis. The problem was that Calabria could not read or write English. The result was a correspondence in Latin that lasted for many years. The book includes both the original Latin text and parallel translations into English. A common theme in these letters is Christian unity beyond the unique features that divide the various Christian denominations. After Calabria's death Lewis continued to correspond with his successor don Luigi Pedrollo (1954–1961).

The Collected Letters of C.S. Lewis. Volume 1: Family Letters, 1905–1931. Walter Hooper, ed. London: HarperCollins, 2000. The first of three volumes. Together with volumes 2 and 3, this work is the most exhaustive collection of Lewis's letters yet published. The three volumes amount to more than 3000 pages of personal correspondence. Part one begins with Lewis's childhood and youth up until the time of his conversion to theism.

The Collected Letters of C.S. Lewis. Volume 2: Books, Broadcasts and the War, 1931–1949. Walter Hooper, ed. London: HarperCollins, 2004. Volume 2 covers the period starting from Lewis's conversion to Christian faith through his maturing ideas as a believer. It includes letters to friends, strangers and known authors as he himself became more well known as a writer.

The Collected Letters of C.S. Lewis. Volume 3: Narnia, Cambridge and Joy, 1950–1963. Walter Hooper, ed. London: HarperCollins, 2007. The last (so far) part of Lewis's correspondence. Here he struggles more and more with the correspondence as greater numbers of readers write fan mail to him after having discovered him through the Narnia books. The letters also cover his time in Cambridge, his relation with Joy Davidman and her cancer and death.

Yours, Jack: Spiritual Direction from C.S. Lewis. Paul F. Ford, ed. New York: HarperOne, 2008. Excerpts from letters by Lewis to a number of correspondents. The selection emphasizes Lewis's thoughts about spiritual guidance. The letters here are all published in their entirety in *Collected Letters.*

Other anthologies

In recent years other editors have tried to follow in the footsteps of Walter Hooper and cash in on Lewis's work by cherry-picking the best bits and repackaging them as collection after collection of Lewis quotes on every imaginable theme: *101 Greater Life Lessons from C.S. Lewis, C.S. Lewis: Best Inspirational Quotes, 50 Best Quotes, 55 Life-Changing Lessons* and *C.S. Lewis: Teachings and Secrets to Success.* Unfortunately the list is almost never ending.

Poems. Walter Hooper, ed. London: Geoffrey Bles, 1964. Unfortunately, Walter Hooper has revised (and – according to some – worsened) many of Lewis's previously published poems. Serious allegations of falsification have been leveled against some of the collection's poems that had never previously been published.

A Mind Awake: An Anthology of C.S. Lewis. Clyde Kilby, ed. Orlando: Harvest / Harcourt, 1968. A somewhat unnecessary collection of Lewis quotes from his previously published books and articles. The quotes are often little more than sound bites. They are organized thematically, but the book *The Quotable C.S. Lewis* is both more practical and more extensive.

Narrative Poems. Walter Hooper, ed. London: Geoffrey Bles, 1969; New York: Harcourt Brace Jovanovich, 1972. Includes "Dymer", "Launcelot", "The Nameless Isle" and "The Queen of the Drum". The book is valuable if for no other reason than the inclusion of the brilliant epic "Dymer."

The Dark Tower and Other Stories. Walter Hooper, ed. London: Collins, 1977; Orlando: Harcourt Brace Jovanovich, 1977. Includes the short stories "The Dark Tower", "The Man Born Blind", "The Shoddy Lands", "Ministering Angels", "Forms of Things Unknown" and "After Ten Years". "The Dark Tower" is said to be the unfinished manuscript of a fourth book in Lewis's science fiction series with a plot that comes immediately after the close of *Out of the Silent Planet*. Researcher Kathryn Lindskoog builds a compelling case for her accusation that "The Dark Tower" is a worthless falsification by Walter Hooper.

The Joyful Christian: 128 Readings from C.S. Lewis. New York: Macmillan, 1977. Excerpts from many well-known books by Lewis.

The Business of Heaven – Daily Readings. Walter Hooper, ed. New York: Collins, 1984. A devotional book with quotes from many previously published works. One drawback with the book is the need to look at the back of the book to find the sources of the quotes.

Boxen – The Imaginary World of the Young C.S. Lewis. Walter Hooper, ed. London: Collins, 1985; Orlando: Harcourt Brace Jovanovich, 1985. As a child Jack Lewis and his brother Warnie created several fantasy worlds. Some of the stories and drawings are included in this book, including the story of Boxen, a land of talking animals, a fascination which stayed with Lewis his entire life. Kathryn Lindskoog has also called into question the authenticity of some of these texts.

The Quotable C.S. Lewis. Wayne Martindale and Jerry Root, ed. Wheaton: Tyndale House, 1990. A very useful reference work with thousands of Lewis quotes organized under hundreds of headings in alphabetical order. A must-have resource for all Lewis nerds and others who wish to pepper their sermons and blogs with suitable Lewis quotes.

All my Road Before Me: The Diary of C.S. Lewis 1922–1927. Walter Hooper, ed. London: HarperCollins, 1991. Lewis's private journal during the 1920s gives some interesting insights into his intellectual and personal development.

Daily readings with C.S. Lewis. Walter Hooper, ed. London: HarperCollins, 1992. A devotional guide with quotes from previously published books. Also published with the title *Readings for Reflection and Meditation*.

Readings for Reflection and Meditation. Walter Hooper, ed. London: HarperCollins, 1992. Also published as *Daily Readings with C.S. Lewis*.

The Visionary Christian. Chad Walsh, ed. New York: Scribners, 1996. Yet another anthology of excerpts from previously published works.

A Year with C.S. Lewis: Daily Readings from His Classic Works. Patricia Klein, ed. New York: HarperCollins, 2003. Yet another devotional that cherry-picks the best from Lewis's key works.

The Complete C.S. Lewis Signature Classics. New York: HarperCollins, 2002. Includes the full-length texts of several Lewis classics: *Mere Christianity, The Screwtape Letters, Letters to Malcolm, The Great Divorce, The Problem of Pain, A Grief Observed* and *The Abolition of Man*. A very handsome book and useful collection in a large format.

Virtue and Vice: A Dictionary of the Good Life. Patricia Klein, ed. New York: HarperCollins, 2005. A reference work with definitions and reflections on a number of topics garnered from Lewis's books and articles.

A Year with Aslan. Julia L. Roller, ed. New York: HarperCollins, 2010.

The Collected Poems of C.S. Lewis. Don W. King, ed. Kent, OH: Kent State University Press, 2015. A good anthology of poems by Lewis with helpful commentaries.

Ray Baker

Essays and other short texts by C.S. Lewis

Lewis published more than 200 short texts during his lifetime. The spectrum includes everything from book reviews and articles to novellas, poems and obituaries over his friends. In addition to the published texts, many manuscripts of his lectures and sermons have been published posthumously. Through the years a bewildering array of anthologies has been published – often edited by Walter Hooper, who built a career on editing and re-editing Lewis's works with a tireless dedication. Most of the short texts appear in several anthologies, and certain anthologies (like *God in the Dock* and *Essay Collection*) have appeared in both abridged and unabridged versions. To add to the confusion, some texts have different titles in British and American editions.

I present here what I believe to be a complete list of Lewis's short prose texts. The works are listed in alphabetical order along with the year of first publication. The letters after each title are the abbreviations for the anthologies in which each text appears. Alternative titles for the same text are given after the most common title, such as "Modern Theology and Biblical Criticism" / "Fern-seeds and Elephants" They key to the abbreviations is found at the beginning of this book.

A Dream (1944)	Comp	EC	EC1	PC
A Lectionary of Christian Prose from the Second Century to the Twentieth Century (1939)	I&I			
A Note on *Comus* (1932)	SMRL			
A Note on Jane Austen (1954)	SLE			
A Panegyric for Dorothy L. Sayers (1958)	EC	EC1	OS	OTOW
A Reply to Professor Haldane (1946)	OS	OOW	OTOW	
A Sacred Poem: Charles Williams, *Taliessin Through Logres* (1939)	I&I			
A Slip of the Tongue (1956)	EC	EC2	Toast	WoG
A Tribute to E.R. Eddison (1955)	EC	EC1	OS	OTOW

A World for Children: Tolkien, *The Hobbit* (1937)	EC	EC1	I&I	OS	OTOW	
Addison (1945)	SLE					
After Priggery – What? (1945)	EC	EC2	PC			
After Ten Years (1959)	DT	EC	EC1	OOW		
Ajax and others: John Jones, *On Aristotle and Greek Tragedy* (1962)	I&I					
Alan M.F. Gunn, *The Mirror of Love: A Reinterpretation of* The Romance of the Rose (1953)	I&I					
Andreas Capellanus, *The Art of Courtly Love* (1943)	I&I					
Answers to Questions on Christianity (1944)	Dock+	EC	EC2	GM	Timeless	Und
Arthuriana: *Arthurian Literature in the Middle Ages: A Collaborative Study* (1960)	I&I					
Arundell Esdaile, *The Sources of English Literature* (1929)	I&I					
Before We Can Communicate (1961)	1&2T	Dock+	EC	EC1	Und	
Behind the Scenes (1956)	Dock+	EC	EC1	Reunion	Und	
Blimpophobia (1944)	EC	EC1	PC			
Bluspels and Flalanspheres: A Semantic Nightmare (1936)	Rehab	SLE				
Boswell's bugbear: Sir John Hawkins, *The Life of Samuel Johnson* (1961)	I&I					
Bulverism (1941)	1&2T	Comp	Dock+	EC	EC1	Und
Charles Walter Stansby Williams (1886–1945): An obituary (1945)	I&I					

Charles Williams, *Taliessin Through Logres* (1946)	I&I						
Christian Apologetics (1945)	Comp	Dock+	EC	EC2	Timeless	GM	Und
Christian Reunion (1944)	EC	EC2	Reunion				
Christianity and Culture (1940)	CR	EC	EC2	SE			
Christianity and Literature (1939)	CR	EC	EC1	Rehab	SE		
Cross-Examination (1963)	Dock+	EC	EC1	GM	Reunion	Und	
Dangers of National Repentance (1940)	Dock+	EC	EC2	GM	Reunion	Und	
Dante's Similes (1940)	SMRL						
Dante's Statius (1957)	SMRL						
De Audiendis Poetis (1958)	SMRL						
De Descriptione Temporum (1954)	Paper	SLE					
De Futilitate (1943)	CR	EC	EC1	SE			
Delinquents in the Snow (1957)	Dock+	EC	EC1	Reunion	Und		
Democratic Education (1944)	Comp	EC	EC1	PC			
Denis de Rougemont, *Poetry and Society* and Claude Chavasse, *The Bride of Christ* (1940)	I&I						
Different Tastes in Literature (1946)	EC	EC1	OS	OTOW			
Dogma and the Universe (1943)	Dock	Dock+	EC	EC2	GM	Und	
Donne and Love Poetry in the Seventeenth Century (1938)	SLE						
Dorothy L. Sayers, *The Mind of the Maker* (1941)	I&I						
Douglas Bush, Paradise Lost *in Our Time: Some Comments* (1947)	I&I						

E.K. Chambers, *Sir Thomas Wyatt and Some Collected Studies* (1934)	I&I					
Edmund Spenser, 1552–99 (1954)	SMRL					
Equality (1943)	Comp	EC	EC1	PC		
Eros on the loose: David Loth, *The Erotic in Literature* (1962)	I&I					
Evelyn Waugh, *Rossetti: His Life and Works* (1928)	I&I					
Evil and God (1941)	Dock+	EC	EC2	Reunion	Und	
Fern-Seed and Elephants (1959) See Modern Theology and Biblical Criticism						
First and Second Things (1942)	1&2T	Comp	Dock+	EC	EC1	Und
Forward to Joy Davidman, *Smoke on the Mountain: An Interpretation of the Ten Commandments* (1955)	I&I					
Forms of Things Unknown	DT	EC	EC1	OOW		
Four-Letter Words (1961)	SLE					
G.A.L. Burgeon (= Owen Barfield), *This Ever Diverse Pair* (1950)	I&I					
Genius and Genius (1936)	SMRL					
George Orwell (1955)	EC	EC1	OS	OTOW		
God in the Dock (1948)	Dock	Dock+	EC	EC2	GM	Und
Good Work and Good Works (1959)	EC	EC2	Toast	WLN		
H.W. Garrod, *Collins* (1929)	I&I					
Hamlet: The Prince or the Poem? (1942)	Paper	SLE				
Hedonics (1945)	Comp	EC	EC1	PC		

Helen M. Barrett, *Boethius: Some Aspects of his Times and Work* (1941)	I&I						
Hero and Leander (1952)	SLE						
High and Low Brows (1939)	EC	EC1	Rehab	SLE			
Historicism (1950)	CR	EC	EC1	FE	SE		
Horrid Red Things (1944)	1&2T	Comp	Dock+	EC	EC2	GM	Und
Howard Rollin Patch, *The Other World, According to Descriptions in Medieval Literature* (1951)	I&I						
Hugh Kingsmill, *Matthew Arnold* (1928)	I&I						
Image and Imagination	I&I						
Imagery in the Last Eleven Cantos of Dante's *Comedy* (1948)	SMRL						
Imagination and Thought in the Middle Ages (1956)	SMRL						
Interim Report (1956)	EC	EC1	PC				
Introduction from *Selections from Lazamon's* Brut (1963)	I&I						
Is English Doomed (1944)	Comp	EC	EC1	PC			
Is History Bunk? (1957)	Comp	EC	EC1	PC			
Is Progress Possible? See Willing Slaves of the Welfare State							
Is Theism Important? (1952)	Comp	Dock+	EC	EC2	Timeless	Und	
Is Theology Poetry? (1944)	EC	EC2	Paper	Toast	WoG		
It All Began With a Picture . . . (1960)	EC	EC1	OOW	OS	OTOW		
J.W.H. Atkins, *English Literary Criticism: The Medieval Phase* (1944)	I&I						
John Vyvyan, *Shakespeare and the Rose of Love* (1960)	I&I						

Kipling's World (1948)	Paper	SLE					
Learning in War-Time (1939)	EC	EC1	FE	Trans	WoG		
Leone Ebreo, *The Philosophy of Love* (*Dialoghi d'Amore*) (1938)	I&I						
Lilies That Fester (1955)	EC	EC2	Paper	Reunion	WLN		
Logan Pearsall Smith, *Milton and his Modern Critics* (1941)	I&I						
Lucretius	I&I						
M. Pauline Parker, *The Allegory of the* Faerie Queene (1960)	I&I						
Man or Rabbit? (1946)	EC	EC2	Dock	Dock+	GM	Und	VSK
Meditation in a Toolshed (1945)	1&2T	Comp	Dock+	EC	EC1	Und	VSK
Meditation on the Third Commandment (1941)	Dock+	EC	EC2	Reunion	Und		
Membership (1945)	EC	EC2	FE	Trans	WoG		
Metre (1960)	SLE						
Ministering Angels (1958)	DT	EC	EC1	OOW			
Miracles (1942)	Dock	Dock+	EC	EC2	GM	Und	
Miserable Offenders (1946)	Dock+	EC	EC1	Reunion	Und		
Modern Man and His Categories of Thought (1946)	EC	EC1	PC				
Modern Theology and Biblical Criticism / Fern-seeds and Elephants (1959)	CR	EC	EC1	FE	SE		
Modern Translations of the Bible (1947)	1&2T	Comp	Dock+	EC	EC1	GM	Und
Must Our Image of God Go? (1963)	Dock	Dock+	EC	EC2	Und		
My First School (1943)	EC	EC1	PC				
Myth Became Fact (1944)	Dock	Dock+	EC	EC2	GM	Und	

Neoplatonism in the Poetry of Spenser (1961)						
Odysseus sails again: *The Odyssey* (1962)	I&I					
Oliver Elton (1861–1945): An obituary (1945)	I&I					
On Church Music (1949)	CR	EC	EC1	EC2		
On Criticism (1957)	EC	EC1	OOW	OS	OTOW	
On Ethics (1942)	CR	EC	EC2	SE		
On Forgiveness (1947)	EC	EC2	FE	WoG		
On Juvenile Tastes (1958)	EC	EC1	OOW	OS	OTOW	
On Living in the Atomic Age (1948)	Comp	EC	EC2	PC		
On Obstinacy in Belief (1953)	EC	EC2	Paper	Toast	WLN	
On Science Fiction (1955)	EC	EC1	OOW	OS	OTOW	
On Stories (1940)	EC	EC1	OOW	OS	OTOW	
On the Reading of Old Books (1944)	1&2T	Dock+	EC	EC1	GM	Und
On the Transmission of Christianity (1946)	1&2T	Dock+	EC	EC1	Und	
On Three Ways of Writing for Children (1952)	EC	EC1	OOW	OS	OTOW	
Our English Syllabus (1939)	I&I	Rehab				
Period Criticism (1946)	EC	EC1	OS	OTOW		
Petitionary Prayer: A Problem Without an Answer (1953)	CR	EC	EC2	SE		
Poetry and Exegesis: Harold Bloom, *The Visionary Company: A Reading of English Romantic Poetry* (1963)	I&I					
Preface from *Essays Presented to Charles Williams* (1947)	I&I					

Preface to Austin Farrer, *A Faith of Our Own* (1960)	I&I						
Priestesses in the Church? (1948)	Dock	Dock+	EC	EC2	Und		
Private Bates (1944)	EC	EC1	PC				
Prudery and Philology (1955)	Comp	EC	EC1	PC			
Psycho-Analysis and Literary Criticism (1942)	Paper	SLE					
Rejoinder to Dr. Pittenger (1958)	Dock+	Timeless	Und				
Religion and Rocketry / Will We Lose God in Outer Space? (1958)	EC	EC2	FE	WLN			
Religion and Science (1945)	Dock	Dock+	EC	EC2	GM	Und	
Religion without Dogma? (1946)	Comp	Dock+	EC	EC2	Timeless	GM	Und
Religion: Reality or Substitute? (1941)	CR	EC	EC2	SE			
Revival or Decay? (1958)	1&2T	Dock+	EC	EC1	Und		
Rhyme and reason: Dorothy L. Sayers, *The Poetry of Search and the Poetry of Statement* (1963)	I&I						
Ruth Mohl, *The Three Estates in Medieval and Renaissance Literature* (1934)	I&I						
Scraps (1945)	Dock+	EC	EC2	GM	Reunion	Und	
Screwtape Proposes a Toast (1959)	EC	Toast	WLN				
Selected Sermons: *A Selection from the Occasional Sermons of Ronald Arbuthnott Knox* (1949)	I&I						
Sex in Literature (1962)	EC	EC1	PC				
Shelley, Dryden, and Mr. Eliot (1939)	Rehab	SLE					

Sir Walter Scott (1956)	Paper	SLE					
Some Thoughts (1948)	1&2T	Dock+	EC	EC1	GM	Und	
Sometimes Fairy Stories May Say Best What's to Be Said (1956)	EC	EC1	OOW	OS	OTOW		
Spenser's Cruel Cupid (1963)	SMRL						
T.R. Henn, *Longinus and English Criticism* (1934)	I&I						
Talking About Bicycles (1946)	EC	EC1	PC				
Tasso (1946)	SMRL						
The Alliterative Metre (1935)	Rehab	SLE					
The Anthropological Approach (1962)	SLE						
The Dark Tower (1938)	DT	EC	EC1				
The Death of Words (1944)	EC	EC1	OS	OTOW			
The Decline of Religion (1946)	1&2T	Comp	Dock+	EC	EC2	GM	Und
The Efficacy of Prayer (1959)	EC	EC2	FE	WLN			
The Empty Universe (1952)	EC	EC1	PC				
The English Prose *Morte* (1963)	I&I						
The Fifteenth-Century Heroic Line (1939)	SLE						
The Founding of the Oxford Socratic Club (1943)	Dock+	EC	EC1	Timeless	Und		
The Funeral of a Great Myth (1945)	CR	EC	EC2	SE			
The Genesis of a Medieval Book (1963)	SMRL						
The Grand Miracle (1945)	Dock	Dock+	EC	EC2	GM	Und	

The Humanitarian Theory of Punishment (1949)	1&2T	Comp	Dock+	EC	EC1	Und
The Idea of an 'English School' (1939)	I&I	Rehab				
The Inner Ring (1944)	EC	EC1	Paper	Toast	Trans	WoG
The Language of Religion (1960)	CR	EC	EC2	SE		
The Laws of Nature (1945)	Dock	Dock+	EC	EC2	GM	Und
The Literary Impact of the Authorized Version (1950)	Paper	SLE				
The Man Born Blind (1928)	DT	EC	EC1			
The Mythopoeic Gift of Rider Haggard (1960) / Haggard Rides Again: Morton Cohen, *Rider Haggard: His Life and Works* (1960)	EC	EC1	I&I	OS	OTOW	
The Morte D'Arthur (1947)	SMRL					
The Necessity of Chivalry (1940)	EC	EC1	PC			
The Novels of Charles Williams (1949)	EC	EC1	OS	OTOW		
The Oxford Book of Christian Verse (1941)	I&I					
The Pains of Animals (1950)	Comp	Dock+	EC	EC2	Timeless	Und
The Parthenon and the Optative (1944)	EC	EC1	OS	OTOW		
The Poison of Subjectivism (1943)	CR	EC	EC1	SE		
The Psalms (1957)	CR	EC	EC2	SE		
The Sagas and Modern Life – Morris, Mr. Yeats, and the originals: Dorothy M. Hoare, *The Works of Morris and of Yeats in Relation to Early Saga Literature* (1937)	I&I					
The Seeing Eye (1963)	CR	EC	EC2	SE		

The Sermon and the Lunch (1945)	1&2T	Dock+	EC	EC2	GM	Und	
The Shoddy Lands (1956)	DT	EC	EC1	OOW			
The Trouble with 'X'. . . (1948)	Dock	Dock+	EC	EC2	GM	Und	
The Vision of John Bunyan (1962)	SLE						
The Weight of Glory (1941)	EC	EC2	Paper	Toast	Trans	WoG	
The World's Last Night / Christian Hope – Its Meaning for Today (1951)	EC	EC2	FE	WLN			
Three Kinds of Men (1943)	Comp	EC	EC2	PC			
Tolkien's *The Lord of the Rings* (1937) is compiled of two earlier reviews: The gods return to earth: J.R.R. Tolkien, *The Fellowship of the Ring* (1954) and The Dethronement of Power: J.R.R. Tolkien, *The Two Towers* (1955)	EC	EC1	I&I	OS	OTOW		
Tragic Ends: George Steiner, *The Death of Tragedy* (1962)	I&I						
Transposition (1944)	EC	EC2	Paper	Toast	Trans	WoG	
Two Lectures (1945)	1&2T	Dock+	EC	EC1	Und		
Two Ways With the Self (1940)	Dock+	EC	EC2	GM	Reunion	Und	
Unreal Estates (1962)	EC	EC1	OOW	OS	OTOW		
Variation in Shakespeare and Others (1939)	Rehab	SLE					
Vivisection (1947)	1&2T	Comp	Dock+	EC	EC1	GM	Und
W.P. Ker, *Form and Style in Poetry: Lectures and Notes* (1928)	I&I						
We Have No 'Right to Happiness' (1963)	Dock	Dock+	EC	EC2	Und		

Werner Schwarz, *Principles and Problems of Biblical Translation* (1957)	I&I					
What Are We to Make of Jesus Christ? (1950)	Dock	Dock+	EC	EC2	GM	Und
What Chaucer Really Did to *Il Filostrato* (1932)	SLE					
What Christmas Means to Me (1957)	Dock+	EC	EC2	GM	Reunion	Und
Who gaf me drink?: Owen Barfield, *Romanticism Comes of Age* (1945)	I&I					
Why I Am Not a Pacifist (1940)	Comp	EC	EC2	Timeless	WoG	
William Morris (1937)	Rehab	SLE				
Willing Slaves of the Welfare State / Is Progress Possible? (1958)	Comp	Dock+	EC	EC1	Timeless	Und+
Work and Prayer (1945)	1&2T	Dock+	EC	EC2	GM	Und
Xmas and Christmas (1954)	1&2T	Comp	Dock+	EC	Und	

Books about C.S. Lewis

One could fill an entire library with books about C.S. Lewis.[1] Some are good; some simply repeat anecdotes and quotes that can be found in scores of other books. Some writers try – sometimes woefully poorly – to find a new, never before discovered angle for *really* understanding Lewis. In this section I separate the monographs from the anthologies and biographies. I have added brief annotations to the books I've read. Especially good books are marked with an asterisk*.

Monographs about C.S. Lewis

Adey, Lionel. *C.S. Lewis: Writer, Dreamer and Mentor.* Grand Rapids: Eerdmans, 1998. Adey focuses on Lewis as a literary critic. The book includes a biographical overview with a special emphasis on *Boxen*.

Aeschliman, Michael D. *The Restitution of Man: C.S. Lewis and the Case Against Scientism.* Grand Rapids: Eerdmans, 1983. Aeschliman emphasizes Lewis's arguments against naturalism with this analysis of the argument from reason and the moral argument.

Barfield, Owen. *Owen Barfield on C.S. Lewis.* Middletown, CT: Wesleyan University Press, 1989. One of the few books about Lewis written by someone who actually knew him.

Beversluis, John. *C.S. Lewis and the Search for Rational Religion.* Buffalo: Prometheus Books, 1985. An unusual work that criticizes Lewis's logic and argumentation.

Boenig, Robert. *C.S. Lewis and the Middle Ages.* Kent, OH: Kent State University Press, 2012. The focus lies on Lewis as literary critic and author of fiction who derived much inspiration from the medieval literature.

[1] And it really exists – The Marion E. Wade Center in Wheaton, Illinois, a research library with an impressive collection of resources related to Lewis and the other Inklings. <http://www.wheaton.edu/wadecenter/Welcome>.

Bremer, John. *C.S. Lewis, Poetry, and the Great War.* Plymouth: Lexington Books, 2012. The author places Lewis's early poems in the historical context of the first world war. His analysis extends to comparing Lewis with contemporary British poets Robert von Ranke Graves and Siegfried Loraine Sassoon.

Bresland, Ronald W. *The Backward Glance: C.S. Lewis and Ireland.* Chester Springs, PA: Dufour Editions, 1999. Bresland tries to set Lewis in his Irish context and focuses on the unfinished manuscript *Ulster Novel.* A rather unnecessary attempt at making Lewis more Irish.

Brown, Devin. *Inside Narnia.* Grand Rapids: Baker Books, 2005.

Burson, Scott R. and Walls, Jerry L. *C.S. Lewis and Francis Schaeffer: Lessons for a New Century from the Most Influential Apologists of our Time.* Downers Grove: InterVarsity Press, 1998. A good analysis of C.S. Lewis and Francis Schaeffer, two influential twentieth-century apologists. The authors show Lewis's and Schaeffer's strengths and weaknesses against the background of our postmodern culture.

* Carnell, Corbin Scott. *Bright Shadow of Reality: Spiritual Longing in C.S. Lewis.* Grand Rapids: Eerdmans, 1999. An early and important presentation of Lewis's thoughts on *Sehnsucht* or longing with special emphasis on *Till We Have Faces* and the space trilogy.

* Christensen, Michael J. *C.S. Lewis on Scripture.* Waco: Word, 1979. Christensen grounds Lewis's bibliology in his views of literature. Probably the most important book on this subject.

Christopher, Joe R. *C.S. Lewis.* Boston: Twain, 1987.

* Como, James. *Branches to Heaven: The Geniuses of C.S. Lewis.* Dallas: Spence, 1999. The author shows Lewis's sometimes complicated relationship to faith, and how it can speak to others who also struggle with their faith.

Connolly, Sean. *Inklings of Heaven: C.S. Lewis and Eschatology.* Leominster: Gracewing, 2007.

Cootsona, Gregory S. *C.S. Lewis and the Crisis of a Christian.* Louisville: Westminster John Knox, 2014.

Cunningham, Richard B. *C.S. Lewis: Defender of the Faith.* Philadelphia: Westminster Press, 1967. Eugene, OR: Wipf & Stock, 2008.

Derrick, Christopher. *C.S. Lewis and the Church of Rome*. San Francisco: Ignatius Press, 1981.

Dickerson, Matthew and O'Hara, David. *Narnia and the Fields of Arbol: The Environmental Vision of C.S. Lewis*. Lexington: University of Kentucky Press, 2009. Environmental issues were not widely discussed during Lewis's lifetime, but they have become all the more important in our day. The authors comb *The Chronicles of Narnia* and the space trilogy for insights into Lewis's attitude to nature and environmental issues.

Donaldson, Mara E. *Holy Places are Dark Places: C.S. Lewis and Paul Ricœur on Narrative Transformation*. Lanham, MD: University Press of America, 1988. Doctoral dissertation from Emory University in literary criticism. The author studies *Till We Have Faces* in light of Ricœur's hermeneutics.

Dorsett, Lyle W. *Seeking the Secret Place: The Spiritual Formation of C.S. Lewis*. Grand Rapids: Brazos Press, 2004.

Downing, David C. *Into the Region of Awe: Mysticism in C.S. Lewis*. Downers Grove: InterVarsity Press, 2005.

Downing, David C. *Planets in Peril: A Critical Study of C.S. Lewis's Ransom Trilogy*. Amherst, MA: University of Massachusetts Press, 1992.

Downing, David C. *Into the Wardrobe: C.S. Lewis and the Narnia Chronicles*. San Francisco: Wiley / Jossey-Bass, 2006. Yet another introduction to *The Chronicles of Narnia*. After a biographical chapter the emphasis is on uncovering the sources of inspiration behind the Narnia books.

Duriez, Colin. *The C.S. Lewis Encyclopedia: A Complete Guide to His Life, Thought and Writings* (Wheaton: Crossway, 2000). Reference book with short texts on all manner of lewisiana.

Edwards, Bruce L., Jr. *A Rhetoric of Reading: C.S. Lewis's Defense of Western Literacy*. Provo, UT: Brigham Young University, 1986. An analysis of Lewis as literary critic with focus on various hermeneutical theories and Lewis's response to them.

Filmer, Kath. *The Fiction of C.S. Lewis: Mask and Mirror*. New York: St. Martin's Press, 1993. The author tries to break the hagiographic tendencies that are found in most books about Lewis and focuses on his fictional works as a mask and mirror for his own views on a number of topics. The most interesting chapters highlight Lewis's views of women without becoming a feminist deconstruction of Lewis's texts.

Freshwater, Mark Edwards. *C.S. Lewis and the Truth of Myth*. Lanham, MD: University Press of America, 1988. Doctoral dissertation from Florida State University with focus on Lewis's interpretations of the Bible as myth – particularly in light of Bultmann's call to demythologize the Christian faith.

Gibson, Evan K. *Spinner of Tales: A Guide to His Fiction*. Grand Rapids: Eerdmans, 1980.

Glover, Donald E. *C.S. Lewis: The Art of Enchantment*. Athens, OH: Ohio University Press, 1981.

Goetz, Stewart. *A Philosophical Walking Tour with C.S. Lewis: Why it did not Include Rome*. New York: Bloomsbury, 2015.

Hannay, Margaret Patterson. *C.S. Lewis*. New York: Frederick Ungar, 1981.

Harries, Richard. *C.S. Lewis: The Man and His God*. London: Fount, 1987.

Hart, Dabney Adams. *Through the Open Door: A New Look at C.S. Lewis*. Tuscaloosa: University of Alabama Press, 1984. Hart follows Lewis's advice to avoid "the personal heresy" and strives to analyze Lewis's books without psychoanalyzing him as a person.

Holbrook, David. *The Skeleton in the Wardrobe: C.S. Lewis's Fantasies: A Phenomenological Study*. Lewisburg, PA: Bucknell University Press, 1991. An extremely critical and controversial book that interprets Lewis's books as symptoms for deep-seated personality disorders and neuroses.

Holmer, Paul L. *C.S. Lewis: The Shape of His Faith and Thought*. New York: Harper & Row, 1976. The strength of Holmer's book is that he does not repeat what has already been written about Lewis in scores of other books. A weakness is that aside from the chapter on Lewis's theology, Holmer is a bit vague, making it difficult to know exactly what he is trying to achieve with his book. An important theme is nonetheless that one cannot easily place Lewis in a box or place neat labels on him and his views.

Honda, Mineko. *The Imaginative World of C.S. Lewis: A Way to Participate in Reality*. Lanham, MD: University Press of America, 2000.

Hooper, Walter, ed. *Past Watchful Dragons: The Narnian Chronicles of C.S. Lewis.* New York: Collier Macmillan, 1971. A classic study of *The Chronicles of Narnia,* but in light of the accusations made against Hooper's veracity, it may be best to take this introduction to the Narnia books with a grain of salt – at least when he recounts personal anecdotes about Lewis.

Hooper, Walter. *C.S. Lewis: Companion and Guide.* New York: HarperCollins, 1998. Hooper gives helpful summaries of all of Lewis's most important books, but presents almost no analysis.

Howard, Thomas. *The Achievement of C.S. Lewis.* Carol Stream: Harold Shaw, 1980.

Howard, Thomas. *C.S. Lewis Man of Letters: A Reading of His Fiction.* San Francisco: Ignatius Press, 2004.

Joeckel, Samuel. *The C.S. Lewis Phenomenon: Christianity and the Public Sphere.* Macon, GA: Mercer University Press, 2013.

Kilby, Clyde S. *The Christian World of C.S. Lewis.* Grand Rapids: Eerdmans, 1964. An introduction to Lewis written shortly after his death.

Kilby, Clyde S. *Images of Salvation in the Fiction of C.S. Lewis.* Carol Stream: Harold Shaw, 1978. Summaries of all fourteen novels Lewis penned, with focus on the Christian message of each.

King, Don. *C.S. Lewis, Poet: The Legacy of His Poetic Impulse.* Kent, OH: Kent State University Press, 2001.

Kort, Wesley. *C.S. Lewis: Then and Now.* Oxford: Oxford University Press, 2001. The author attempts, from a skeptical and liberal starting point, to "rescue" Lewis from the evangelical Christians who have beatified him.

Kreeft, Peter. *C.S. Lewis: A Critical Essay.* Grand Rapids: Eerdmans, 1969. A short early work which serves as a good introduction to Lewis's life and writings.

Kreeft, Peter. *C.S. Lewis for the New Millennium: Six Essays on* The Abolition of Man. San Francisco: Ignatius, 1994. Six essays with occasionally very loose ties to *The Abolition of Man*. The essays are of varying quality; some seem more like newspaper editorials and lack references for the Lewis citations.

Kreeft, Peter. *The Shadow-Lands of C.S. Lewis: The Man Behind the Movie.* San Francisco: Ignatius Press, 1994. A presentation of Lewis's thoughts on love, suffering and grief against the background of the film *The Shadowlands*. Was perhaps more relevant when the film was first released.

* Kreeft, Peter. *Between Heaven and Hell*. Downers Grove: InterVarsity Press, 1982, 2008. Three famous people died on November 23, 1963: C.S. Lewis, President John F. Kennedy and author Aldous Huxley. In this clever book Kreeft presents an imaginary conversation on the other side of the grave, where these three men represent three worldviews: Lewis – Christian theism; Kennedy – secular humanism; Huxley – Eastern mysticism.

Lawlor, John. *C.S. Lewis: Memories and Reflections.* Dallas: Spence, 1998.

Lindskoog, Kathryn Ann. *The Lion of Judah in Never-Never Land: God, Man and Nature in C.S. Lewis's Narnia Tales.* Grand Rapids: Eerdmans, 1973. Lindskoog sifts through *The Chronicles of Narnia* in search of pearls about God, humanity and nature. The book seems rather irrelevant in light of Michael Ward's groundbreaking *Planet Narnia.*

Lindskoog, Kathryn A. *C.S. Lewis: Mere Christian.* Chicago: Cornerstone Press, 1987.

* Lindskoog, Kathryn Ann. *The C.S. Lewis Hoax*. Portland, OR: Multnomah Press, 1988. A very controversial book that has rocked C.S. Lewis studies. Lindskoog accuses Walter Hooper of falsification and claims that a number of posthumously published texts were not written by Lewis at all. She strengthens her case in the sequels *Light in the Shadowlands* (1994) and *Sleuthing the Real C.S. Lewis* (2001).

Lindskoog, Kathryn A. *Light in the Shadowlands: Protecting the Real C.S. Lewis.* Pasadena: Hope Publishing House, 1994.

Lindskoog, Kathryn A. *Finding the Landlord: A Guidebook to C.S. Lewis's* The Pilgrim's Regress. Chicago: Cornerstone Press, 1997.

Lindskoog, Kathryn A. *Sleuthing the Real C.S. Lewis: More Light in the Shadowlands.* Macon, GA: Mercer University Press, 2001. The last book in Lindskoog's witch-hunt against Walter Hooper. She builds a strong case, but this book feels more like a diary as she works through the reviews and consequences of her earlier books.

Lindsley, Art. *C.S. Lewis's Case for Christ: Insights from Reason, Imagination and Faith.* Downers Grove: InterVarsity Press, 2005.

Lindvall, Terry. *Surprised By Laughter: The Comic World of C.S. Lewis.* Nashville: Thomas Nelson, 1996.

Loconte, Joseph. *A Hobbit, a Wardrobe and a Great War: How J.R.R. Tolkien and C.S. Lewis Rediscovered Faith, Friendship, and Heroism in the Cataclysm of 1914–18.* Nashville: Thomas Nelson, 2015.

Lovell, Steven Jon James. *Philosophical Themes from C.S. Lewis.* Unpublished doctoral dissertation, University of Sheffield, 2003.

McCusker, Paul. *C.S. Lewis and* Mere Christianity*: The Crisis that Created a Classic.* Carol Stream: Tyndale House, 2014.

Macdonald, Michael H. *The Riddle of Joy.* London: HarperCollins, 1989.

McGrath, Alister. *If I Had Lunch with C.S. Lewis: Exploring the Ideas of C.S. Lewis on the Meaning of Life.* Wheaton: Tyndale House, 2014.

* McGrath, Alister. *The Intellectual World of C.S. Lewis.* Oxford: Wiley-Blackwell, 2014. An outstanding and detailed overview of the most important themes in Lewis's work.

* Manlove, Colin. *The Chronicles of Narnia: The Patterning of a Fantastic World.* New York: Twain, 1993. Yet another introduction to *The Chronicles of Narnia,* this time directed to literature teachers. The book includes helpful tips for teachers who would use the Narnia books in the classroom.

Markos, Louis. *Lewis Agonistes: How C.S. Lewis Can Train Us to Wrestle with the Modern and Postmodern World.* Nashville: Broadman & Holman, 2003. Markos argues that Christians have not presented an effective critique against modernism and postmodernism, but that Lewis can help us in meeting the challenges raised by these two dominant worldviews.

Martindale, Wayne. *Beyond the Shadowlands: C.S. Lewis on Heaven and Hell.* Westchester IL: Crossway, 2005. The strength of this book is that Martindale collects in one volume all the relevant Lewis texts on heaven and hell. The weakness is that he presents almost no analysis of Lewis's creative thoughts on the afterlife.

* Martindale, Wayne and Root, Jerry. *The Quotable Lewis.* Wheaton: Tyndale House, 1990. A very useful reference work with thousands of Lewis quotes organized under hundreds of headings in alphabetical order. A must-have resource for all Lewis nerds and others who wish to pepper their sermons and blogs with suitable Lewis quotes.

* Meilaender, Gilbert C. *The Taste for the Other: The Social and Ethical Thought of C.S. Lewis.* Grand Rapids: Eerdmans, 1978. Meilaender focuses on Lewis's thoughts about social ethics, morality, pride and Christian fellowship and emphasizes Lewis's longing for a community built on love.

Milward, Peter. *A Challenge to C.S. Lewis.* Madison, NJ: Fairleigh Dickinson University Press, 1995. A critical book where the author maintains that Lewis has misunderstood medieval literature since Lewis interprets it as heathen and neglects the Catholic context of the middle ages.

Meuller, Stephen P. *Not a Tame God: Christ in the Writings of C.S. Lewis.* St. Louis: Concordia Publishing House, 2002.

Myers, Doris T. *C.S. Lewis in Context.* Kent, OH: Kent State University Press, 1994.

* Nicholi, Armand J., Jr. *The Question of God: C.S. Lewis and Sigmund Freud Debate God, Love, Sex, and the Meaning of Life* (New York: Simon & Schuster, 2003). Nicholi compares Lewis's and Freud's philosophies and interpretations of life. This book was the inspiration to the theater play *Freud's Last Session* by Mark St. Germain.

Payne, Leanne. *Real Presence: The Holy Spirit in the Works of C.S. Lewis.* Grand Rapids: Baker, 1979.

Pearce, Joseph. *C.S. Lewis and the Catholic Church.* Charlotte: St. Benedict Press, 2003.

Peters, John. *C.S. Lewis: The Man and His Achievement.* Attic Press, 1985.

* Peters, Thomas C. *Simply C.S. Lewis.* Wheaton: Crossway, 1997. A good book that can be used as an overview of Lewis's work or as a preparation for a reading of Lewis's books themselves. The book gives a helpful introduction to the intellectual climate of late nineteenth-century England as a background to C.S. Lewis.

Phillips, Justin. *C.S. Lewis at the BBC: Messages of Hope in the Darkness of War.* New York: HarperCollins, 2003.

Purtill, Richard L. *C.S. Lewis's Case for the Christian Faith.* San Francisco: HarperOne, 1981.

Reed, Gerald. *C.S. Lewis and the Bright Shadow of Holiness.* Kansas City: Beacon Hill Press, 1999.

Reed, Gerald. *C.S. Lewis Explores Vice and Virtue.* Kansas City: Nazarene Publishing House, 2001. A systematic presentation of Lewis's interpretation of both the seven deadly sins and the seven virtues.

* Reppert, Victor. *C.S. Lewis's Dangerous Idea: A Philosophical Defense of Lewis's Argument from Reason.* Downers Grove: InterVarsity Press, 2003. Reppert presents probably the best analysis and defense of Lewis's argument from reason.

Ryken, Leland and Marjorie Lamp Mead. *A Reader's Guide Through the Wardrobe: Exploring C.S. Lewis's Classic Story.* Downers Grove: InterVarsity Press, 2005.

Sammons, Martha C. *A Guide Through Narnia.* Wheaton: Harold Shaw Publishers, 1979, 2004.

Sammons, Martha C. *A Guide Through C.S. Lewis's Space Trilogy.* Chicago: Cornerstone Press, 1980.

Schakel, Peter J. *Reading with the Heart: The Way into Narnia.* Grand Rapids: Eerdmans, 1979, 2005.

Schakel, Peter J. *Reason and Imagination in C.S. Lewis: A Study of* Till We Have Faces. Grand Rapids: Eerdmans, 1984. The first part of this book is a summary and analysis of *Till We Have Faces.* In the second (and in my opinion inferior) part, the author tries to force Lewis into a number of categories that correspond to the various decades of his life: 1910–20 Lewis was a poet; in the 1930s an author of fiction; in the 1940s an apologist; in the 1950s an autobiographer and in the 1960s someone who tried to unify reason and imagination. This schematization does not fit the historical evidence – *The Chronicles of Narnia* were written in the 1950s and Lewis only wrote one autobiography.

Schakel, Peter J. *Imagination and the Arts in C.S. Lewis: Journeying to Narnia and Other Worlds.* Columbia, MO: University of Missouri Press, 2002.

Schakel, Peter J. *Is Your Lord Large Enough?: How C.S. Lewis Expands Our View of God.* Downers Grove: InterVarsity Press, 2009.

* Schwartz, Sanford. *C.S. Lewis on the Final Frontier: Science and the Supernatural in the Space Trilogy.* Oxford: Oxford University Press, 2009. One of the better analyses of the space trilogy.

Smith, Robert H. *Patches of Godlight: The Pattern of Thought in C.S. Lewis.* Athens, GA: University of Georgia Press, 1981.

Taliaferro, Charles C. *Praying with C.S. Lewis.* Frederick, MD: Word Among Us Press, 1998.

Vaus, Will. *Mere Theology: A Guide to the Thought of C.S. Lewis.* Downers Grove: InterVarsity Press, 2004.

Wagner, Richard. *C.S. Lewis and Narnia for Dummies.* Hoboken: Wiley, 2005.

Walsh, Chad. *C.S. Lewis: Apostle to the Skeptics.* New York: Macmillan, 1949; Eugene, OR: Wipf and Stock 2008. The first analysis of C.S. Lewis, written even before a large portion of Lewis's own books were written (including *The Chronicles of Narnia*).

* Walsh, Chad. *The Literary Legacy of C.S. Lewis.* New York: Harcourt Brace Jovanovich, 1979. A good analysis of Lewis's fictional works by a skilled literary critic.

* Ward, Michael. *Planet Narnia.* New York: Oxford University Press, 2008. Michael Ward's groundbreaking discovery that medieval cosmology is both the inspiration and the hidden key to understanding the unity of *The Chronicles of Narnia.* The details in this book are an "extra credit course" for all Narnia nerds who wish to go deep into the esoteric roots and hidden symbolism of the Narnia books.

* Ward, Michael. *The Narnia Code: C.S. Lewis and the Secret of the Seven Heavens.* Carol Stream, IL: Tyndale House, 2010. Not quite as detailed as *Planet Narnia.* Good for those who will be satisfied with an "introductory course".

White, William Luther. *The Image of Man in C.S. Lewis.* Nashville: Abingdon Press, 1969.

Williams, Rowan. *The Lion's World: A Journey into the Heart of Narnia.* Oxford: Oxford University Press, 2012. A light introduction to *The Chronicles of Narnia* by the former Archbishop of the Church of England.

Willis, John Randolph. *Pleasures Forevermore: The Theology of C.S. Lewis.* Chicago: Loyola Press, 1983. Perhaps the first book by a Roman Catholic priest to present a Catholic perspective on Lewis's ecclesiology and theology.

Anthologies about C.S. Lewis

Abate, Michelle Ann and Weldy, Lance, ed. *C.S. Lewis: The Chronicles of Narnia.* New York: Palgrave Macmillan, 2012. Yet another anthology with essays on various aspects of the Narnia books, including questions of sexism, gender studies and what happens to the books' theology when they become games for electronic consoles.

* Baggett, David J. and Walls, Jerry L., ed. *C.S. Lewis as Philosopher: Truth, Goodness and Beauty.* Downers Grove: InterVarsity Press, 2008. One of the better anthologies about Lewis.

Bassham, Gregory and Walls, Jerry L., ed. *The Chronicles of Narnia and Philosophy: The Lion, the Witch, and the Worldview.* Chicago: Open Court, 2005.

* Edwards, Bruce L., ed. *C.S. Lewis: Life, Works, and Legacy, Vol. 1: An Examined Life.* Westport, CT: Praeger, 2007. This is the first part of a four-book series that make up one of the better anthologies about Lewis's life and works.

Edwards, Bruce L., ed. *C.S. Lewis: Life, Works, and Legacy, Vol. 2: Fantasist, Mythmaker and Poet.* Westport, CT: Praeger, 2007.

Edwards, Bruce L., ed. *C.S. Lewis: Life, Works, and Legacy, Vol. 3: Apologist, Philosopher abd Theologian.* Westport, CT: Praeger, 2007.

Edwards, Bruce L., ed. *C.S. Lewis: Life, Works, and Legacy, Vol. 4: Scholar, Teacher, and Public Intellectual.* Westport, CT: Praeger, 2007.

Ford, Paul F. *Companion to Narnia.* San Francisco: Harper & Row, 1980. This is not the kind of book one reads from cover to cover, but it has a certain value as a reference work that gives introductions to many subjects related to *The Chronicles of Narnia.*

Gibb, Jocelyn, ed. *Light on C.S. Lewis.* New York: Harcourt Brace & World, 1965. An early anthology.

Graham, David. *We Remember C.S. Lewis: Essays and Memories.* Nashville: Broadman and Holman, 2001. A collection of less academic texts where people relate what Lewis has meant to them.

Keefe, Caroline. *C.S. Lewis: Speaker and Teacher.* Grand Rapids: Zondervan, 1971. A collection of essay that focuses on Lewis as a rhetorician and teacher.

* MacSwain, Robert and Ward, Michael, ed. *The Cambridge Companion to C.S. Lewis.* Cambridge: Cambridge University Press, 2010. A very good collection of serious essays.

Marshall, Cynthia. *Essays on C.S. Lewis and George Macdonald: Truth, Fiction, and the Power of Imagination.* Lewiston, NY: Edwin Mellen Press, 1991. Six authors reflect on Macdonald's influence on C.S. Lewis.

Martin, Thomas L. *Reading the Classics with C.S. Lewis.* Grand Rapids: Baker Academic, 2000. A collection of essays by literature scholars that focus on Lewis's contacts with classical literature.

Menuge, Angus J.L. *Lightbearer in the Shadowlands: The Evangelistic Vision of C.S. Lewis.* Wheaton: Crossway, 1997. A collection of essays with an occasionally irritating tendency to repeat already cited quotes and anecdotes on Lewis's view of evangelism. The texts are of varying quality and have the lamentable tendency of trying to force Lewis into a North American evangelical mold.

Mills, David. *The Pilgrim's Guide: C.S. Lewis and the Art of Witness.* Grand Rapids: Eerdmans, 1998.

Piper, John and Mathis, David, ed. *The Romantic Rationalist: God, Life, and Imagination in the Work of C.S. Lewis.* Wheaton: Crossway, 2014. Essays of mixed quality on Lewis's views of biblical inerrancy, salvation, heaven and hell.

Schakel, Peter J., ed. *The Longing for a Form: Essays on the Fiction of C.S. Lewis.* Kent, OH: Kent State University Press, 1976.

Schakel, Peter J. and Huttar, Charles A., ed. *Word and Story in C.S. Lewis: Language and Narrative in Theory and Practice.* Eugene, OR: Wipf & Stock, 1991.

Schofield, Stephen, ed. *In Search of C.S. Lewis.* South Plainfield, NJ: Bridge, 1983. Interviews with a number of people who knew Lewis in different capacities.

Schultz, Jeffrey D. and West, John G., ed. *The C.S. Lewis Readers' Encyclopedia.* Grand Rapids: Zondervan, 1998.

Skinner, Andrew C. and Millet, Robert L., ed. *C.S. Lewis: The Man and His Message.* Salt Lake City: Deseret Books, 1999. A collection of essays written by Mormons focusing on Lewis's influence on the Church of Jesus Christ of Latter-day Saints.

Watson, George. *Critical Essays on C.S. Lewis.* Aldershot: Scholars Press, 1992. An unusual anthology of early texts about Lewis, including many original reviews of his books.

Wolfe, Judith and Wolfe, Brendan, ed. *C.S. Lewis's* Perelandra*: Reshaping the Image of the Cosmos.* Kent, OH: Kent State University Press, 2013. An anthology of texts that use *Perelandra* as a starting point.

Biographies about C.S. Lewis

There are several problems with writing a biography about C.S. Lewis. In the first place, Lewis wrote a definitive autobiography, *Surprised by Joy,* even though it ends with his conversion in the early 1930s. Secondly, many biographies have a regrettable hagiographic tendency. The man could simply do no wrong. Other biographers, who refuse to bow the knee at the altar of St. Jack of Oxford, often end up in the ditch of iconoclasm on the other side of the road. It is difficult to find the right balance.

Arnot, Anne. *The Secret Country of C.S. Lewis.* London: Hodder & Stoughton, 1974. A short, relatively early biography with an easy-going, less serious style.

Bleakley, David. *C.S. Lewis: At Home in Ireland.* Bangor: Strandtown Press, 1998. Written in connection with the Lewis centennial in 1998,

Bleakley focuses on Lewis's childhood in Northern Ireland along with his Irish roots and influences.

Brown, Devin. *A Life Observed: A Spiritual Biography of C.S. Lewis.* Grand Rapids: Brazos, 2013.

Carpenter, Humphrey. *The Inklings.* New York: HarperCollins, 1979.

Como, James, ed. *C.S. Lewis at the Breakfast Table and Other Reminiscences.* New York: Macmillan, 1979. an anthology memoirs by people who had some contact with Lewis in various capacities. The texts are of varying quality and value; some were written by people who were close friends or colleagues of Lewis. Others were written by people who had studied under Lewis at Oxford and only knew him in a professional role. Still others were written by people who did not have a personal relationship with him, and who may only have met him during temporary visits in Oxford.

Cording, Ruth James. *C.S. Lewis: A Celebration of His Early Life.* Nashville: Broadman & Holman, 2000. A short biography with lots of photos.

Coren, Michael. *The Man Who Created Narnia: The Story of C.S. Lewis.* Toronto: Lester Publishing, 1994. A biography written for children. Includes many pictures.

* Dorsett, Lyle W. *And God Came In: The Extraordinary Story of Joy Davidman, Her Life and Marriage to C.S. Lewis.* Peabody, MA: Hendrickson, 1983. The definitive biography of Lewis's wife Joy Davidman. Dorsett did extensive research and interviews with friends, family members and unpublished letters. Also published with the title *A Love Observed.*

Downing, David C. *The Most Reluctant Convert: C.S. Lewis's Journey to Faith.* Downers Grove: InterVarsity Press, 2002. A rather unnecessary book in light of *Surprised by Joy.*

Duriez, Colin. *C.S. Lewis: A Biography of Friendship.* Oxford: Lion Hudson, 2013.

Gilbert, Douglas. *C.S. Lewis: Images of his World.* Grand Rapids: Eerdmans, 1973, 2005. A popular book with many beautiful and interesting photos.

Gilchrist, K.J. *A Morning After War: C.S. Lewis and World War I.* Bern: Peter Lang International Academic Publishers, 2005.

Glaspey, Terry W. and Grant, George, ed. *Not a Tame Lion: The Spiritual Legacy of C.S. Lewis.* Nashville: Cumberland House Publishing, 1996.

Gormley, Beatrice. *C.S. Lewis: Christian and Storyteller.* Grand Rapids: Eerdmans, 1997. A biography written for children.

* Green, Roger Lancelyn and Hooper, Walter. *C.S. Lewis: A Biography.* Orlando: Harcourt Harvest, 1974, 1994. One of the definitive biographies. This early book builds to a large degree on Green's previous book *C.S. Lewis* (1963).

* Gresham, Douglas H. *Lenten Lands: My Childhood with Joy Davidman & C.S. Lewis.* New York: HarperCollins, 1988. Gresham focuses on his mother Joy Davidman, but also presents many interesting and unusual insights into Lewis as a private person.

* Gresham, Douglas H. *Jack's Life: A Memory of C.S. Lewis.* Nashville: Broadman & Holman, 2005. This book focuses more specifically on Gresham's step-father Lewis, who was part of his life for approximately ten years.

* Griffin, William. *Clive Staples Lewis: A Dramatic Life.* San Francisco: Harper & Row, 1986. This novel-like biography is well-written and enjoyable to read. Griffin begins his narrative in 1925 and skips Lewis's childhood. A discrete system of references contributes to a more fluid reading experience.

Griffin, William. *C.S. Lewis Spirituality for Mere Christians.* Eugene, OR: Wipf & Stock, 1998. A narrative biography where Lewis "comments" on his own life through his texts.

Hooper, Walter, ed. *Through Joy and Beyond: A Pictorial Biography of C.S. Lewis.* New York: Macmillan, 1982; London: Collier Macmillan, 1982. An accessible introduction with many photos of Lewis, his friends and the environments in which they moved.

* Jacobs, Alan. *The Narnian: The Life and Imagination of C.S. Lewis.* San Francisco: Harper San Francisco, 2005. One of the better biographies. A good combination of the story of Lewis's life with quality introductions to all of Lewis's books.

* McGrath, Alister. *C.S. Lewis – A Life: Eccentric Genius, Reluctant Prophet.* Wheaton: Tyndale House, 2013. McGrath succeeds in finding the

balance between iconoclasm and hagiography. Some of McGrath's interpretations may nonetheless raise a few eyebrows, such as his critical take on Joy Davidman.

Morris, A. Clifford. *Miles and Miles: Some Reminiscences of an Oxford Taxi Driver and Private Care Home Service Chauffeur.* St. Meinrad, IN: Abbey Press, 1964.

* Sayer, George. *Jack: A Life of C.S. Lewis.* New York: Harper & Row, 1998; Wheaton: Crossway, 1994. One of the best biographies, written by a personal friend of Lewis's who collected material from interviews and primary sources.

Sibley, Brian. *C.S. Lewis through the Shadowlands: The Story of His Life with Joy Davidman.* Old Tappan, NJ: Revell, 1994. This book was the inspiration to the play and the films called *Shadowlands.*

Wilson, A.N. *C.S. Lewis: A Biography.* New York: W.W. Norton, 1990, 2002. Wilson attempts to provide a counterbalance to the hagiographic biographies that fill the bookshelves. Wilson accuses Walter Hooper of having exaggerated his friendship with Lewis and points out the historical impossibility of Hooper's anecdote about celebrating an Easter Sunday service together with Lewis. Hooper met Lewis for the first time June 7, 1963 when Lewis was already seriously ill; Lewis subsequently passed away in November 1963, which makes the Easter service a fabrication. Wilson also points out the fraudulent nature of the blurb on an early edition of *God in the Dock* that Hooper was "a long-time friend and for some years personal secretary of C.S. Lewis." (p 302).

Articles about C.S. Lewis

The number of articles about C.S. Lewis has grown exponentially in recent years. Several serious journals publish only articles about Lewis and the other Inklings. Among others, one may mention *The Journal of Inkling Studies, Inklings Forever, VII: An Anglo-American Literary Review, The C.S. Lewis Chronicle* and *The Canadian C.S. Lewis Journal.* I will list here only the articles I have quoted in this book.

Anonymous, "Don v Devil" *Time* 50/10 (September 8, 1947): 65–74.

Baker, Ray. "Ske min vilja: Helvetet enligt C.S. Lewis" *Theofilos* 1 (2011): 16–29.

Holyer, Robert. "The Argument from Desire" *Faith and Philosophy* 5/1 (1988): 61–70.

Kreeft, Peter. "C.S. Lewis's Argument from Desire" in M.H. Macdonald and A.A. Tadie, ed. *The Riddle of Joy*. London: Collins, 1989.

Neuhaus, Richard John. "C.S. Lewis and Postmodernism" *First Things* (December 1998).

Poe, Harry Lee. "C.S. Lewis was a Secret Government Agent" *Christianity Today* (December 10, 2015).

Reppert, Victor. "Several Formulations of the Argument from Reason" *Philosophia Christi* 5/1 (2003): 9–33.

Stephen Schofield, "Professor Anscombe Corrects Father Hooper" *Canadian C.S. Lewis Journal* (December 1979): 5–10.

Svahn, Martin. "Längtan till ett förlorat paradis". *Moderna tider* 12/132 (Oct 2001): 44–50.

Walker, Andrew. "Scripture, revelation and Platonism in C.S. Lewis" *Scottish Journal of Theology* 55/1 (2002): 19–35.

Ward, Michael. "How Lewis Lit the Way to Better Apologetics" *Christianity Today* 57/9 (October 22, 2013).

Wright, N.T. "Simply Lewis: Reflections on a Master Apologist After 60 Years" *Touchstone Magazine* 20/2 (2007). <http://www.touchstonemag.com/archives/article.php?id=20-02-028-f>.

Other referenced works

Aitken, Jonathan. *Charles Colson: A Life Redeemed*. Colorado Springs: Waterbrook Press, 2005.

Anscombe, G.E.M. "A Reply to Mr. C.S. Lewis's Argument that 'Naturalism' is Self-Refuting" *Socratic Digest* (nr 4) in *The Collected Philosophical Papers of G.E.M. Anscombe, Vol 2: Metaphysics and the Philosophy of Mind.* Minneapolis: University of Minnesota Press, 1981.

Bauckham, Richard. *Jesus and the Eyewitnesses.* Grand Rapids: Eerdmans, 2008.

Beisner, Frederick. "Romanticism, German" in Edward Craig, ed. *Routledge Encyclopedia of Philosophy*, vol. 8. London: Routledge, 1998.

Blocher, Henri. "Everlasting Punishment and the Problem of Evil" in Cameron, Nigel M. de S., ed. *Universalism and the Doctrine of Hell.* Carlisle: Paternoster, 1992.

Carson, Thomas L. and Moser, Paul K. *Moral Relativism: A Reader.* Oxford: Oxford University Press, 2001.

Chesterton, G.K. *The Everlasting Man.* Seaside, OR: Rough Draft Printing, 2006.

Cioran, Emil. *Histoire et utopie.* Paris: Gallimard. 1987.

Corbineau-Hoffman, A. "Sehnsucht" in *Historisches Wörterbuch der Philosophie,* vol. 9. Basel: Schwabe Verlag, 1971–1998.

Craig, William Lane. *Reasonable Faith: Christian Truth and Apologetics.* Wheaton: Crossway, 1994.

Eco, Umberto. *Art and Beauty in the Middle Ages.* New Haven: Yale University Press, 1986.

Ehrman, Bart D. *Jesus, Interrupted: Revealing the Hidden Contradictions in the Bible (and Why We Don't Know About Them).* New York: HarperCollins, 2009.

Geisler, Norman L., ed. *Inerrancy*. Grand Rapids: Zondervan, 1980.

Gustavsson, Stefan. *Skeptikerns guide till Jesus, Vol. 2: Om Jesu identitet och uppståndelse*. Stockholm: CredoAkademin, 2015.

Hasker, William. *Metaphysics: Constructing a World View.* Downers Grove: InterVarsity Press, 1983.

Hitchens, Christopher. "In the Name of the Father, the Sons…". *The New York Times.* July 9, 2010. <http://www.nytimes.com/2010/07/11/books/review/Hitchens-t.html?_r=0>.

Hume, David. "Concerning Moral Sentiment", Appendix 1 in *An Enquiry Concerning the Principles of Morals.* Indianapolis: Hackett, 1983.

Hume, David. "Section X: Of Miracles" in *An Enquiry Concerning Human Understanding*. Oxford: Oxford University Press, 2007.

Kreeft, Peter and Tacelli, Ronald. *Handbook of Christian Apologetics.* Downers Grove: InterVarsity Press, 1994.

Kvanvig, Jonathan L. *The Problem of Hell.* New York: Oxford University Press, 1993.

Maudlin, Michael. "1993 Christianity Today Book Awards" *Christianity Today* (April 5, 1993).

Mayhew, Robert, ed. *Ayn Rand's Marginalia: Her Critical Comments on the Writings of over 20 Authors.* Irvine, CA: Second Renaissance Books, 1998.

Moltmann, Jürgen. "The Logic of Hell" in Richard Bauckham, ed. *God Will Be All in All: The Eschatology of Jürgen Moltmann.* Minneapolis: Fortress, 2001.

Muggeridge, Malcolm. *Jesus Rediscovered.* New York: Doubleday, 1979.

Parrinder, Geoffrey. *Mysticism in the World's Religions.* Oxford: Oneworld Publications, 1976, 1995.

Plantinga, Alvin. *Warrant and Proper Function.* New York: Oxford University Press, 1993.

Plato, "Symposium" in Louise Ropes Loomis, ed. and B. Jowett, trans. *Plato: Apology, Crito, Phaedo, Symposium, Republic.* Roslyn, NY: Classics Club, 1942.

Stackhouse, John G. "By Their Books Ye Shall Know Them" *Christianity Today* (September 16, 1996): 58–59.

Steinbeck, John. *East of Eden.* New York: The Viking Press, 1952.

Wright, Ronald Selby, ed. *Asking Them Questions.* Oxford: Oxford University Press, 1950.

Questions for Study and Discussion

Surprised by Joy, chapter 14 – "Checkmate"

1. Lewis uses the analogy of chess to describe his journey towards faith. What four moves converged to rouse his interest in belief in God?
2. What did Lewis mean by *joy*? How did it impact him?
3. What happens when we focus our attention on joy? Why?

Mere Christianity, first book, chapters 1–5

1. How does Lewis argue for the existence of God in these chapters?
    a. How does Lewis answer the objection that different views of morality in different cultures at different times in history are an argument against an objective moral law?
    b. Why does Lewis dismiss herd instinct as an explanation of the moral law?
    c. How does Lewis answer the objection that the truths we learn about the laws of nature are categorically different than what we learn about ethics and morality?
2. How does Lewis argue for the transition from the observation that people have moral values to the idea that there is an objective moral law?
3. Which of God's attributes can we understand through the moral argument, according to Lewis?
4. How do we know that Satan is not the cause or explanation of the moral law?
5. What weaknesses do you see in Lewis's argument? Is his argument logically valid? Is it true?

Miracles, chapter 8 – "Miracles and the Laws of Nature"

1. Assuming that there is a force *outside* of nature, how can that force perform miracles *within* the natural realm?
2. Of the three interpretations of the laws of nature Lewis presents, which alternative does Hume's perspective represent?
3. How does Lewis use the billiard illustration to explain what happens with a miracle?

4. Why is Lewis critical of Hume's definition of miracle as a violation of the laws of nature?
5. What does Lewis mean when he writes that some people confuse a certain system within reality with reality as a whole?

The Problem of Pain, chapter 4 – "Human Wickedness"

1. Lewis says that we need to recover the old sense of sin. What does he mean by that?
2. In light of this, how should we understand:
    a. The wrath of God against sin?
    b. Lewis's explanation about why we need to be saved?
    c. "The proof" of the reality of sin that can be found outside Christianity in other religions and philosophies?
    d. Lewis's argument against the total depravity of humanity?

The Screwtape Letters, letter 1

In this text, a senior demon Screwtape begins to write to his nephew Wormwood, who is a novice at the art of tempting humans. In the book all the values are turned on their head. The "Enemy" is God.

1. How does Screwtape view logic? Why?
2. How do the demons use "real life" in their work?
3. Why does Screwtape want to direct his target away from the natural sciences?

The Great Divorce, chapters 3–4

In these chapters the narrator has just left hell along with other "ghosts" (damned souls) on a bus trip to the outskirts of heaven.

1. What are the narrator's impressions of nature when he first arrives? How does this fit in with Lewis's overall ontology?
2. How does the ghosts' willingness to return to the gray city illustrate Lewis's view of hell?
3. Why is the murderer in heaven and why is it so difficult for his friend to grasp that? Why doesn't he want to go along to the mountains?

A Grief Observed, chapter 1

A Grief Observed was Lewis's last book. In it Lewis processes his grief after the passing of his wife Joy Davidman Gresham. She is called H (from her first name Helen) in the book.

1. How does Lewis describe the struggle between emotions and what he knows to be true?
2. How does one arrive at new perspectives on life when one is in mourning?
3. How did Lewis's faith in God change in the face of his grief?
4. Why is Lewis convinced that religion is not merely a projection of subconscious, unsatisfied desires?
5. Lewis writes that the memory of H can easily become some sort of weapon of coercion. How?
6. What does Lewis think about the awkwardness his friends feel when they run into him?

Acknowledgements

I would like to thank Mark Nelson and the Baltic Methodist Theological Seminary in Tallinn, Estonia. My lectures there form the foundation of this book. I still feel a pang of sympathy for the poor women whose unenviable task it was to provide simultaneous interpretation into Estonian and Russian during the lectures. They're probably still lying there in a fetal position in the interpreters' booths.

I am also grateful Anna and Lasse Axelsson for the use of your cabin on an island in the Stockholm archipelago while I was writing this book. Unfortunately, I see your cabin more often than I see you.

My friends, family and students also deserve a medal for putting up with me peppering almost any conversation with a relevant quote or anecdote from C.S. Lewis.

Finally, special thanks are due to the enormously talented Phil Mendez. The *joie de vivre* in your artwork gives this book the magic that the creator of Narnia deserves.